THE POLITICAL
RECONSTRUCTION OF
AMERICAN TOBACCO,
1862–1933

Reconstructing America
Andrew L. Slap, series editor

The Political Reconstruction of American Tobacco, 1862–1933

Patrick Mulford O'Connor

FORDHAM UNIVERSITY PRESS
NEW YORK 2025

Copyright © 2025 Fordham University Press

All rights reserved. No part of this publication may be reproduced, stored in a retrieval system, or transmitted in any form or by any means—electronic, mechanical, photocopy, recording, or any other—except for brief quotations in printed reviews, without the prior permission of the publisher.

Fordham University Press has no responsibility for the persistence or accuracy of URLs for external or third-party Internet websites referred to in this publication and does not guarantee that any content on such websites is, or will remain, accurate or appropriate.

Fordham University Press also publishes its books in a variety of electronic formats. Some content that appears in print may not be available in electronic books.

Visit us online at www.fordhampress.com.

For EU safety / GPSR concerns: Mare Nostrum Group B.V., Mauritskade 21D, 1091 GC Amsterdam, The Netherlands, gpsr@mare-nostrum.co.uk

Library of Congress Cataloging-in-Publication Data available online at https://catalog.loc.gov.

Printed in the United States of America

27 26 25   5 4 3 2 1

First edition

For my family,
and in memory of Robert H. Greene

Contents

Introduction 1

1 "An Acknowledged Power in the Land": Tobacconists, Taxation, and the Politics of Market Creation, 1862–1872 | 10

2 "A Hard Law at Best": The Political Economy of Tobacco Taxation from Depression to Surplus, 1873–1890 | 40

3 Tobacco's "Imperfect Knowledge": Governance, Classification, and Conflict in the World Tobacco Market, 1865–1890 | 65

4 "The Road to Prosperity": Power and the Politics of Quality on the Bright Tobacco Frontier, 1865–1900 | 88

5 The Health of the State: The USDA, Agricultural Hegemony, and the Federal Improvement of Tobacco Quality, 1890–1933 | 113

Conclusion: Revising Tobacco Politics in the Twentieth Century | 144

Acknowledgments 151
Notes 153
Bibliography 203
Index 219

THE POLITICAL
RECONSTRUCTION OF
AMERICAN TOBACCO,
1862–1933

Introduction

In the decades following the Civil War, the American tobacco economy underwent a period of profound growth and change. Unbound from the slave labor regime that had dominated it for centuries, tobacco agriculture came to depend on thousands of smallholders, tenants, and sharecroppers. Tobacco's agricultural frontiers spread rapidly following emancipation, permeating much of the Southern countryside as well as river valleys in the Northeast and Midwest. By the early twentieth century, American growers produced roughly forty percent of the world's tobacco supply, more than double the output of any other nation, although they chronically struggled under low prices and political marginality.[1] In search of buyers, growers hauled their crops to auction warehouses that sprung up in cities and small towns wherever tobacco was grown. Feeding on this supply were dozens of powerful manufacturing firms in cities such as Cincinnati, Detroit, Durham, New York, and Richmond that, between 1865 and the turn of the century, produced four and half billion pounds of chew and hand-rolled tobacco, in addition to more than 100 billion cigarettes and cigars.[2] By 1890, the nation's largest manufacturers would form the American Tobacco Company—the so-called Tobacco Trust—and eventually control much of the global manufacturing market. In seemingly every sphere of its postbellum political economy, from law to agriculture to consumerism, tobacco was utterly reconstructed, "comparatively a new industry," as one analyst put it.[3] This book tells the story of how tobacco's reconstruction came to be. It argues that during the final decades of the nineteenth century, diverse political developments across tobacco's commodity chain created the power and poverty that defined tobacco's reconstruction.

Tobacco's political reconstruction began during the Civil War when Congress selected tobacco as a cornerstone of internal taxation. This decision made tobacco into a uniquely politicized commodity, driving tobacco manufacturers across the country, and particularly in New York City and Cincinnati, to create a political infrastructure to shape fiscal policy in their favor. In 1865, a group of New York tobacconists established a weekly trade journal, *Tobacco Leaf*, which provided a forum for inter-industry debates and a platform for policy proposals. Throughout the 1860s, tobacco manufacturers—or tobacconists, as they often called themselves—routinely organized trade conventions to showcase their organizational prowess and vigorously petitioned Congress for alterations of the tax system. They did most of this work through dozens of local trade associations and unions, which confederated as the National Tobacco Association (NTA) in 1869. "The tobacco industry is especially placed in a peculiar situation," noted one industry observer in 1874. "In one sense it has been singled out and placed apart from the other great industries of the country. It has been honored by being made the object of onerous taxation."[4] Although few rejoiced at this "honor," tobacconists came to recognize the advantages of embracing taxation rather than fighting it. Through their burgeoning political infrastructure, tobacconists forged partnerships with the federal government, which was happy for the help. By 1872, tobacconists and their allies in Congress and the Bureau of Internal Revenue had created a tax system in which tobacco generated as much as thirty-five percent of all internal revenue and fifteen percent of *total* federal revenues.[5] Tobacco taxes thus fortified the postbellum federal government's military and administrative capacities, as well as its solvency, particularly in the lean years following the Panic of 1873.[6]

The tobacconist-designed revenue system provided the foundations for tobacco's reconstructed commodity chain. It obliterated tobacco's more flexible antebellum "commodity web," which had enabled growers to shift their crops strategically to different markets—industrial, urban, and overseas as well as agrarian and local. Antebellum growers sold their tobacco for money, but they could also exchange it for "produce, groceries, and handcrafted articles, including woven cloth."[7] The antebellum commodity web had left room for growers to incorporate tobacco culture into makeshift economies that were not entirely dependent on money.[8] The postbellum revenue system, by contrast, compelled the tobacco market's participants into what Steven Stoll has called "monetized circuits of production and exchange."[9] It created a strictly regulated commodity chain marked by legally bounded categories such as growers, brokers, and dealers of tobacco, as well as cigar makers and tobacconists. Each category had unique responsibilities while some—brokers, tobacconists, and dealers—paid license fees to enter the market. Federal prohibitions on the sale of unmanufactured tobacco ensured that the nation's supply—"every leaf," as the revenue system's proponents often proclaimed—was sold only to federally licensed brokers or tobacconists.[10]

It was in this context that emancipation came to the tobacco-growing regions of the South. In the decades following the Civil War, the number of tobacco

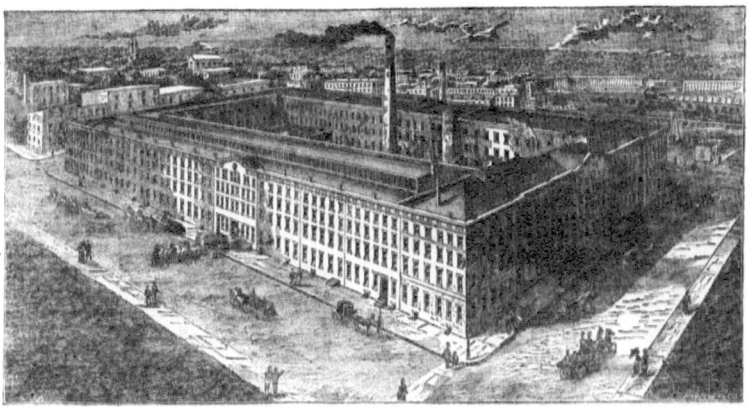

Figure 1. Jersey City's P. Lorillard & Co. played a major role in the creation of the federal tobacco tax system. In this 1875 advertisement, they boasted that they were the "Largest Tax Payers in U.S." From *Tobacco Leaf*, December 1, 1875.

growers increased rapidly as freeholders—particularly prevalent in Virginia—and sharecroppers attempted to bolster household economies by selling tobacco.[11] Freedpeople and their descendants supplied much of the tobacco that crowded postbellum auction floors and supplemented their incomes by working in tobacco factories from Danville to Durham. It was these families who provided the base for Black political mobilizations, such as the Readjuster movement that challenged white Democratic rule in Virginia during the 1870s and 1880s.[12] At the same time, many white growers and their self-proclaimed spokesmen in racist organizations such as the Democratic Party and the Grange frequently argued that the revenue system shared an origin story with emancipation, when the Republican Party overthrew the foundations of Southern political economy and racial hierarchy.[13] For this reason, the tobacco tax remained contested even after federal Reconstruction had ended in 1877. During the 1880s, dozens of new growers' associations emerged to protest the tax. These waves of dissension expanded the political consciousness and infrastructure of various trade sectors, but they had little effect on the tax system. For national political leaders in the 1880s and 1890s, it was import revenue—the tariff—that determined legislative agendas, and competing factions exploited the tobacco tax for potential leverage over other issues. It was through this tortuous process, from war and business politics to agricultural protest and partisan wrangling, that the tax and its profound structural consequences for the tobacco industry became a permanent feature of federal public finance, ensuring that tobacco and the players along its commodity chain would remain highly politicized.

Tobacconists took the lead in the political reconstruction of the commodity chain, but the revenue system they created did not address more substantive questions about conditions within that chain. Most notably, the tax system entirely avoided questions about leaf tobacco's standards of quality. This was significant because ideas about tobacco's quality were inextricable from any discussion of tobacco's supply and demand. Changing definitions of tobacco quality illuminated broader transformations in governance during the postbellum period.[14] "Quality" was a means of standardizing tobacco—a frequently unwieldy and illegible crop—by assessing traits such as color, elasticity, and oiliness.[15] Growers sought quality in their months-long cultivation of crops, while buyers demanded it, auctioneers announced it, trade journals and scientific treatises interpreted it,

Figure 2. An 1887 engraving depicts Black tobacco growers journeying to the auction houses of Danville, Virginia. Under the federal revenue system, growers had to bring tobacco to licensed buyers—typically manufacturers—who gathered in the auction houses of burgeoning tobacco towns. From *The New South: Supplement to Harper's Weekly*, January 29, 1887.

and the emergent fertilizer industry promised their products would deliver it. Although interpretations of quality appeared to describe nature objectively, they were always embedded in political and economic contexts, and thus subject to revision. Throughout the late-nineteenth and early-twentieth centuries, these revisions produced more exacting quality demands, thereby making tobacco culture, in the words of one agronomist, "a more intensive system of cultivation than any other general farm crop."[16] As the second half of this book argues, the distribution of wealth and power in the tobacco market thus depended, in no small part, on the politics of quality: who determined what it was and what it was worth.

The description of quality was a political act that seemed entirely apolitical. Unlike the standards that governed most global commodities, tobacco quality was untethered to universal grades. Tobacco was a difficult crop to know, and thus to govern; "quality" made it more knowable, and thus more governable. In the decades following the Civil War, a concept I call the "quality principle" unified various powerful actors' efforts to standardize leaf quality, scale up agricultural production, and disenfranchise growers. Among these actors were American tobacconists; foreign tobacco buyers, particularly government tobacco monopolies from around the world; boards of trade and other public institutions in emerging tobacco warehouse towns; and a new class of "tobacco capitalists"—fertilizer manufacturers, banks, and railroads—who altered the forces and relations of production throughout the Southern tobacco frontier. For these institutions, the quality principle became a powerful instrument of governance: a means of projecting expertise within abstruse leaf tobacco markets, leveraging economic advantage, and disciplining labor across thousands of small farms.[17] When disempowered growers challenged this situation, their antagonists could justify poor prices by explaining that growers had simply not produced a quality crop. More insidiously, they could enflame the racial resentments of white growers by accusing Black growers of undermining prices by raising, as one tobacco analyst wrote in the 1880 national census, "as a rule, an inferior grade."[18]

By the end of the nineteenth century, quality ideals had become synonymous with elite calls for a "scientific" approach to tobacco agriculture. Scientific expertise was yet another political authority to emerge in tobacco's chain. This was most apparent among agronomists with the U.S. Department of Agriculture (USDA), whose tobacco studies during the 1890s culminated in the creation of a federal office committed exclusively to tobacco science—the Office of Tobacco Investigations (OTI)—in 1907. OTI's mission was to introduce "more profitable and permanent systems of farming with tobacco as the central money crop."[19]

OTI drew upon intensive analysis of tobacco's physiology and its relation to various soils for the purpose of improving the national crops' consistency and quality. This process was intended to secure American hegemony in global tobacco markets against increasing international competition. Yet, as agronomists embedded nineteenth-century quality ideals into the plant genetics and soils of the tobacco frontier, they also reinforced structural inequities that had been forming in tobacco's commodity chain since the Civil War.

The Political Reconstruction of American Tobacco shows that a range of actors, working within political contexts that spanned decades, created and governed tobacco's turn-of-the-century political economy. Their work intersected only occasionally, as key developments came through diverse corners such as taxation, fertilizer production, warehouse governance, and scientific agriculture. When taken together, these processes made possible the so-called "cigarette century" to come.[20] Tobacco's postbellum political history challenges long-standing assumptions among business and economic historians about the post-Civil War political economy. The supposedly apolitical innovations of firms and trusts, for example, has traditionally dominated analysis. In fact, tobacco history has its own rendition of this story, centering the American Tobacco Company, with its internalized supply chains and managerial coordination, as the agent of industrial development. No monograph has illustrated this approach more fully than Alfred Chandler's *The Visible Hand*, which emphasized the entrepreneurial innovations of James Buchanan Duke. More recent scholarship has foregrounded American Tobacco's racial and imperial contexts, but has continued to emphasize the Trust's primacy in the creation of the tobacco market.[21] Even scholars looking beyond the Trust have explained tobacco's prominence through the actions of firms, including their advertising, their technological ingenuity, and their exploitation of tobacco's addictive qualities to create mass consumption.[22] Firms and trusts no doubt mattered a great deal in this era, but they did not operate in a vacuum. Rather, their triumphs occurred in the context of major contestations for power across tobacco's commodity chain.[23]

By identifying the political foundations of the tobacco economy, *The Political Reconstruction of American Tobacco* contributes to broader reassessments of the nature and diversity of politics in the nineteenth-century United States.[24] Central to this scholarship has been an interpretive expansion of the "political" beyond the realms of parties, courts, regional coalitions, and elite intellectuals.[25] Moreover, recent political histories have highlighted the inseparability of nineteenth-century Americans' political activations and their economic concerns.

The Political Reconstruction of American Tobacco builds upon these insights by emphasizing figures whose economic identities—as tobacconists, growers, warehousemen, scientists, and so forth—drove their political innovations. At the same time, this book pushes beyond a common tendency among historians of the late nineteenth century to associate politics with reactions against the reigning political economy, or, inversely, to associate market creation with "corruption."[26] The political movements across tobacco's commodity chain were activated by the possibility of producing—not merely resisting—the market, and for the most part they sought to accomplish their political goals through modes of democratic activism, including interest-group formation, conventions, and petitioning.

Perhaps the most consequential outcome of postbellum tobacco politics was institutional development, particularly of the American state. From the Civil War to the Progressive Era, tobacco's political economy demonstrated the centrality of the federal state in the orchestration of economic life. Reconstructing tobacco's commodity chain, promoting the power of manufacturers, and achieving global dominance of tobacco production required dramatic public intervention into the tobacco market as well as the cultivation of a reliable partnerships between policymakers, public administrators, trade associations, corporations, and farmers.[27] This was not, then, the "battle between state and society" that one group of scholars has ascribed to the postbellum years; rather, tobacco's history suggests a dynamic and associational, albeit contested, partnership between "state" and seemingly "non-state" actors.[28] The political history of postbellum tobacco therefore provides a compelling case for what Stefan Link and Noam Maggor have called "an American developmental state," which managed to "forge, mobilize, and ring-fence markets" and thereby "fueled the reorientation of American capitalism from agrarian exports to domestic industrialization."[29] The history of the tobacco tax exemplifies this situation. Historians have long characterized the postbellum fiscal regime based on what it lacked, including an income tax, an inheritance tax, and most of the war-era excises. It was, scholars have suggested, a product of "cutting back" and "phasing out" the comprehensive war tax system.[30] But such cutting back was only possible because policymakers and their tobacco industry partners created a new revenue system of unprecedented peacetime scope, forging in the process an entirely new structure for tobacco's commodity chain.

The reconstruction of tobacco's commodity chain likewise illustrates the global context of American state development. Contrary to Americanists' ambivalence about the postbellum state, scholars such as Charles Maier and Jürgen Osterhammel have pinpointed the latter half of the nineteenth century as the springboard of modern statehood.[31] Amid the global reconstructions of the 1860s and 1870s, every developing state made tobacco a source of public revenue. Tobacco was thus important not only for commercial purposes but as a source of geopolitical influence, a means by which states assured the sovereignty of their public finances or even, as the United States was able to do, linked other nation's tax systems to their own agricultural production.

In emphasizing agriculture's centrality to postbellum political economy and state development, this book stresses the rural basis of American power after the Civil War. Indeed, a defining characteristic of postbellum tobacco culture was the rapid expansion of tobacco's growing frontier. This "tobacco frontier" included regions that knew little or no tobacco farming prior to the 1870s and 1880s but by the twentieth century were either dominated by tobacco culture or were the sites of state experimentation in developing it.[32] As the tobacco frontier grew, the total national acreage planted in tobacco expanded from 395,000 acres during the 1860s to nearly two million by the early twentieth century.[33] The increasing total production was especially notable because it did not coincide with an increase in pounds per acre. In other words, tobacco growers were not becoming more efficient during this period—there were simply more of them, devoting more and more acres to tobacco. For those growers, life on the burgeoning tobacco frontier meant earning their livings from the land, struggling to pay landlords, and relying on household economies in addition to wage labor. These realities do not mean, however, that tobacco growers were anti-modern, but rather, as Christopher Clark has noted, that rural, household production remained central to American capitalist development amid the industrialization of the late-nineteenth and early-twentieth centuries.[34]

The Political Reconstruction of American Tobacco provides a new beginning to a well-known story. Between the 1920s and the middle of the twentieth century, tobacco companies made cigarettes into a product "so popular, so profitable, and so deadly" as to defy imagination.[35] Enjoying a degree of power almost unparalleled in corporate America, these companies captured regulatory power, manipulated science, innovated the field of public relations, and oversaw public policies that bolstered supply chains and expanded global consumption. For their part, tobacco growers charted a path quite different from their turn-of-the-century predecessors. Between the New Deal and the end of the twentieth century, they forged corporatist relations with the Department of Agriculture, land-grant colleges, and numerous other state institutions that promoted and protected tobacco culture.[36] The costs were—and remain—astounding, as global pandemics of lung cancer, heart disease, and emphysema killed roughly one hundred million people in the twentieth century. Yet the origins of that story are in the Civil War era, as policymakers and business leaders began reimagining the place of tobacco in American society.

1

"An Acknowledged Power in the Land"

Tobacconists, Taxation, and the Politics of Market Creation, 1862-1872

During the autumn of 1878, a commission of German dignitaries visited the United States to study the country's unusual tobacco tax system. Prompted by Bismarck's drive to monopolize the domestic tobacco trade, the commission—whose members included prominent public finance officials and tobacconists—hoped the "American system" might offer another option, one that increased tobacco revenue while preserving private industry.[1] They had reason for optimism. Federal tobacco receipts had risen rapidly during the preceding decade, from four percent of total federal income in 1868 to fifteen percent in 1878.[2] In the tumultuous age of Reconstruction and economic depression, tobacco had rapidly become a productive staple of public finance.

To understand the system, the commissioners embedded themselves at the Bureau of Internal Revenue (BIR) to pore over account books and assessment lists. Guided by Israel Kimball, BIR's Tobacco Division leader, they toured factories in Baltimore, Richmond, Chicago, and New York, observing the entwined processes of tobacco manufacture and tax collection. They explored the Lorillard factory in Jersey City, New Jersey, a facility so large its annual tax payments accounted for nearly three percent of total internal revenue. Along the way, they interviewed revenue officials and farmers, warehouse proprietors and tenement-house cigar makers. Before leaving, they met Edward Burke, editor of *Tobacco Leaf*, "the recognized organ of the trade," whose office enjoyed "a direct communication with the departments in Washington." Through each of their stops, the commissioners marveled at the cooperation that seemed to define the tobacco revenue system. "You have a good class of tax-payers here," noted one commissioner. "We have seen the highest and the lowest, and nowhere any one who wanted to evade the tax."[3]

What the commissioners could not account for, however, were the political origins of this "American system" of tobacco taxation. How had such a distinct and apparently well-functioning bureaucracy come to be, particularly amid the upheavals of war and Reconstruction? They studied the bills that created the tax, but found no evidence of "the motives nor the reasons assigned for the measure." The debates compiled within the *Congressional Globe* offered little of substance. "In many instances," they concluded in a final report of their tour, "the details have never been subject to a public debate."[4]

This was inaccurate. The tax had been "subject" to debate—years of it, in fact—but those debates had largely occurred outside the formal institutions of law, bureaucracy, and politics, such as Congress or the parties. Rather, the creation of the tobacco excise tax—a process that lasted from 1862 to 1872, included four major legislative overhauls, and nearly annual amendments—demonstrated the political mobilization and influence of business during the Civil War era. Frustrated by market instability under the earliest versions of the tax, tobacco manufacturers—whom I refer to as "tobacconists"—bemoaned the limits of democratic governance within an industrializing economy and a powerful, bureaucratic central state.[5] Throughout the 1860s, they repeatedly asked of themselves, as the journal *Tobacco Leaf* put it in 1868, "What does the man of business do when his agents act contrary to his wishes, and in consequence involve him in difficulties?"[6] Their responses to this question turned the decade-long creation of the tax into a decisive moment in the political economy of the late-nineteenth-century United States.

In pursuit of revenue reform, tobacconists embraced a wide range of democratic practices. Most visibly, they formed dozens of local trade associations that comprised a coherent, albeit bewildering, national network.[7] Among that network's most prominent constituents were the Tobacconists' National Association, the Association of the Tobacco Trade of Cincinnati, and the tobacco boards of trade of several major cities. Throughout the decade, these associations gathered for mass conventions and elected leaders who represented their members' regional and trade diversity. They published their opinions and debates in a trade journal, *Tobacco Leaf*, which claimed to be "The Largest Special Trade Paper in the World." They organized mass petition drives and influenced public opinion by publishing their criticisms of tax policy in major national newspapers. And as they struggled to outline a vision of tax reform that would suit the industry's various constituencies, they composed competing theories of business-state relations, bitterly challenged one another's positions, and forged coalitions and compromises. By the early 1870s, they would overcome their differences and devise the legal framework that buttressed federal public finance throughout the late-nineteenth and early-twentieth centuries.[8] That framework also created a new national tobacco market, defined in part by legal distinctions between trade sectors and, most clearly, federal protections for tobacconists as the only legal purchasers of leaf tobacco. This market was the foundation upon which the turn-of-the-century tobacco industry—integrated, monopsonistic, and global—was built.[9]

If it seems difficult to imagine business leaders, particularly tobacco interests, as exemplars of democratic practice, it was no less surprising to tobacconists themselves. Tobacconists held no special affinity for democracy, and political ideals rarely informed their actions.[10] Rather, they embraced democracy out of economic necessity. During the antebellum period, the tobacco industry was fractured along two faults: trade sector and region. As this chapter details, the agricultural sector of the tobacco trade asserted its political influence by rejecting tobacconists' earliest calls for reform and forcing tobacconists to embrace more sophisticated political mobilization. Yet regional divisions within their own ranks proved equally challenging for tobacconists. During the Civil War era, the key sectional division of the manufacturing trade was between the East, with its trade hub in New York City, and the West, where business gravitated toward Cincinnati. In other words, tobacco's sectional division mapped closely onto the Republican Party's own fault line—a reality that precluded a single firm or faction from legitimately speaking for the entire industry and dictating the terms of reform.[11] And so tobacconists organized, publicized, and petitioned their way to reform.

Tobacconists' politicization exemplified the associational nature of state building during the Civil War era. As they gathered in convention halls, established organizations, published a trade journal, petitioned Congress, and articulated competing visions of political economy, tobacconists were building state power by acting as mediators, as historian Brian Balogh has put it, "between citizen and state."[12] Tobacco manufacture was a "private sector," but its political activation and policy proposals had profoundly public consequences. That these developments occurred more than half a century before the developments most historians identify with associationalism suggests that this approach to governance emerged much earlier than scholars have previously understood.

This chapter considers tobacconists' democratic engagement from their initial political mobilization in the early 1860s until their triumph with the passage of the 1872 Internal Revenue Act. It begins following Congress's maladroit early attempts with internal taxation in 1862, which ignited controversy when analysts, such as Revenue Commissioner Joseph Lewis, recommended shifting tobacco taxes from the sale of manufactured products to the sale of raw leaf tobacco. The chapter then explores a significant 1864 convention of predominately Eastern tobacconists at New York's Cooper Union, during which delegates endorsed Lewis's leaf tax plan and launched their political movement. The Cooper Union convention initiated an intense period of politicization throughout the tobacco industry, as tobacconists, growers, and commission merchants attempted to shift the revenue debate in their favor. Amid this scramble, tobacconists increasingly criticized the government's failure to police "fraud," or the sale of untaxed tobacco. Tobacconists exploited the publicity surrounding frauds to promote their theory of business-state relations, which held that taxation necessitated a federal partnership with tobacconists to oversee every transaction in the tobacco economy while guaranteeing tobacconists' right to the nation's supply of raw leaf tobacco. At a series of conventions in 1867, tobacconists turned this theory into a policy proposal, which Congress adopted as part of the 1868 Revenue Act. Following that victory, tobacconists combined their organizations under an umbrella association—the National Tobacco Association (NTA). The NTA's signal achievement, the 1872 Internal Revenue Act, marked the culmination of this era of tobacco politics. Under the 1872 law, the federal state generated unprecedented tobacco revenues and tobacconists enjoyed political influence and market stability. Their critics in other sectors of the tobacco industry, however, would come to interpret the tobacconists' democracy as a corruption of the policymaking process.

Civil War Taxation and the Search for Tobacco's Value

When Congress passed its first internal revenue legislation of the Civil War era in 1862, the new law's tobacco provisions received scant attention. The law appeared in response to the fiscal crises of the early war years, as Union policymakers worried that bond sales and tariff revenue could not support the conflict's mounting costs.[13] The first internal revenue system was remarkable for its breadth, drawing from "almost all monetary transactions" through a sweeping tripartite system of income, excise, and ad valorem taxes.[14] Under this system, the newly established Bureau of Internal Revenue extracted levies from cigars, snuff, and chewing and smoking tobacco, while tobacconists (manufacturers and dealers) paid license fees of ten dollars—essentially the same taxes applied to all manufactured goods and professions.[15] As Congress debated the law throughout the spring of 1862, tobacco interests remained mostly aloof. Few tobacco-related petitions found their way to relevant congressional committees and debate over the law rarely focused on tobacco—a stark difference from later tax debates that suggested a lack of political organization among the tobacconists who would pay the tax, as well as a general lack of concern among tobacco growers.[16]

The earliest tobacco tax returns were a disappointment, generating only three million dollars in 1862 and eight million dollars in 1863. These failures vexed revenue analysts such as Internal Revenue Commissioner Joseph Lewis, who pointed out that tobacco taxation had been far more remunerative in other nations.[17] In Britain, a tobacco import duty generated more than thirty million dollars annually and tobacco and alcohol alone accounted for nearly half of all public revenue.[18] The French government's tobacco monopoly enjoyed profits of nearly five hundred percent on tobacco sales—most of that, as Lewis indignantly reminded policymakers, from "the manufacture and sale of that product of American soil."[19] If European models suggested the bright possibilities of tobacco taxation, however, they also highlighted the differences between the tobacco economies of Europe and North America.

A successful tobacco tax in the United States required a legal framework that suited the country's producer-driven, export-heavy, regionally diverse tobacco economy, as opposed to one that looked like the import-dependent systems of Britain or France. Revenue Commissioner Lewis's proposed framework would shift the point of payment from the sale of manufactured tobacco to the sale of raw leaf tobacco. It would also eliminate differentiated, quality-dependent rates in favor of a universal rate, thereby disregarding questions of quality and value. If Lewis had his way, tobacco would be treated like most other commodities: whether grown in Connecticut or Kentucky, for domestic consumption or export, for chew or cigars, revenue officials would assess a single value for it all. In his annual reports to Congress in 1863 and 1864, Lewis argued that his plan would simplify collections, improve revenue returns, and protect domestic manufacturers by increasing the cost of tobacco importation for foreign governments.[20]

Lewis's "leaf tax" proposal was the spark that animated tobacco tax politics in the Civil War era. Soon after its publication, the proposal provoked frantic responses from exporters and growers who viewed tobacco as one of the Union's only true cash crops, and as such, an important conduit between the Union states and the global economy. "These southern states who ... have left us, have left us comparatively without a market," remarked one congressional opponent of Lewis's proposal. "We have nothing to sell but tobacco, comparatively speaking, and that we sell abroad."[21] Lewis's critics charged that he had exaggerated the primacy of American tobacco in foreign markets. In December 1863, a group of New York tobacco exporters countered the leaf tax proposal with a detailed analysis of the global tobacco market that suggested foreign governments had become reliant on "home growth" since mid-century. If the federal government burdened U.S. growers and their global consumers with a tax, tobacco culture "would be largely increased in other countries where they cultivate the article already, and new regions would make the experiment."²² One month later, Commissioner of Agriculture Isaac Newton expanded upon the exporters' conclusions. In a letter to John Sherman, Chair of the Senate Committee on Agriculture, Newton argued that foreign governments were "rapidly" developing tobacco culture "to the substitution of their own tobacco for American."²³ As Lewis's critics understood the situation, a tax on leaf tobacco would hinder domestic growers while promoting competition abroad.

Opposition to the leaf tax demonstrated the political support tobacco growers enjoyed within the northern agricultural reform movement and border state agricultural associations that had organized during the antebellum period.²⁴ Leaders of state agricultural societies, such as the Kentucky State Agricultural Society's L.J. Bradford, fumed the tax would "annihilate" tobacco exports.²⁵ A representative of the Ohio State Board of Agriculture, meanwhile, contended it "would put an end to tobacco culture in Ohio."²⁶ Editors of agricultural periodicals were equally defiant. *Moore's Rural New Yorker* argued that a leaf tax would establish a precedent for more taxes on "products of the soil," while Chicago's *Prairie Farmer* celebrated widespread opposition to the leaf tax as evidence of agriculturists' "ascendent" [sic] political fortunes.²⁷ These arguments resonated among Northern farmers, including those who did not grow tobacco, had spent decades constructing a position of influence within the federal state, and were well situated to resist fiscal interference in their trade.²⁸

The Republican Congress, itself imbricated in northern agricultural politics, refused to adopt Lewis's proposal. Instead, facing a fiscal crisis and desperate for greater revenue in the spring of 1864, lawmakers simply raised taxes on manufactured tobacco.²⁹ For the highest grossing categories of "cavendish," "plug," and "fine cut" tobacco, the new law increased the tax from fifteen cents per pound to forty cents; on "smoking" tobacco, generally considered a lower quality, the tax rose from five cents per pound to thirty-five cents. Cigar rates, which had ranged between $1.50 and $3.50 per thousand under the 1862 law, reached forty dollars per thousand.³⁰ Yet few legislators were confident in the new rates or, for that matter, in the categories by which the system distinguished tobacco products' values.

Congressional debate over the new rates was entangled by the problem of "thing uncertainty," or the distinction of "one type of good from the others."³¹ This was precisely the issue Lewis had sought to circumvent when he proposed a universal rate for leaf tobacco. During the 1864 debates, legislators repeatedly asked what made "plug" or "fine cut" tobacco more valuable than "smoking."

Others wondered how—and by whom—these differences could be identified and measured. On one side of the debate, men like New Hampshire's Senator Daniel Clark argued that tobacco could be divided into a small number of categories that generally corresponded to the socioeconomic statuses of consumers. Clark was especially interested in levying a higher tax (at one point he suggested 45 cents per pound) on "fine-cut" tobacco, a second tier of 35 cents per pound for plug (chewing) tobacco, and a lower tax of 25 cents per pound for tobacco with the "stem in," which was commonly considered a quality only selected by the poorest consumers. By taxing types of tobacco manufacture as opposed to qualities of tobacco, Clark and others chose a simplified, predictable, universal system of reading the tobacco market. At the same time, they were willing to risk attaching relatively high taxes—as much as 600 percent, in one estimate—to cheaper tobaccos that happened to be manufactured as "fine-cut" or "plug." On the other side of the debate, Western senators such as Michigan's Zachariah Chandler and Missouri's John Henderson called for lower rates and feared Clark's distinctions exaggerated differences in quality and value among tobacco types. These men believed the important distinctions in tobacco emerged in the soil; what happened after was merely a matter of aesthetics or personal taste, but not integral to the value of the commodity. Henderson claimed that "the very moment tobacco is sent to New York and looked at by a purchaser there, he can tell the exact quality of the tobacco, and precisely what to pay for it." The state could harness that expertise by using those already "acquainted with the business" to gauge tobacco quality prior to its manufacture. Clark, meanwhile, remained deeply skeptical of distinctions. When Henderson asserted there was a "first quality, second quality, third quality" inherent in tobacco, Clark retorted that the boundaries in those distinctions were so unclear that no assessor could consistently identify them.[32] In the end, a version of Clark's proposal triumphed. Congress raised the tax on plug, twist, Cavendish, and fine-cut to 40 cents per pound, on smoking tobacco to 35 cents, and on smoking tobacco with stems to 15 cents.

The significance of this debate transcended the problem of tax rates. In debating the tax, policymakers were compelled to ponder more fundamental questions about this enigmatic commodity.[33] Where did tobacco find its value? Were there distinct differences in the qualities of tobaccos, and if so, how significant were those differences? Were the rich man's "fine-cut" and the poor man's "stem-in" truly distinct? How—and by whom—could their differences be identified and measured? Did price matter, or should the tax code emphasize differences in tobacco's region of growth, its style of manufacture, or its appeal to varying classes of consumers? Congress could debate these questions endlessly, enlisting all the expertise they could find, but they would never objectively "know" tobacco because tobacco was not objectively knowable—at least not by any individual, firm, or trade sector. Rather, the cultural and economic values associated with different "types" of tobacco could only become knowable through a dynamic policymaking process that produced a legal framework to govern the industry—a reality that attracted flocks of tobacconists, growers, and speculators to Washington's lobbies throughout 1864 as they attempted to shift debate in their favor.[34] Yet lobbyists failed to influence debate because they lacked sophisticated political organizations and promoted their narrow self-interest. The result was confusion and exasperation, feelings New Hampshire Senator John Hale captured when he announced, after nearly a week of debate, "I give up. I see I do not know anything about tobacco."[35]

The confusion surrounding the tobacco provisions of the 1864 Internal Revenue Act produced yet another ineffective law. Although the new rates generated eleven million dollars in their first fiscal year—three million more than in 1863—collections were spectacularly inefficient.[36] Under the original rates in 1863, the government collected taxes on more than thirty-eight million pounds of plug, twist, and cavendish tobacco and twenty-four million pounds of smoking tobacco. In 1864, however, those totals plummeted to 14.5 million pounds and 7.7 million pounds, respectively.[37] Either Americans had given up their tobacco habits, or the new rates had badly distorted the market, allowing vast quantities to avoid taxation.

"Anxiety, Perplexity, Doubt": The Tobacconists' Mobilization

In response to the agricultural backlash against Lewis's leaf tax proposal and Congress's incomprehension of the tobacco economy, a group of New York tobacconists called for the political organization of the nation's tobacco manufacturers and dealers.[38] In December 1864, three months after the second revenue act became operative, "three thousand persons connected with the cigar and tobacco trade" heeded that call by convening at New York City's Cooper Union.[39] Prior to this gathering, manufacturers and dealers had lacked the sort of political infrastructure that growers and exporters harnessed in their response to Lewis: they had no established associations, no trade journals, and no high-profile federal official, such as the Commissioner of Agriculture, to endorse their case. But manufacturers and dealers were not entirely without political assets.

Most importantly, the Cooper Union convention displayed the extensive business and personal relationships that connected elite tobacconists, smaller proprietors, and government officials. Among the elite delegates at Cooper Union were the wealthiest tobacconists in the country, including the convention's president, William E. Lawrence, son-in-law of a former New York City mayor and senior partner of the chewing tobacco firm A.H. Mickle & Sons; David Hunter McAlpin, whose manufacturing operation dominated "seven or eight city lots" in lower Manhattan; Joseph Hall, a cigar manufacturer "of wealth and eminence" whose firm "contributed as much toward the development of the Cigar Trade in the United States as any one engaged in the pursuit"; and Pierre Lorillard, scion of one of New York's wealthiest families and director of the nation's oldest tobacco business, P. Lorillard & Co.[40] While New Yorkers dominated the proceedings, they were joined by allies from smaller eastern markets in Connecticut, Massachusetts, New Jersey, Pennsylvania, and Rhode Island, as well as the border cities of Baltimore and St. Louis. Hundreds of smaller manufacturers and dealers joined as well, including a New York cigar manufacturer named Edward Burke, who became the convention's leading spokesperson and the author of its resolutions. At the convention and banquet that followed, delegates welcomed their allies in government, including New York City's revenue assessor and several inspectors. The relationships between delegates and their guests almost certainly extended back to the internal revenue era's inauguration in 1862, and, in many cases, into the antebellum period.

The Cooper Union convention empowered tobacconists to leverage their business and personal relationships into political capacity. It did so by providing a venue for tobacconists to identify shared interests and an opportunity to produce a statement of shared purpose; an organizational structure in which delegates assumed official posts, such as president, secretary, or membership in various committees; and a high-profile platform from which they could announce their goal of reforming tax policy to Congress, the press, and the general public. As Edward Burke announced to the convention, "we are henceforth to be regarded as an acknowledged power in the land; a vital force; one of the main arteries of national life!"[41]

Cooper Union delegates' primary argument was that the 1864 Revenue Act placed excessive burdens on their trade.[42] Under the first revenue act in 1862, Congress had regulated tobacco as it had other industries. Tobacconists had to obtain a license before continuing their business, submit monthly returns, provide statements regarding the place and style of manufacture, and declare their intended markets. Under the second revenue act in 1864, Congress intensified regulations upon tobacconists. Proprietors now had to report specific buyers as opposed to proposed ones; they were to notify assessors of "every change or

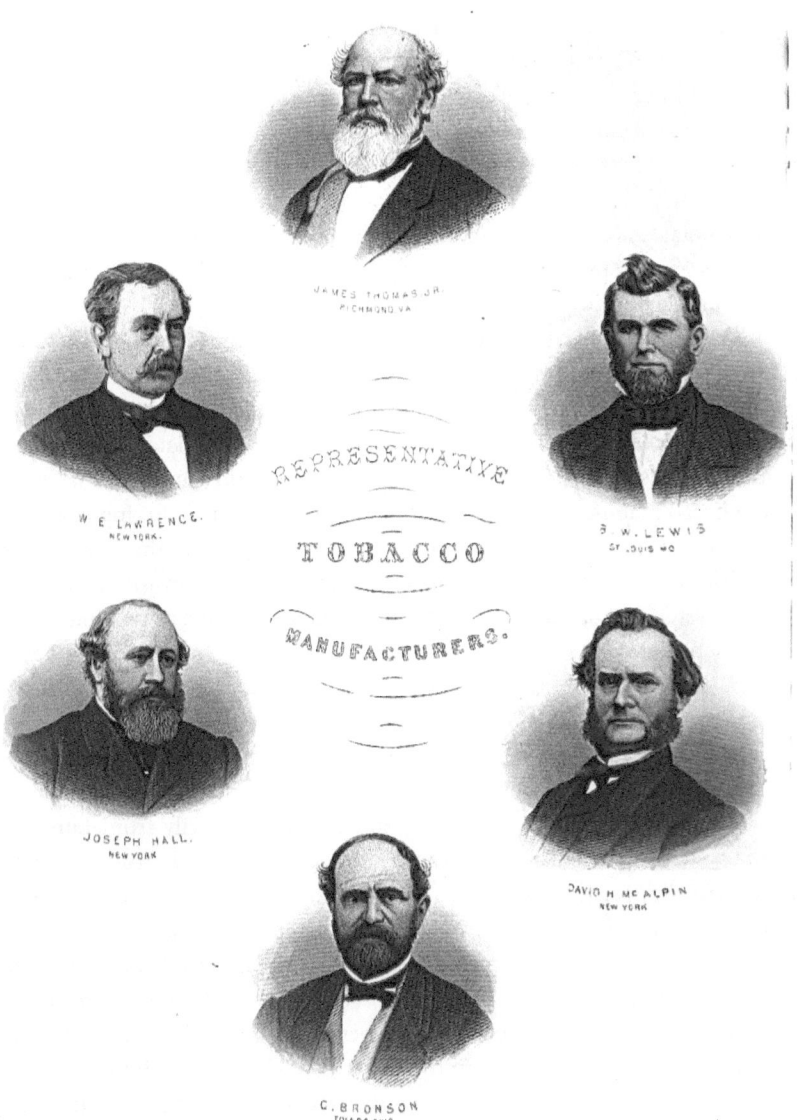

Figure 3. Several of the Cooper Union convention's elite delegates appeared as "Representative Tobacco Manufacturers" in J. Leander Bishop's *A History of American Manufactures*. Pictured above are William E. Lawrence (upper left), Joseph Hall (lower left), and David Hunter McAlpin (lower right). Lawrence would eventually become the first president of the National Tobacco Association.

removal made" on their premises; their records were to be open "to the inspection of any person"; and, for violation of these regulations, tobacconists faced severe fines or imprisonment.[43] For most tobacconists, these regulations may have been acceptable if Congress had not also imposed such staggeringly high rates. It was an article of faith among the Cooper Union delegates that Congress had invented a value that tobacco could not bear—a mistake Edward Burke compared to selling potatoes for the price of diamonds.[44] High rates coupled with punitive regulations trapped manufacturers in a cycle of "stagnation," and, as Burke put it, "anxiety, perplexity, doubt."[45]

Burke detailed these grievances in a lengthy report of the tobacco market since the 1850s, which delegates subsequently printed and distributed to one thousand legislators, newspapers, and tobacco interests across the country.[46] Drawing on evidence gathered from tobacconists' testimonials as well as data from the Census and Agricultural bureaus, Burke sought to convince his audience that established tobacco manufacturing firms, and the Treasury, were suffering under the new law. Yet Burke's report did not reject taxation outright. Rather, the Cooper Union delegates' position was that the only way to avoid tax evasion, ensure an equitable system of collection, and generate as much revenue as possible was to revive Joseph Lewis's proposal to place the tax on leaf tobacco. Unlike Lewis, however, Cooper Union delegates suggested an audacious legal framework that would support the leaf tax.

At the center of this proposed framework was strict federal management of tobacco's commodity chain. G.W. Gail, a partner in the Baltimore firm Gail & Ax, had devised the plan in early 1864 and borrowed heavily from European revenue systems, particularly the French monopoly.[47] Growers would obtain a tobacco-growing permit from local collectors, to whom they would declare the number of acres they had devoted to tobacco. Following harvest and curing, they would transport their crop to bonded warehouses, which the federal government would establish in every tobacco district. There, tobacconists could purchase tobacco, paying the tax simultaneously.[48] In essence, the federal government would channel every leaf of tobacco from the soil to the tobacconist. Burke favorably compared the plan to European tobacco monopolies, writing in 1865 that "[w]herever there has been a government monopoly, the result has been of the most satisfactory character."[49] This proposed monopoly, however, differed from European models in that it relied on a partnership between federal regulators and private tobacconists, who would pay the tax but enjoy dominion over the nation's supply of raw leaf tobacco.

The Cooper Union convention marked a turning point in the politics of tobacco taxation. The widespread distribution of the convention's resolutions, the wealth and influence of its delegates, and the audacity of its proposal sparked an organizational surge among tobacco interests. Throughout 1865, newly formed unions and trade associations in Connecticut, Illinois, Massachusetts, Missouri, New York, and Pennsylvania flooded the House Ways and Means Committee with petitions supporting the Cooper Union leaf tax plan.[50] These petitions tended to reiterate the convention's resolutions while reminding representatives that smaller manufacturers, and not merely industry elites such as Lorillard, supported the leaf tax. Groups including the Cigar Makers' Union and its affiliated branches, New York's German Cigar and Tobacco Manufacturers and Dealers, and the Tobacco and Cigar Manufacturers of the City of Saint Louis begged policymakers to place the tax "where it unmistakably belongs on the RAW MATERIAL."[51]

Yet the post-Cooper Union organizational surge also reinvigorated agricultural opposition to the leaf tax, as growers' associations derided the plan from regions as varied as Ohio's Miami Valley, West Virginia's Kanawha Valley, and New England's Connecticut Valley.[52] Resistance was especially vehement in the rural West and Border States, where tobacco growers tended to produce a cheaper leaf than their counterparts in other regions. They offered two rebuttals to the Cooper Union plan. First, they rejected the logic of a regressive single tax on the all-leaf tobacco, which would burden growers of cheaper tobaccos with the same taxes as growers of expensive fine leaf in, for instance, Connecticut. Second, growers argued that although tobacconists appeared to pay the tax under the Cooper Union plan, they would surely shift the tax incidence to their suppliers and consumers. "Say the average value of our tobacco … is 20 cents per pound, subject to a tax, to be paid before removal, of 20 cents per pound," wrote a group of West Virginia growers. "Will the manufacturer give us 40 cents per pound, being the value and the tax combined? Certainly not." Likely drawing upon the lessons of their decades-long conflict with Virginia's planter elite, West Virginia growers presciently realized that tobacconists would likely "combine and monopolize" to keep leaf prices low, a problem the tax would only exacerbate.[53]

In addition to attacks from the agricultural sector, the Cooper Union proposal aroused sectional conflict among tobacconists. One Quincy, Illinois manufacturer contended that the Cooper Union plan would "destroy the Western tobacco interest," and that perhaps such destruction was the convention delegates' goal all along.[54] A petition from Chicago accused the Cooper Union convention's "heavy

Capitalists" of seeking "every opportunity ... for monopolizing and controlling the market."[55] One Kentucky critic suggested that the "real object" of the Cooper Union plan was "to throw the entire manufacturing business into the hands of large capitalists."[56] According to these petitioners, the leaf plan was but an opening gambit in the construction of a national tobacco economy dominated by major Eastern firms. H.S. Gunkel, a Miami Valley grower and president of the Ohio Tobacco Growers' Association, warned Westerners that "This tobacco business is only a 'drop in the bucket' compared with the stupendous system of infamous class legislation for the sole and exclusive benefit of New England manufacturers."[57] Although Cooper Union delegates had ostensibly hoped to transcend the tobacco economy's sectionalism, anti-leaf tax petitions suggested that unity was improbable.

By the spring of 1865, the debate over the leaf tax had become a struggle for control of the industry. The struggle intensified when Congress created a Revenue Commission to analyze and recommend changes to the revenue system. Chaired by political economist David Ames Wells, the commission studied the operations of the internal revenue system, gathered testimony from industry experts, and framed legislation.[58] For the industry's competing factions, Wells' willingness to hear testimony, along with his influence in Congress, represented the clearest opportunity yet to shape tax law in their favor.

Cooper Union delegates took notice and reconvened in November 1865 under a new title, the Tobacconists' National Association [TNA]. In addition to renewing their call for a leaf tax, TNA adopted a sophisticated organizational scheme that included an Executive Committee, a Committee on Resolutions, and a Committee of Conference. They also elected a slate of officers, including Lorillard, the Detroit manufacturer and future Michigan governor John J. Bagley, and, as president, William E. Lawrence. New Yorkers dominated the association's leadership, but officers also represented eleven other states, even anti-leaf strongholds such as Illinois, Kentucky, Missouri, and Ohio. With David Wells and the Revenue Commission in mind, the new arrangements emphasized TNA's professional legitimacy and reinforced their claim to representation of the "Northern, Eastern, Western, and Middle States" and support among "the oldest, wealthiest, and most respectable leaf and manufacturing firms in the United States."[59]

The agricultural opponents of leaf taxation likewise attempted to broadcast their political legitimacy to the Revenue Commission. From Kentucky, L.J. Bradford—president of the state's agricultural society— convened the "National Tobacco Convention" in September 1865. Backed by delegates from Virginia, Kentucky, and throughout the West, the convention's organizers claimed this would be the first public discussion of revenue policy to include representatives from every sector of the industry, including growers, manufacturers, commission merchants, and dealers. Edward Burke attended in hopes of generating Western and agricultural support for the leaf tax, but the convention lasted only one hour—just enough time for a few Kentuckians to rebuke the Cooper Union proposal before endorsing plans for modest rate reductions and a shift to *ad valorem* taxes that would reflect tobacco's fluctuating values.[60] Not that Bradford and other agriculturists rejected any federal role in the tobacco industry. Rather, they encouraged Congress to continue promoting tobacco through protection from foreign competition, "endowments of agricultural colleges, experimental farms, national fairs," and the distribution of tobacco seeds. As another Kentucky analyst put it, "The planter and the farmer should be invited and encouraged to extend [tobacco] culture, rather than be annoyed with the vexatious requirements involved in a direct tax upon its production."[61] In other words, in opposition to the TNA's preference for federal surveillance of tobacco growers, Bradford offered a theory of a promotional state in which farmers would sustain a booming domestic tobacco market.

Bradford and other agriculturists situated their opposition to the leaf tax within the broader politics of Reconstruction and emancipation. While Eastern manufacturers almost never discussed these issues, leaf tax opponents rightly understood that the interests of ex-masters and wage labor proponents would influence the reconstruction of tobacco's political economy.[62] For ex-masters, the leaf-tax proponents' vision of a federal tax bureaucracy dictating where, when, and to whom they could sell tobacco was anathema. As Bradford explained for the Revenue Commission, such a bureaucracy would burden growers with "surveys, permits to plant, returns of growth, inspections, shipping permits" policed by an "outlying army of guerilla attachés selected to … convey the crops to these Government receptacles."[63] Increased government oversight was particularly disconcerting because it enabled federal leverage over tobacco farmers and, by necessity, their labor practices. For free labor proponents, the TNA plan threatened the cultivation of a major cash crop, potentially hampering the tobacco South's embrace of wage labor. This concern was most poignant in Virginia, where Freedmen's Bureau officials struggled to coax freedpeople, who prioritized the preservation of household economies, as well as planters fighting to retain their mastery, into wage labor contracts. A profitable tobacco crop might help this process along, but it would be difficult to achieve such a crop if tobacco were bound up in a complex machinery of tax collection.[64] As the tobacco South approached its first planting season since emancipation, Bradford and other agricultural opponents emphasized these concerns, which they knew weighed heavily upon policymakers and the Revenue Commission.

Aware that "a vast majority of the trade" opposed the leaf tax, Wells and his colleagues hedged against the leaf tax proposal. In its January 1866 report to Congress, the Revenue Commission offered no analysis of tobacco taxation other than the opinion *"that the tax should not be laid upon the leaf."*[65] TNA president William E. Lawrence criticized the commission for "so summary a conclusion," suggesting that the commission had not taken the "requisite" time to consider tobacco taxation.[66] Although some sectors of the trade continued making pro-leaf overtures in 1866, the Revenue Commission's declaration effectively ended the leaf tax debate.

Two years of struggle over the leaf tax, however, had produced a tobacco industry of unprecedented political consciousness and organization. The TNA was the most conspicuous example of this development, but others soon followed. In 1866, the New York City Tobacco Board of Trade [TBOT] formed to represent the interests of businesses operating between tobacconists and consumers, such as "receivers, commission merchants, and dealers in manufactured plug tobacco."[67] The TBOT's primary interests were the reduction of taxes and the reform of trade regulations, particularly surrounding the operations of bonded warehouses. Commission merchants prioritized their opposition to high tax rates that they argued would reduce profits for every sector of the trade—not just the manufacturers who paid them. Commission merchants were especially concerned that high rates would keep small manufacturing firms out of business. Because tobacconists relied on commission merchants for sales, more manufacturers in business meant commission merchants could play them off one another for higher commissions.[68]

Also in 1866, the tobacconists of Covington, Kentucky and Cincinnati founded the Association of the Tobacco Trade of Cincinnati [ATTC]. A powerful counter to the New York-based TNA and TBOT, the ATTC represented the West's most important tobacco hub and its business allies throughout the region. The ATTC challenged the political influence of Eastern tobacco associations by organizing multiple sectors of the trade, including tobacconists but also dealers, commission merchants, and growers.[69] Further, the Ohio General Assembly had empowered the ATTC to govern the Ohio River Valley's tobacco trade under an 1866 act authorizing "the incorporation of boards of trade and chambers of commerce." Under that law, the Association established a central Tobacco Exchange for the region; appointed inspectors of leaf warehouses, factories, and dealerships; collected bonds for its members' "faithful discharge" of duties; investigated "charges of misconduct"; and brokered disputes.[70]

This governing authority enabled the ATTC to gather extensive "statistical information relative to the trade" and craft detailed analyses of the federal tax system. For example, in an effort to prove that rates under the 1864 revenue law were "disproportionate" to the value of smoking tobacco, ATTC leader J.P. Spence compiled the average leaf price for tobacconists in the West, estimated the value added by various manufacturing processes, and thus the rate of taxation relative to the costs of producing plug, Cavendish, and smoking.[71] Like the Cooper Union report in 1864 and TNA report in 1865, these analyses were intended to render tobacco "legible" for policymakers, thereby reducing the official confusion many manufacturers blamed for the unpopular 1864 law.[72]

Fraud, Gaming, and the Tobacconists' "Perpetual Lien"

Legibility had also been the goal of leaf tax supporters like Joseph Lewis and the Cooper Union delegates, who had hoped to sidestep their industry's complexities with a single, universal tax. With the demise of that proposal, associations such as TNA and ATTC dedicated themselves to the production of ever more detailed statistical analysis for the benefit of Congress, the Treasury, and the newly appointed Special Commissioner of Revenue, David Wells.[73] As one TNA leader declared in 1865, "we must educate Congress."[74]

The primary goal of this "education" was to convince policymakers and revenue administrators that the tobacco tax was failing because of widespread tax reduction behaviors tobacconists referred to as "frauds." Cooper Union delegates in 1864 were the first to protest revenue frauds publicly, but the term had been a popular "rhetorical club" among tobacco interests for decades.[75] Since the eighteenth century, tobacco growers and merchants in Virginia, Maryland, and other tobacco-producing states had defended government inspection regimes to limit fraud among their colleagues and ensure their commodity's international "merchantability."[76] Tobacconists, meanwhile, were among the most common victims of the counterfeit currencies that proliferated during the antebellum era.[77] Not that "fraud" was unique to tobacco: as tobacconists surely understood, the urban press had long cultivated a popular fascination with counterfeits, embezzlers, and other deceitful beneficiaries of antebellum capitalism.[78] As Civil War-era tobacconists fumed against the consequences of taxation, they drew on this rhetorical heritage in a potent condemnation of the Internal Revenue system's shortcomings. Predictably, the press caught on. In the years after Cooper Union delegates first propagated the idea of tobacco frauds, newspapers throughout the country offered regular descriptions of "tobacco swindles" so widespread that, as the *New York Times* asserted, the "uninitiated will be lost in astonishment."[79]

Tobacconists blamed the 1864 revenue law for the proliferation of fraud. The regulatory system developed under that law, they argued, forced "legitimate" businesses to pay high taxes but failed to prohibit illicit competition.[80] And as the illicit market drew customers away from tax-paying tobacconists, it depressed prices, distorted values, and, according to Edward Burke, rendered "everything uncertain and insecure."[81] "The law," according to one petition, "affords such opportunities for fraud that our business will soon pass entirely into the hands of irresponsible men and fraudulent combinations."[82] David Wells' analysis of the revenue system supported these claims: under the 1864 law, he alerted Congress, more than fifty percent of all tobacco—roughly forty-five million pounds each year—evaded the tax.[83] Yet revenue officials struggled to identify, much less prosecute, illicit manufacturers. A congressional committee empowered to investigate tobacco and whiskey frauds in December 1866 turned up paltry evidence.[84] Revenue inspectors in New York City, according to Burke, were continually "discouraged" by their inability to check the flood of untaxed tobacco.[85]

The failure to prosecute evasion was at least partly due to the law's vulnerability to "gaming."[86] Although any tax system presents opportunities for gaming, or quasi-legal reduction strategies, tobacco's epistemological uncertainties left the tax especially vulnerable to these evasions. Drawing on the complaints of tobacconists, David Wells catalogued a litany of common gaming practices. For example, because revenue law based tax rates on the sale price of finished tobacco products, tobacconists often reduced their prices below their "proper net cost."[87] Similarly, Wells notified Congress that some tobacconists asked revenue officials to inspect packages of smoking tobacco and then replaced the contents with chew, "thus enabling chewing tobacco to escape with a fifteen cent tax, when by law it is required to pay forty cents."[88] A number of tobacconists also complained of "speculators" who, in anticipation of a tax rate change, stockpiled their tobacco under the old rate and then flooded the market with cheap tobacco after Congress increased the tax.[89]

Tobacconists' associations seized on the controversies surrounding "frauds" to advance their evolving theories of taxation and the state. As they had been during the struggle over the leaf tax, Edward Burke and other TNA leaders were at the forefront of this development. While they complained about numerous gaming strategies, Eastern manufacturers specifically criticized farmers for cutting or pressing tobacco from their own fields instead of purchasing tax-paid market tobacco. This practice was so widespread that several major agricultural journals even promoted it by marketing tobacco seeds and providing instructions for building a tobacco press. "If men will use [tobacco]," opined the editors of Albany's *Country Gentleman*, "they had better grow it than pay their money for it."[90] In the wake of the failed leaf tax campaign, this practice infuriated TNA leaders. As Burke and his allies understood it, home production was simply fraud. Growers and other "country people," he protested, "have no more right to use tobacco in the natural state than residents of the city have to manufacture it and evade the tax, or either do to smuggle goods through a custom-house, or rob a bank."[91] If the federal government were to tax tobacco, this logic suggested, then *all* tobacco must be taxed. And if taxes were to be extracted from tobacco in its manufactured state, then tobacconists had an "indefeasible right" to all tobacco in the land.[92] These conclusions returned the TNA and other leading political associations to the core principle of the leaf tax proposal: that the collection of the tax necessitated extensive federal control over tobacco's commodity chain, and that tobacconists deserved a privileged position within that chain.

The monopolistic implications of the tobacconists' logic were not lost on critics, particularly those in the agricultural community. Drawing from the political tradition of antimonopolism, agriculturists such as Kentucky's L.J. Bradford warned David Wells that tobacconists were attempting to "realize in the tobacco trade that odious thing to Americans—a monopoly."[93] Lewis Bollman, a Pennsylvania farmer and chief statistician in the Department of Agriculture, likewise complained that concerns about the "public debt" among the TNA and other lobbies was but a "disguise" to promote the "prerogative of the manufacturer" and render growers "tributary to the manufacturing interests."[94] These criticisms rested on the pillars of nineteenth-century antimonopolism: that monopolies favored one class to the disadvantage of all others, and that such favoritism distorted competition and manipulated the natural value of goods.[95]

According to tobacconists, however, antimonopolists' worst fears had already been realized under the 1864 revenue law. The federal government's simultaneous extraction of revenue from major tobacconists and failure to police evasions favored one class—"knaves" and "dishonest persons"—over all others.[96] The proliferation of fraud, meanwhile, had destroyed the tobacco economy's natural competition. As Burke put it, fraud "unsettles prices, it deranges values, it demoralizes customers, it undermines the very foundations of the trade, and renders everything uncertain and insecure."[97] The answer to this monopoly of fraud was an "honest" tobacconists' monopoly on the purchase of leaf tobacco, which could provide the security, and revenue, that had been lost since 1864.[98] That is, according to tobacconists, the Bureau of Internal Revenue would have to eliminate forms of tobacco exchange that had existed for decades and instead channel all supply and demand to tax-paying tobacconists.[99] As Burke argued in 1865, "To direct this interest aright, the Government must take hold of it—must grasp it—must clutch it with hooks of steel and bands of iron."[100]

Their theory of taxation led Burke, Cincinnati's J.P. Spence, and other industry spokesmen to see tobacco manufacturing as an auxiliary operation of the federal government. Spence, for example, characterized tobacconists as "the agents who stand between the revenue department that receives the tax, and the consumer who pays it." And as "agents" of revenue collection, tobacconists were entitled to dominion over every leaf grown and every ounce consumed in the country. "We are the taxpayers of tobacco," Spence argued, "and must be protected."[101] Burke called this tobacconists' "perpetual lien," which he claimed extended over "the entire consumption of the country."[102] "On every pound raised and consumed in the country," he argued, "the Government, first, to the extent of the tax sought from it, and the manufacturers, second, have a prior claim; and whatever impairs the value of that claim defrauds the one and robs the other."[103]

Several postwar conditions prepared legislators to accept this formulation. For one, the federal government faced significant fiscal challenges, including the funding of expanded military and administrative capacities; the production of a large enough surplus to inject greenbacks into financial markets during seasonal contractions; and the servicing of the nation's $1 billion debt.[104] Further, as tobacconists constructed their argument for monopoly, most other industries were demanding retrenchment.[105] Tobacco interests expressed their share of anti-tax sentiment as well, the editors of *Tobacco Leaf* going so far as to protest that tobacconists had "the best plucked pockets" in the country.[106] But a third factor—tobacco's status as a "luxury"—led tobacconists to expect continued taxation as the war drew to a close. As House Ways and Means chairman Justin Morrill put it in 1866, "all civilized nations requiring large revenues" must extract "the largest sums" from luxuries—namely, tobacco, beer, and spirits.[107] In this context, so-called tobacco "frauds" threatened much more than tobacconists' bottom lines—they represented a challenge to the fiscal viability of the Reconstruction-era state and the Republican coalition that ruled it.

More broadly, by constructing a commodity chain in place of the antebellum tobacco "web," with its many options of exchange, the tobacconists' plan provided the structure for a national tobacco economy—as opposed to local, and particularly rural economies that tobacco culture might also have supported—and thereby complimented Republicans' vision for state and market development. Thus, although their monopolistic theory of taxation departed dramatically from antebellum norms, tobacconists found themselves in a potential position of leverage.[108] Their burden was to turn that leverage into policy.

"The Union and Head-Centre" of American Tobacco

An essential voice in this process was New York City's Charles Pfirshing, a Bavarian immigrant and founder of the trade journal *Tobacco Leaf*. Since establishing the journal in 1865, Pfirshing had sought to instill a sense of shared interest throughout the industry's competing sectors and regional sections. In *Tobacco Leaf*'s inaugural issue, he described his papers' determination to "promote the development of the tobacco interest in all its branches" and "to serve as an organ of communication between the different classes engaged" in the business.[109] In an attempt to familiarize competing sections with one another, he compiled a *Directory of Tobacco Men*, which listed hundreds of manufacturers and dealers as well as auctioneers, box makers, brokers, licorice paste dealers, and tin foil manufacturers.[110] Familiarity and communication, Pfirshing believed, would promote political organization and, eventually, legislative reform. But if the trade remained fractured, its members alienated from legislators who did "not know how to make laws for taxing tobacco," tobacco's depression would continue.[111]

In other words, Pfirshing believed that for the federal government to meet its obligations and for tobacco to flourish, legislators and tobacconists alike would have to embrace a new vision of representative governance. "Every large industrial interest," Pfirshing suggested, "should be entrusted to the hand of those who are practically as well as theoretically acquainted with its requirements, and to no others." The elected officials of the people, ignorant of the tobacco trade, were ill suited to govern such an industry. Or, as Pfirshing suggested in 1867, "Tobacconists only can faithfully represent tobacconists."[112]

In February 1867, roughly forty leading tobacconists and commission merchants gathered at Washington's Masonic Hall to move closer to Pfirshing's vision. Called by Pfirshing and the ATTC, convention delegates came primarily from the West and, in a first for Civil War-era tobacco politics, Virginia. While the TNA, ATTC, and TBOT each sent several delegates to represent their views, more than a dozen Virginians came.[113] In a show of postwar sectional unity, the convention selected Richmond manufacturer and Confederate partisan Robert Atkinson Mayo as its chairman.[114] From the beginning, however, it was clear that Pfirshing's vision of a unified trade faced other challenges. F.A. Prague, the convention's president and a spokesman for ATTC, challenged "the right" of commission merchants from the New York TBOT to join a convention "intended for manufacturers only"; Philadelphia's fine-cut manufacturers and cigar makers, who hoped to revive the leaf tax debate, walked out on the second day. Others expressed surprise that more tobacconists had not attended, which Edward Burke attributed to a widespread sense that convention delegates cared only for "a portion of the trade."[115] Even among delegates who attended for the full three days, consensus was elusive. Delegates bickered over issues such as the ideal rate of taxation for each tobacco type and the wisdom of a universal tax rate for all types. In the end—and only after losing much of the Eastern delegation—delegates agreed to propose a universal tax of fifteen cents per pound and salaries for government inspectors. Although these proposals lacked the audacity of the leaf tax plan, they did suggest the trade's embrace of compromise and coalition building. Further, the convention's election of a committee to present their proposals to Congress and the Commissioner of Internal Revenue marked a step toward the representative political action envisioned by Pfirshing.

The Washington convention demonstrated a tension within the trade that characterized tobacco politics throughout 1867. On one hand, the convention revealed potential for cross-sectional "appreciation," "fraternity," and "liberality," which Edward Burke—now a reporter for *Tobacco Leaf*—believed was cause enough to celebrate. "The Convention," he boasted, "can not fail to be remembered as one of the most significant ... trade meetings ever held in the United States."[116] On the other hand, it was clear that trade sectors still viewed each other suspiciously. Thus, as representatives sought to build on the proposals of the Washington convention, two paths emerged among the industry's prominent leaders in the East and West.

Eastern manufacturers and commission merchants opted to pursue "insider" politics. The TNA demonstrated this approach in a TNA fete of their president, William E. Lawrence, in May 1867. Held at Astor House, the celebration brought together leading figures of the Eastern trade with government officials, including revenue collectors, the Deputy Commissioner of Internal Revenue, and David Wells' chief lieutenant. Over dinner and toasts, gatherers listened as New York's most influential tobacconists celebrated Lawrence and the fruitful partnership he helped construct between their trade and federal officials. As Deputy Commissioner of Internal Revenue Isaac Messmore put it, "no man stood higher than [Lawrence] in the estimation of the Revenue Department."[117] New York TBOT leaders likewise convened a series of meetings in the summer and fall of 1867, which gathered the tobacco boards of trade of Baltimore, Boston, New York, and Philadelphia and made overtures to Treasury Secretary Hugh McCulloch and various revenue officials. In addition to the TNA and TBOT, one individual personified this "insider" approach: Pierre Lorillard. As competing industry sectors squabbled to convince revenue officials and lawmakers of their legitimacy, Lorillard repeatedly reminded his competitors and the general public that he was the face of American tobacco. "The Lorillard factory," noted one friendly article, "pays more in revenue tax to the Government than a score of any other shops combined." This refrain, which became common throughout Reconstruction, suggested that Lorillard's market dominance—and thus his significant tax burden—entitled him to special access.[118]

Alternatively, Western firms under the leadership of Cincinnati's ATTC opted for popular politics. This was evident in two notable events in the summer of 1867. The first was the ATTC's second-annual Tobacco Fair, which brought thousands of tobacco growers, manufacturers, and dealers to Cincinnati for several days of festivities in July. Inspired by the state agricultural fairs that had proliferated since the antebellum era, the Tobacco Fair tempted tobacco growers to enter their crops in various competitions in the hope of winning prizes such as gold watches, diamond rings, and even a college scholarship.[119] As the festivities concluded, F.A. Prague capitalized on his huge audience by announcing ATTC's vehement opposition to the revenue system. The tax, he claimed, had destroyed "all equality before the law"; it had turned tobacconists into "holders of Government securities" while granting them no protections; and, by increasing the price of tobacco, it placed "the luxuries of life beyond the reach of the poor, and exclusively within the reach of the rich." To remedy these ills, Prague announced that the ATTC would host a national convention, this time in Cleveland.[120]

In the weeks preceding the Cleveland convention, tobacconists publicized their impending meeting to a national audience. They held public meetings in their home cities, elected delegates for the national convention, and encouraged local newspapers to broadcast their grievances and goals. Throughout the late summer of 1867, papers throughout the country published brief reports on the progress toward the convention. "Delegates are already appointed from Richmond, Cleveland, Chicago, and other points," noted a Memphis paper, "and the meeting promises to be very largely attended."[121] "Everything is in readiness for the Convention," reported Philadelphia's *Evening Telegraph*.[122] These notices appeared repeatedly throughout September, suggesting that the ATTC and its affiliates had strategized to maximize exposure. When delegates convened on September 17, correspondents from the *New York Herald*, *New York Times*, *Chicago Tribune*, and *Washington Star* joined them and transmitted their proposals to the public.

Rather than risk appearing like a "lobby," creeping through the hotels of Washington in search of special privileges, Cleveland delegates depicted themselves as a legitimate, democratically organized interest; their concerns were the nation's concerns. The choice to meet in Cleveland, and not Washington, was itself part of this strategy. As W.B. Pierce, a Utica manufacturer and Cleveland delegate, put it, "[I]t is disreputable to be seen in Washington," for lobbies had "become a stench in the nostrils of Congress and of the country." "To dance attendance in the anterooms of our servants is beneath the dignity of an American citizen," he announced. On the other hand, to organize a public convention in a centrally located city; to publicize efforts in dozens of newspapers; and to invite delegates from as many cities and towns as possible, was to perform the duties of American citizenship.[123]

The convention's proceedings emphasized these themes. Delegates claimed "to speak for the entire tobacco manufacturing interest of the country."[124] To that end, they devised an Executive Committee of fifteen manufacturers that included prominent leaders of ATTC, such as Prague and Spence, three Virginians, and three TNA members—Pierre Lorillard among them.[125] Their resolutions, and the press coverage drawn from them, asserted that delegates arrived "from all the principal cities of the Union" and represented "a capital of fifty millions dollars invested in the tobacco trade."[126] They hoped to defend their interests as well as those of "the great mass of tax-paying consumers." They convened, they suggested, only out of grudging necessity because the law offered "bounties" for tax evasion and consigned "to poverty those who are faithful in discharging all the burdens imposed by law."[127] They demanded Congress incorporate "the pecuniary interests of this important branch of manufacturing industry" into future tax debates.[128] And, most importantly, they set to work outlining policy proposals for a new tax system.

In the weeks before the convention, a number of delegates discussed adopting a system in which all tobacco sold would be packaged uniformly, with revenue officials affixing a tax-paid stamp upon each package. Cleveland delegates quickly took to the idea. They proposed that tobacconists prepay for stamps, meaning the system required an outlay of capital prior to any trade. Collectors would affix stamps to uniform packages; they would also affix tobacconists' names—later switched to their government-assigned factory numbers—upon every package of tobacco. Finally, before purchasing any stamps or registering with a collector, tobacconists would pay a minimum bond of ten thousand dollars.[129] If carefully administered, the system would make all tobacco sold in the United States "traceable," as one proponent put it.[130]

It would also move the industry closer to the monopolism favored by Burke, Spence, and other trade reformers. Unlike the explicit monopoly of the leaf tax proposal, however, the monopolistic tendencies of the stamp system were implicit: prepayment, along with mandatory manufacturers' bonds of thousands of dollars, created significant capital barriers to the manufacturing business. The proposals did not guarantee that Cleveland delegates themselves would exclusively profit, but by defining a "tobacco manufacturer" as someone who had paid in advance for the privilege of selling tobacco, it ensured that "small capitalists" would struggle to compete.[131] In effect, the proposals would integrate tobacco manufacture into a single, national market—a first in American history. And Cleveland delegates—"representing a capital of fifty millions dollars"—would have an enormous advantage in securing the expensive access necessary to compete.[132]

As the convention adjourned, delegates empowered the Executive Committee to build upon their newfound sense of organization by calling trade conventions "whenever deemed necessary" and raising funds for the support of a permanent association of tobacconists. The convention also charged committee members with promoting the delegates' proposals.[133] To that end, Prague, Lorillard, J.P. Spence, and other committee members spent the fall enlisting the support of other trade interests, such as the Eastern TBOTs, who had not attended the Cleveland convention.[134] Particularly critical in this process was Prague, who published the Cleveland proposals as a small pamphlet for David Wells, who subsequently republished them almost verbatim in his January 1868 report to Congress.[135] Several weeks later, the Executive Committee—"all united"—joined representatives of the New York TBOT and TNA in a meeting with the House Ways and Means Committee to review their proposal and display their unified support.[136] For the first time in the decade, the industry, revenue officials, and Congress were on the verge of an agreement. It seemed years of debate and strife had finally yielded a unified, politically effective tobacco industry, prepared to assert its role as the federal state's partner in revenue administration.

For Burke, Pfirshing, and other advocates of organized tobacco politics, the Executive Committee meeting stood as an answer to a question *Tobacco Leaf* had posed to its readers in early 1868: "What does the man of business do when his agent [in government] acts contrary to his wishes, and in consequence involves him in difficulties?"[137] As tobacconists understood it, their "difficulties" under the revenue system uniquely suited them to respond, and their response came in the form of democratic action: frustrated business leaders had to organize their trade across economic and sectional barriers; publicize their cause; develop concrete policy proposals and defend them with rigorous statistical analysis; and elect representatives to carry those proposals through committee and into law. The 1868 Revenue Act illustrated the potential viability of tobacconists' democratic organization by enshrining most of the Cleveland convention's proposals—most conspicuously the stamp system.[138]

Nonetheless, the 1868 law was not a complete victory. To the frustration of many manufacturers, Congress had no plan for addressing tobacco on which taxes had been paid prior to the passage of the law, meaning tobacconists faced paying a second tax on millions of pounds of stock. Legislators also retained a relatively high rate—thirty-two cents per pound—on chewing and fine-cut tobaccos, thus burdening many tobacconists with presale outlays they would struggle to offset.[139] Further, that rate was twice as high as the tax on "smoking" tobacco—a distinction that opened a door to the fraudulent practice of reporting chewing tobacco as smoking tobacco.[140]

In addition to the law's shortcomings, the impeachment of Andrew Johnson in the spring of 1868 created a long legislative delay that exposed fault lines in the tobacconists' political coalition. These divisions were especially evident in the voluminous letters, memorials, and petitions tobacconists sent to Congress between January and July. Southern and Western businesses were especially worried that the Cleveland convention's proposals would benefit only "a very small portion" of the trade. "No man of moderate means," protested a group of North Carolina tobacconists, "can command the capital [to prepay the tax] and consequently it will drive out of business all but men of unlimited means."[141] Even figures who had embraced the convention's implicit monopolism, such as Thomas R. Spence, the brother and business partner of ATTC leader J.P. Spence, expressed concerns that Congress might "sacrifice the entire trade … to add to the already large wealth" of men such as Lorillard and McAlpin.[142] There was good reason to be concerned, as Lorillard undertook a regular correspondence with Ways and Means Chair Robert Cumming Schenck. Lorillard aggressively advocated for tweaks in the law, such as a ban on the bulk packages ubiquitous among Western producers, which would force his competitors to overhaul their operations. At the same time, he reminded Schenck and other legislators that as the industry's largest taxpayer—"who pays twice the amount of tax that the forty Cincinnati manufacturers combined"—it was in the government's best interests to indulge him.[143]

Aware of their coalition's fragility, tobacconists worked to assuage anxieties among small competitors following passage of the 1868 law. In a pamphlet signed by Thomas Spence, Frank Prague, and—somewhat reluctantly—Lorillard ally and former TNA President William E. Lawrence, tobacconists attempted to reframe their proposed monopoly in a manner more favorable to antimonopolistic small manufacturers.[144] In an extensive analysis of the 1868 law, they called for a lower rate of tax, more generous rules for bonded warehouses, and the printing of "free" stamps for tobacco taxed before the law's passage—all necessities for "ninety-five out of every hundred manufacturers in Virginia, Kentucky, North Carolina, and the West." These propositions were also crucial for maintaining the tobacco industry's fragile political equilibrium. In particular, in order to counter Lorillard's influence, the industry's Western leaders needed the support of small manufacturers. In an effort to convey that support to Congress, J.P. Spence wrote to Schenck, "I am daily in receipt of letters from our trade in all quarters (St. Louis Chicago Detroit Toledo Cincinnati Rochester Syracuse +c +c)" opposing Lorillard's propositions.[145] As long as they represented small Western interests, Spence and his colleagues could exploit the Republican Party's East-West division to keep their seats at the legislative table. At the same time, Western leaders still shared Lorillard's priority of eliminating "fraud." Thus, even after Congress adopted most of the industry's suggestions with the 1868 Revenue Act, existential questions—about protecting "legitimate" manufacturers, and even what constituted legitimacy—continued to define tobacco politics.

These questions led to a series of meetings held in Washington during January and February 1869. The most conspicuous issue for tobacconists was the industry's need for "free stamps" on unstamped but tax-paid tobacco, but other matters of business quickly emerged.[146] In early February, the Executive Committee that had formed at Cleveland in 1867 reconvened to argue that tobacco stamps were conducive to counterfeits and proposed a more intricate and traceable design that extended "the same scrupulous care" to tobacco stamps as the "securities and money of the nation."[147] Most significantly, the Executive Committee decided to form a permanent organization representing the trade's diverse interests before Congress. The industry's continuing political turmoil, even in the wake of landmark legislation, had clearly disturbed industry leaders enough to institutionalize their relationships. They accomplished that goal in August 1869, at a meeting that coincided with the ATTC's annual trade fair, when Executive Committee members constituted the National Tobacco Association of the United States (NTA).

The NTA incorporated the industry's sectional and trade diversity into its organization. Its Executive Committee, for instance, was comprised of two representatives elected from every tobacco manufacturing state; its Finance Committee, which raised funds for annual meetings, members' legal defense expenses, and mass petition campaigns, likewise included a member from each tobacco state. In 1870, the NTA also formed committees specially charged to address issues in the industry's five major sectors: cigars, fine cut, manufactured (or plug), dealers, and snuff. Further, the NTA incorporated the infrastructure of dozens of extant organizations, including the ATTC and TNA, which elected members to the NTA Executive Committee and, in coordination with the NTA president, addressed issues germane to their local trades.[148] As *Tobacco Leaf* put it, the NTA was the "union and head-centre" of the American tobacco industry, its constitution the "consolidation of interest in one common cause."[149] That unity implied political stability throughout the industry—a welcome circumstance for the trade's national leaders in Cincinnati, New York City, and Richmond. They fortified that stability by sharing authority with local leaders in cities such as St. Louis, Chicago, or Lynchburg, Virginia. With a national organization in place, NTA members imagined a lucrative and influential future for their industry. "The whole boundless continent is ours," claimed Connecticut NTA member James Gallagher, and manufacturers could look forward to "customers not only from every portion of the United States, but from every portion of the world."[150]

Through the early 1870s, the NTA organized dozens of campaigns in favor of amendments to the revenue system. Campaigns focused on creating a single rate for all tobacco types, reducing taxes, and establishing bonded warehouses in every tobacco-manufacturing city. Unlike prior to the NTA's founding, when a slew of conflicting letters, petitions, and memorials poured into Congress, the NTA could rally thousands of tobacconists into uniform positions on every tobacco issue. They accomplished this by printing form petitions and encouraging local leaders to simply collect signatures from proprietors and laborers in their cities. They also paired with other associations, such as the Cigarmakers' Union, to coordinate a political message across tobacco's trade sectors.

The climax of the NTA's authority came in 1872, when Congress passed its fourth major internal revenue bill since 1862. The 1872 law refined the stamp system and incorporated the NTA's desire for a uniform rate on all manufactured tobacco. Critically, it also expanded the license tax system. Previously, the Bureau of Internal Revenue had issued licenses (for a fee) to either dealers or manufacturers in tobacco. In addition to those categories, the new law imposed license fees on "peddlers" of tobacco—presumably smaller, rural dealers—and "dealers in leaf tobacco." The latter was the NTA's greatest triumph—and it represented the culmination of tobacco politics since the Cooper Union Convention eight years earlier. By licensing leaf dealers and barring them from selling to anyone without a manufacturing license, Congress effectively guaranteed tobacconists'

TO THE CIGAR AND TOBACCO TRADE OF THE UNITED STATES.

We would call your attention to the proposed reduction of the Tariff on Cigars, and ask you to get the following Remonstrance signed by all parties interested in your vicinity, and forward the same to your Representative in Congress. The time is short. The bill has been reported, and will come up for action on the 15th of February. Your immediate and hearty co-operation is earnestly requested.
NEW YORK, February 1, 1870.
WM. E. LAWRENCE,
President National Tobacco Association of the United States,
OFFICE, 108 WATER STREET, NEW YORK.

CUT OFF THE ABOVE BEFORE SENDING THE PETITION.

PETITION.

To the Honorable the Senate and House of Representatives, in Congress assembled:

We, the undersigned,—Cigar Manufacturers, Journeymen Cigarmakers, Dealers in Cigars, Growers of and Dealers in Seed Leaf Tobacco,—would most respectfully represent to your Honorable Bodies that the present depressed condition of the industrial interests connected with the Cigar Interest of the country, is owing largely to the change made in the Tariff on Cigars, by the reduction of the duties from $3 per pound and 50 per cent. *ad valorem* to $2.50 per pound and 25 per cent. *ad valorem*, which we have found to work disastrously to our several interests. We do therefore pray your Honorable Bodies to restore the Tariff rates on imported cigars to $3 per pound and 50 per cent. *ad valorem*, as we are fully persuaded that it will prove both advantageous to the Revenue and our several industries. We are also persuaded that the duty should not be reduced until all of our industrial relations are more fixed and reliable.

Figure 4. During the early 1870s, the National Tobacco Association circulated form petitions for redress of a range of revenue related issues. The NTA printed thousands of these petitions with spaces for local trades to add signatures. Although most detached the NTA's instructions, several failed to—an oversight that reminded legislators of the NTA's influence within tax debates. Records of the Committee on Ways and Means; Records of the House of Representatives, RG233. National Archives Building, Washington, D.C.

dominion over the nation's raw leaf production. Congress—under pressure from the NTA, and, for years earlier, other tobacco associations—had oriented tobacco's commodity chain around tobacconists.

The results were startling: in the first year under the 1872 system, the federal government collected a record thirty-four million dollars in tobacco taxes. By the end of the decade, the total consistently reached forty million dollars, or more than thirty percent of total internal revenue collections.[151] The NTA had thus become an indispensable partner for the federal government. In a move that would have seemed impossible during the leaf tax debate, Edward Burke even "secured" appointment as a revenue collector. Throughout the decade, he "made several successful raids against ... 'moonshine' distillers'" while continuing his work for *Tobacco Leaf*.[152] Burke, who had built his career advocating for the symbiosis of the federal state and the tobacco industry, had come to personify that very reality.

Not everyone was pleased with tobacco's revamped political economy. In December 1872, several months after Congress passed the new revenue bill, a Kentucky Democrat named John McConnell Rice denounced the law before the House of Representatives. Rice was incensed with the provision requiring tobacco growers to sell exclusively to "persons ... who have paid a special tax as

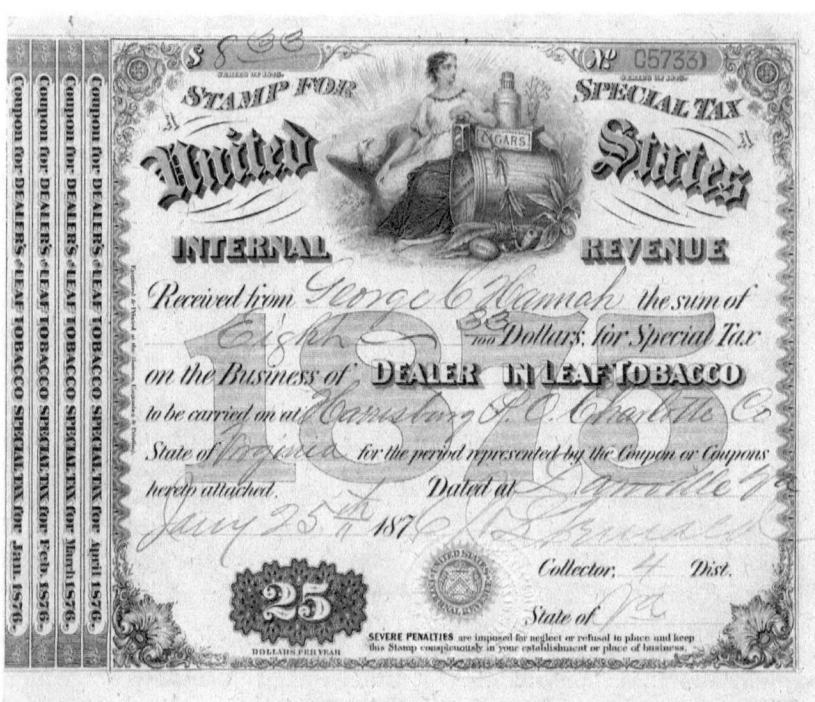

Figure 5. A license to deal leaf tobacco for the year 1875 belonging to George Cummington Hannah of Charlotte County, Virginia. Such licenses were the National Tobacco Association's greatest legislative triumph, as they guaranteed tobacconists' "dominion" over all leaf tobacco cultivated in the country. By numbering stamps and identifying collection districts, the stamps enhanced the Bureau of Internal Revenue's surveillance powers and made tobacco "traceable." Hannah Family Papers 1760-1967, Virginia Museum of History and Culture, Richmond, Virginia.

leaf-dealers or manufacturers of tobacco … or to persons purchasing leaf-tobacco for export."[153] As Rice admitted, growers who paid a license tax could sell to anyone they wished, but that tax was "so outrageously high" that it forced growers into business with "moneyed" manufacturers and dealers. Worse yet, Rice recalled that the provision in question emerged after "a swarm of manufacturers of tobacco" had descended on Washington, "flooding the desks of members of Congress with printed circulars explaining how the proposed tax would operate." That Rice delivered his speech days after the House began its investigation of the Crédit Mobilier affair made the subtext of his remarks all the more clear: the new tax bill was "pure class legislation," the work of a nefarious special interest and its patrons in Congress.[154]

Rice's criticism harkened back to tobacco growers' and small manufacturers' responses to a range of issues during the 1860s, from the leaf tax to the pre-paid stamp system. Yet they also anticipated the NTA's troubles in the years to come. During the 1870s, several issues imperiled the revenue system. The return of the Democratic Party to national influence disturbed the peace between the tobacconists and Republicans, forcing the Association to choose sides as its members and its benefactors in government grew alienated from one another. New trade journals, including New York's *United States Tobacco Journal* and Cincinnati's *Western Tobacco Journal*, emerged to criticize both the NTA and *Tobacco Leaf*. The *United States Tobacco Journal* took special pleasure in attacking the NTA's "idiotic harlequins" who "depart for Washington, and dine and wine, and squibble and squabble with the Committee of Ways and Means."[155] As different sectors of the trade increasingly criticized the NTA and called for reduction, or even abolition, of the tax, the National Tobacco Association struggled to retain its influence. The political processes that had produced the NTA were overlooked in the arguments of the 1870s and 1880s, and the picture painted by John McConnell Rice seemed increasingly accurate: tobacco's leading men were little more than a "moneyed" lobby.

2

"A Hard Law at Best"

The Political Economy of Tobacco Taxation from Depression to Surplus, 1873-1890

In 1891, economist Frank Olmsted published a detailed history of the federal tobacco excise tax since the Civil War. Although Olmsted recognized the turbulence of the tax's early years, he argued that since the creation of the stamp system in 1868 and its reinforcement in 1872, the tax had been a steady and uncontroversial boon for the federal treasury.[1] Olmsted marveled at tobacco's efficiency as a source of revenue. During the 1870s, he wrote, "the single item of tobacco yielded nearly one-third as much as the customs, and somewhat more than one-sixth of the total revenue received by the government."[2] Cautious of overestimating the tax's importance, Olmsted was nonetheless effusive in his estimation of the often overlooked levy. Throughout the "whole period since the war," he argued, "the revenue from tobacco is a constant and growing quantity, little affected by the fluctuations of trade."[3] For Olmsted, the evidence of two decades of tobacco taxation had verified a principle of political economy. "As an object of taxation, [tobacco] is obviously a stable source of revenue, and the surest in times of great necessity. It has met high taxation without apparent injury to the growers or to the manufacturers; while, as far as consumers are concerned, its use in steadily increasing quantities indicates that the burden is easily borne."[4]

Olmsted was right about the tax's performance. Since the National Tobacco Association's legislative victory in 1872, the tobacco excise generated an annual average of 35 million dollars and, along with the various excises on alcohol, funded nearly half of the federal budget. Yet Olmsted's portrayal of tobacco taxation's "obvious" and inevitable progress mischaracterized the contentious political debates that accompanied the federal government's retention of the tax in the decades following the war. Subsequent generations of historians have tended to echo Olmsted's portrayal, suggesting that excise taxes on alcohol and tobacco "faced little resistance because of their hidden and insidious application."[5] From this perspective, the NTA's triumphs between 1868 and 1872 were the final political upheavals in the construction of the tobacco revenue system, and from that point forward the tax became an uncontestable feature of the postbellum federal bureaucracy.

The tax's subjects—tobacco growers, leaf dealers, retail dealers, and tobacconists—would not have agreed with such a portrayal. For tobacco interests, the preservation of the federal tobacco tax during the 1870s and 1880s was as politically turbulent as its creation during the 1860s. For nearly two decades, large tobacconists found it necessary to defend the system they had created, while most other sectors of the industry, from smaller tobacconists to growers and leaf dealers, used their resentment of the revenue system to forge political movements that challenged the tax and, more broadly, federal authority. The *Norfolk Virginian* captured these interests' perspectives when it argued, in 1875, that the revenue system was "an unmixed evil" that made "necessary to business twice, and often thrice, the capital needed for manufacture," and thus prevented "the poor from competing with the rich manufacturer."[6] As a group of Louisville warehousemen and leaf dealers proclaimed, the tax was "a hard law at best," which depressed prices, distorted competition, and subjected every trade interest to the Bureau of Internal Revenue's "autocratic" administrative oversight.[7]

In the wake of its victories, the National Tobacco Association receded into latency for several years following 1872. In its place, agitated interests from the tobacco fields of Virginia to the warehouses of Kentucky organized hundreds of new county and state tobacco associations to abolish the tax. At times, even tobacconists in the urban North and West—core supporters and one-time members of the NTA—endorsed abolition. Through their emergent associations, growers, dealers, and tobacconists petitioned their representatives in Congress and state legislatures. They also contributed to and learned from a growing tobacco press, including such outlets as New York's *United States Tobacco Journal*, founded in 1876 and edited by the cigar maker (and, later, theater impresario) Oscar Hammerstein, and the *Western Tobacco Journal*, the organ of the Association of the Tobacco Trade of Cincinnati.[8] In the process, they raised critical questions of the tobacconists' revenue system and, more broadly, the era's political economy. Like the National Tobacco Association before them, the tax's opponents understood that the reconstruction of tobacco's commodity chain signified a major shift in the relations of business and the state. What right, they asked, supported the government's creation of a national tobacco market and, more specifically, the Bureau of Internal Revenue's authority to inspect their businesses, oversee their labors, and extract their profits? What purpose informed the government's perpetuation of a "war tax" years, even decades, after the war had ended? And who benefited from tobacco's reconstruction? As figures like Lorillard defended the tax throughout the 1870s, critics increasingly depicted the revenue system as a privilege for the nationally powerful and connected. Boards of Trade, small tobacconists' associations, and growers' organizations—themselves influential within their own regions—attacked the regressive character of tobacco taxation. "Is it better," asked members of Louisville's tobacco trade, "that the poor should grow poorer" under a regressive excise system, and the "rich richer?"[9]

This chapter begins in the years following the Panic of 1873, when import duties declined and the tobacco tax became even more essential to federal public finance. During those years, the Bureau of Internal Revenue honed its administration of the tax, a process that eliminated alternate means of exchange and forced tobacco commerce into a national market. It then explores the industry's political organization against the tax during the late 1870s and early 1880s, which culminated in a series of rate reductions but never the abolition that tax opponents desired. Finally, it suggests explanations for the tax's ultimate survival—an outcome that seemed unlikely for much of the postbellum period but was ultimately ensured by both the industry's internal divisions and external factors within the national party system. After 1890, the tax seemed less like an odd holdover from the Civil War and increasingly like the natural element of the federal tax system that Frank Olmsted praised.

The Structural Foundations of Tobacco Taxation

The Bureau of Internal Revenue operated an extensive administrative network for the collection of public revenue throughout the postbellum period. At the top of that network was the position of Commissioner of Internal Revenue, a presidential appointment within the Treasury Department. The Commissioner supervised seven internal "divisions," including a Division of Tobacco, each of which specialized in a different area of revenue collection.[10] The commissioner and division heads oversaw dozens of "collection districts" staffed by collectors, assessors, and their numerous assistants and deputies. During the 1870s, Congress and the Bureau enhanced accountability by creating a fourth bureaucratic layer of salaried agents charged with supervising several collection districts each. Effectively free of judicial oversight, this vast network aggressively pursued the government's revenue, particularly as tax evasion rose and import duties fell in the wake of the Panic of 1873.[11] Green Berry Raum, commissioner from 1876 until 1883, personified the Bureau's administrative accountability and single-minded pursuit of the revenue. Following his appointment, Raum empowered deputy collectors to assemble "raiding parties" to patrol and inspect tobacco factories, distilleries, and breweries.¹² His agents, as well as the U.S. marshals and district attorneys they worked alongside, were especially notorious among "moonshiners" in the mountain South, of whom they arrested more than 7,000 between 1876 and 1880.¹³

Tobacconists likewise felt the press of federal authority, with one North Carolinian claiming it was "a common thing for the Government to close Tobacco Factories."¹⁴ In a particularly dramatic episode, revenue agents "seized" fourteen tobacco factories in North Carolina and arrested twenty-three tobacconists for "re-using, altering, forging, and counterfeiting tobacco stamps."¹⁵ Nor were Southern tobacconists the only target of the Bureau. In 1878, revenue officials in Pennsylvania broke up a ring of tobacco farmers who had hired professional "segar" makers to roll their tobacco for home consumption.¹⁶ Several weeks later, officials in Brooklyn impounded the factory of Buchanan & Lyall, "one of the oldest and most respected" tobacco firms in the country. The *United States Tobacco Journal* and *Tobacco Leaf* complained that agents had soiled Buchanan & Lyall's reputation over an "irregularity," and Raum "released" the factory after conferring with its owners, but the event symbolized the Commissioner's determination to collect every tobacco dollar due.¹⁷

At the same time, that determination likely came easily because tobacconists themselves so frequently asked for enforcement of the law. In the South, where "blockading," or the sale of untaxed goods, was rumored to be widespread, well-established tobacconists formed associations to petition the Bureau for greater enforcement. Claiming that their competitors avoided the tax, the Richmond Tobacco Exchange demanded "the proper authorities of the United States … remedy this blockading of manufactured tobacco at once."¹⁸ A group called the North Carolina Tobacco Manufacturers' Association formed in 1874 to "unite with the honest manufacturers of the United States in all honorable efforts to bring violators to speedy punishment for infraction of the revenue laws."¹⁹ The North Carolina Association was especially notable because its membership included W.T. Blackwell, manufacturer of Durham Smoking Tobacco, which was among the era's best known brands, and because it held its meetings in Durham, a city that would, because of its association with James B. Duke's American Tobacco Company, become synonymous with manufacturers' power over tobacco's commodity chain. It was clear, not even ten years after Appomattox, that larger Southern manufacturers had no problem asking federal authorities to increase law enforcement in their districts. For these tobacconists, the revenue system was a vital tool for controlling trade.

In addition to the Bureau's policing, a constellation of regulatory mechanisms, such as occupational licensing and records surveillance, proved essential to the collection of tobacco revenue. With the Internal Revenue Acts of 1868 and 1872, Congress had surrounded tobacco growers, exporters, dealers, and tobacconists with regulations on everything from factory signs ("painted in oil or gilded") to the type of paste affixing revenue stamps to packages ("dissolve one pound of gum Arabic in one and three fourths pints of boiling water, add from two to four ounces of acetic acid, and keep it corked").[20] The Bureau's Tobacco Division interpreted these regulations—often publicly, in the *United States Tobacco Journal* and *Tobacco Leaf*—and enforced them. These measures further realized the objective of Civil War-era policymakers and their partners in the tobacco trade: to make tax collection efficient by structuring the industry around a series of traceable exchanges.

The most conspicuous aspect of revenue regulation was the occupational license system. As one legislator noted, the license system was the essential administrative safeguard for tobacco revenue, enabling the state "to trace the entire production from the field to the spittoon."[21] A product of the partnership between tobacconists and policymakers I explored in chapter 1, the system defined the industry's sectors—growers, exporters, dealers, and tobacconists —and imposed distinct obligations on each.[22] A fairly simple formula determined each designation: to whom an entity sold tobacco; from whom they purchased it; and what they did to it, if anything, after purchase. For example, a grower, who cultivated and cured a crop, sold that crop to a "leaf dealer," who in turn could sell to other leaf dealers or to a "manufacturer" (tobacconist). Aside from the grower's curing, only the tobacconist could manipulate tobacco for consumption. When they finished their products, tobacconists could sell to "peddlers" or "dealers" in manufactured tobacco, who sold to consumers.[23] The license system undergirded all other transformations in tobacco's postbellum political economy, from sharecropping to monopsony, significantly influencing who would, or would not, benefit from the industry's late-century growth.

The experience of tobacco growers, the only link in the commodity chain who did not require a license, demonstrates the system's influence. Under the 1872 Revenue Act, growers could technically sell their tobacco to any buyer. However, if growers sold to unlicensed buyers they became taxable as "retail dealers in leaf tobacco," a class that was effectively prohibited by an annual license tax of five hundred dollars.[24] The license system, in other words, confined growers to three potential markets: exporters, leaf dealers, and manufacturers.[25] In the tobacco regions of Kentucky, North Carolina, Tennessee, and Virginia, leaf dealers could exploit this captured market and keep prices low. This consequence became

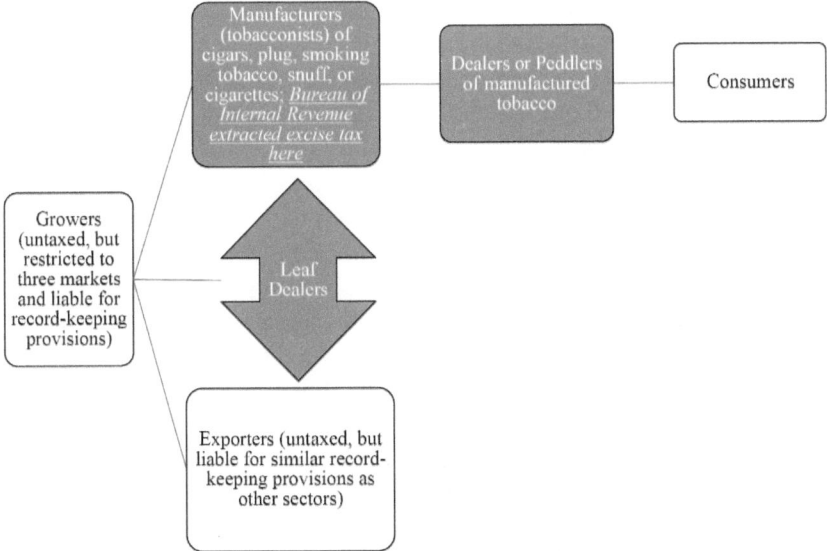

Figure 6. Tobacco's postbellum commodity chain as dictated by the occupational licensing system. Sectors in grey paid an annual license tax. Growers could technically sell their crop to anyone, but they were effectively prohibited from selling to anyone besides exporters, leaf dealers, and manufacturers by a prohibitively expensive tax on "retail dealers in leaf tobacco."

apparent as early as the mid-1870s, as leaf dealers forged combinations, such as Virginia's Danville Tobacco Association, to suppress prices paid to growers.[26]

Growers suffered under this system, but planter-landlords, who grew tobacco and rented land to other growers, made out better because the law did not consider tobacco paid as rent a "sale."[27] This rule accommodated the crop lien laws that proliferated in the South after the Civil War. In the cash- and credit-poor tobacco-growing regions of the South, larger growers maximized their properties' values and reasserted control over freedpeople's labor by claiming a share of their crop in exchange for supplies and land. Small merchants—a critical source of credit in the postbellum South—could likewise claim a share of crops and subsequently enter the tobacco trade without ever growing tobacco or paying a license tax.[28] Postwar credit scarcity and reactionary state legislatures produced crop-lien laws, but they would not have spread through the tobacco South without this critical accommodation.

To trace tobacco sales, Congress also imposed record-keeping provisions on growers, exporters, dealers, and manufacturers. These provisions drew on capitalist innovations that had emerged before the Civil War by prioritizing the labor of clerks.[29] For instance, dealers in leaf tobacco had to keep two "identical" books of daily inventory and sales. One book remained with the dealer, "to be open at all hours to the inspection of any internal revenue officer or agent," while the other became the property of the Bureau at the end of the fiscal year.[30] Growers, fearing the legal and financial threat of an audit, often relied on leaf dealers' clerks as well. "Any farmer selling at our warehouse," claimed one Virginia auction house, "need only carry home with him and preserve the statement of sales furnished by us, and he will be always prepared to answer the inquiries of United States officials."[31] Manufacturers had to keep similar records, but the law also forced them to synthesize their data into a monthly "abstract."[32] Revenue officials then compared manufacturers' abstracts with the records of leaf dealers and growers, a painstaking process that guaranteed, as nearly as possible, that the nation's supply of raw leaf tobacco had been accounted for. "Thus," wrote Raum, "should any one deliberately or accidentally omit recording the correct ... amount of tobacco by him manufactured, a comparison of his account with that of the leaf dealer's will show that a mistake or an attempt to defraud the Government has been made."[33] As Raum recognized, thousands of tobacco industry clerks, bookkeepers, and accountants performed the critical public function of tracing tobacco from the soil to the consumer.

Federal record-keeping provisions accelerated the managerial revolution within the tobacco industry, a process that small tobacconists found especially exhausting.[34] Even those who managed to comply with Bureau demands groaned under the law, claiming that the potential for a violation frightened potential investors. For instance, credit analysts reported that a small North Carolina tobacconist named Erastus Mitchell "may be d[oin]g well but a seizure"—always likely under the Bureau's byzantine regulations—"might ruin him."[35] Lacking financing, Mitchell and others like him not only struggled to compete with larger firms, but also struggled to pay the clerks whose labor had become so consequential.

The Bureau's regulatory framework also reshaped the relationship between employers and labor. Raum was especially concerned that employers exert maximum "control" over employees to limit discrepancies in their tax returns. It was common, for instance, for firms to blame a discrepancy on employee oversight—whether the intentional removal of untaxed tobacco or a mistake in measurement or packing. Facing a seizure, firms denied responsibility by arguing that employees retained their autonomy and the responsibilities associated with it.

Self-possession was a dominant principle of nineteenth-century labor law, but Raum argued that "the interest of the Government" superseded workers' autonomy.[36] Firms, he claimed, assumed their workers' risks when dealing in taxable goods. That determination pressured employers to advance surveillance and control of employees, backed with the power of the federal state.

Bureau regulations also fueled the development of ancillary businesses surrounding the tobacco trade, including publishers, bookbinders, and stamp printers. *The Internal Revenue Record and Customs Journal*, a weekly periodical founded in 1865 "for the guidance of Government officers and taxpayers," published relevant judicial decisions, queries from tobacco interests, and revenue officials' interpretation of the law. For tobacco interests who chose not to subscribe to the *Internal Revenue Record*, trade journals such as *Tobacco Leaf* and *United States Tobacco Journal* were especially adept at using revenue data to publish "everything of a statistical character calculated to be of interest or use to tobacco representatives."[37] A number of entrepreneurs, such as New York's William Vidal, profited from the Bureau's record-keeping provisions by selling fresh revenue books to tobacconists each year.[38] Another, Orlando Bump, sold tobacconists annotated copies of the 1872 Internal Revenue Act alongside relevant court decisions, Bureau interpretations, and "all changes affecting previous Laws ... carefully noted."[39] Other businesses secured lucrative government contracts to print the revenue stamps tobacconists attached to every package of tobacco. For a time during the 1870s, New York's Graphic Company, already well known among tobacco manufacturers for printing labels, also enjoyed the exclusive privilege of printing revenue stamps alongside those labels.[40] John J. Crooke and Company, the New York firm that invented tinfoil and supplied packaging to most Northeastern tobacconists, monopolized stamp printing for tinfoil packages between the Civil War and the turn of the century.[41] Crooke's deal was somewhat unique: rather than pay him for printing tax stamps, the Bureau simply allowed him to charge tobacconists for the privilege of getting their tax stamps from their packaging supplier—thereby saving them the trouble of attaching stamps separately. In return for that privilege, Crooke reimbursed the Bureau for the salaries of two revenue agents permanently stationed in his factory.[42] Although Crooke's deal was exceptional, his ability to profit from federal tax regulation illustrated the ways the revenue system shaped every aspect of the tobacco business.

The revenue system's thicket of regulations—and the BIR's presence in tobacconists' manufacturing operations—made relations between the Bureau and tobacconists vital to the system's success. At times, particularly in the years immediately following the Panic of 1873, tobacconists bristled against the system they

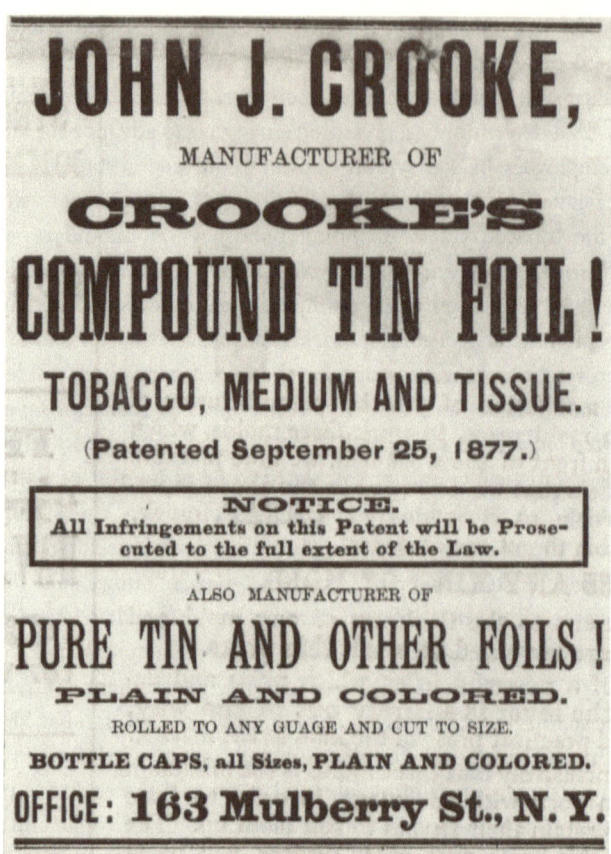

Figure 7. John J. Crooke monopolized the printing of revenue stamps for tinfoil packaging during the 1870s. *Tobacco Leaf*, January 21, 1878.

had created, as revenue agents seemed too eager to find violations and Raum's predecessors sought to alter the law without their consultation. "The moment a merchant joins the ranks of the tobacco trade," observed a frustrated Edward Burke in 1874, "the Government takes a very fatherly interest in him, is especially anxious on the subject of his personal honesty and his general habits and modes of life." Such paternalism, Burke continued, robbed tobacconists of the dignity due to white, male proprietors whose work produced "forty-millions annually towards the support of Government." In its place, the government seemed to suspect that tobacconists' "'ways are dark,' like those of the 'Heathen Chinee,'" thereby necessitating "strict surveillance in the strong expectation of detecting certain 'tricks that are vain.'" Perhaps unsurprisingly, given his leadership during earlier legislative battles, Burke believed the only option was to "stay politically engaged" and to remind legislators and regulators of tobacconists' "tremendous power."[43]

Relations improved significantly under Raum, who used the intimacy between the BIR and their tobacconists to cultivate a cooperative, even affectionate, relationship.[44] As with many of the era's heavily politicized industries, from railroads to alcohol, homosocial camaraderie eased the tension between regulators and their subjects and facilitated the daily labors of both.[45] Collectors grew especially close to tobacconists, with whom they worked daily and shared an interest in the industry's economic success.[46] In turn, tobacconists offered effusive praise in order to nourish their relationships with Bureau leaders. One group of "segar" manufacturers lauded Commissioner Raum's "painstaking, conscientious" collection of the revenue.[47] As his tenure neared its conclusion, the *United States Tobacco Journal* claimed that "in spite of occasional fault being found with his rulings," most tobacconists believed Raum had perfected the revenue system, gaining "the good graces and respect of the trade" in the process.[48] Tobacco Division leader Israel Kimball enjoyed even greater respect. "His knowledge of the internal revenue laws, dating back to the organization of the Department," noted a glowing industry profile, "has made him invaluable to the service."[49] When he addressed the National Tobacco Association in 1882, "deep silence filled the room" as Kimball thanked his "friends" in the industry for the "privilege of operating, in my humble way, in your interest."[50] The proliferation of cooperation, affection, and praise suggested that tobacconists recognized the legal and economic value of friendship. In instances such as Kimball's speech before the NTA, however, those qualities also suggested how faint the distinction between the Bureau and tobacconists often appeared.

By the end of the 1870s, tobacco frauds had become so rare that the *United States Tobacco Journal* could accurately remark that "the gross abuses" of the early revenue system had "ceased to exist."[51] The lack of frauds suggested that alternate forms of exchange, such as those offered by the antebellum commodity web, had disappeared. The government had, as Edward Burke had wished back in 1865, "take[n] hold" of the tobacco market and "clutch[ed] it with hooks of steel and bands of iron."[52] By 1880, tobacco's commodity had been fully reconstructed by the revenue system and absorbed into the national economy.

Figure 8. Israel Kimball, head of the Bureau of Internal Revenue's Tobacco Division, developed productive "friendships" with the industry's leading manufacturers. The *U.S. Tobacco Journal* featured this image in a glowing summary of Kimball's career in its March 12, 1881 issue.

Economic Decline, Racist Reaction, and the Anti-tax Movement

Despite some tobacconists' camaraderie, however, tobacco tax politics were suffused with hostility toward the Bureau. Much of this hostility came from small tobacconists or non-manufacturing interests, such as growers and leaf dealers, who viewed the revenue system as a corrupt agreement between the state and a privileged class of wealthy tobacconists. During the 1870s, this hostility took the form of three persistent criticisms: that the Bureau was autocratic and corrupt, that tobacconists were using the revenue system to monopolize the trade, and that the tax benefited one section—primarily the industrial Northeast—to the detriment of another—the South. Anti-corruption, antimonopolism, and sectionalism were among the dominant strains of political thought throughout the era, and the tobacco revenue system proved a powerful wellspring for each as small manufacturers and growers, as well as journalists and policymakers, relied on their criticisms of the system to make more general points about the iniquities of the era's political economy.[53]

Criticism of the Bureau's autocracy and corruption drew upon widespread assumptions, particularly among Democrats and Southerners, that Republican governance was simply institutionalized malfeasance.[54] According to one Richmond critic, it was "self-evident" that the Bureau existed "for the exclusive benefit of the favored few who are represented in official rings and other combinations, against the mass of the people as tax-payers."[55] J.P. Spence, a Cincinnati tobacconist who had helped lead the National Tobacco Association several years earlier, now complained that Israel Kimball "gets up bills to suit the views of New York City, and the East, ignoring entirely the views of the West and South."[56] Although the *United States Tobacco Journal* would later offer praise for Bureau leaders, during the mid-1870s it claimed that tobacconists were haunted by Bureau officials' "rowdyism and autocratic rulings."[57] Even as reports of corruption declined under Raum's administration, this criticism persisted. Indeed, one of the Government's solutions to corruption, paying officers salaries rather than commissions, only reinforced the popular suspicion of Bureau officials' "jobbery," or personal gain through coercion instead of productive labor.[58] The average Bureau officer, wrote the *Western Tobacco Journal*, "considers it high treason to put him out of a $4,000 or $5,000 a year salary and the pickings made on the sly."[59] The inevitable result of such a situation, suggested one cigar maker, was that "officialism begins to make its mark upon brain and action," and agents begin to "regard the Government as something apart from the people."[60] Accusations of the tax system's corruption reflected broader concerns about Gilded Age political economy: that industrial Northerners, with their unparalleled access to policymakers, tilted economic policy in their favor; that bureaucrats, immune from oversight, enriched themselves at businesses' expense; and that the entire system had become so entrenched as to preclude reform. Knowing such criticisms would find a receptive audience, opponents of the tobacco tax deployed these attacks for a variety of reasons, from defending themselves following a seizure to generating political support for revenue reform.

As it funneled the nation's tobacco supply through licensed tobacconists, the revenue system was particularly vulnerable to charges of monopolism. Alongside Congress and Bureau officials, the tobacconists who had organized the National Tobacco Association and designed the revenue system between 1868 and 1872 were the most common targets of this criticism. Surveying the manufacturing industry of the late 1870s, the *United States Tobacco Journal* suggested that the system had "stamped out of existence" tobacconists who operated on a "limited scale." In their place, the tax "farm[ed] out industries to wealthy people ... to make monopolies," thereby transforming large tobacconists' would-be competitors into a pool of wage laborers.[61] From the South came the charge that forcing growers to sell "only ... to three classes of buyers" served "monopolists and add[ed] to their wealth and power."[62] At least in the case of chewing and smoking ("manufactured") tobacco, critics were correct that the system did exhibit consolidating—monopsonistic, if not monopolistic—tendencies.[63] In the year following the system's renovation in 1868, the number of manufacturers nationwide had dropped precipitously, from 2,400 to 963; after that, however, the number hovered between 850 and 1,000 for the next two decades.[64] During the same period, national tobacco crop production surged from roughly sixty million pounds per year to more than two hundred million pounds annually.[65] As tobacconists took control of this rapidly growing supply, they claimed unprecedented profits. By 1890, tobacconists and cigar makers were adding eighty million dollars to the value of tobacco crops annually—making tobacco the thirteenth largest industry in the country, in terms of value-added—profits they did not distribute back down the commodity chain to growers.[66] Analysts who condemned manufacturers' "monopoly" recognized that things would be different without the revenue system: as the *United States Tobacco Journal* noted in 1882, if the tax were abolished, every tobacco dealer would "purchase a cutting machine and cut large quantities of tobacco on his premises, as was the custom before the internal revenue system was organized, and, as then, he [would] push the sale of goods of his own manufacture."[67] Instead of that diverse, decentralized economy, however, the revenue system limited access to a commodity cultivated by hundreds of thousands of farmers while helping a stable, relatively small number of tobacconists extract record profits from that commodity.[68]

Dismay over the revenue system's perceived corruption and monopolism coincided with protests that the tax discriminated against Southern businesses and farmers. Although tobacconists paid the tax when they purchased revenue stamps, critics argued that they shifted tax incidence to Southern growers by paying less for leaf tobacco. In an 1878 petition, the Louisville Tobacco Board of

Trade argued that because "tobacco as an article of commerce is not co-extensive with the United States," a tax on its sale—at any stage of production—was "unjust" and "contrary to the original spirit of our institutions."[69] Other critics were more resentful. Southern economic boosters, such as the Southern Fertilizing Company's Robert Ragland, believed their section (and their businesses) had a right to "the many millions that were snatched away by the treasury." Writing for *The Southern Review* in 1879, Ragland suggested the tax was a relic of "an evil hour, when the jealous eye of a partizan congress looked with envious hate on their late conquered foe, and when the South was powerless and unrepresented."[70] "The only fair analogy [to a tax on manufactured tobacco]," reasoned an editor for the *Richmond Whig*, "would be a tax on bread, cake, and other forms of wheat; and such a tax would be manifestly impolitic and unjust, although it would be a more general, and therefore fairer, tax than this one tobacco."[71] "To levy a tax upon the staple product of any portion of our country," echoed a National Grange memorial, "is relieving the other portions from their just share of the burdens of a common Government."[72] This sectional disparity inverted the era's prevailing "benefit theory" of taxation, which held that taxes were the price paid for government services.[73] But under the tobacco revenue system, taxpaying Southern tobacco growers received no clear benefits while Northern manufacturers, industrialists, and veterans enjoyed monopoly, tariff protection, and pensions.[74]

Nowhere was the sectional hostility toward the tax more virulent than in Virginia. During the antebellum period, Virginia had "almost a monopoly of the manufacture [of tobacco] in this country." Between 1860 and 1870, however, the number of manufacturers in the state declined from 261 to 96, and sales dropped from more than $12 million to $6.9 million annually.[75] The situation deteriorated further following the Panic of 1873, as prices for the state's tobacco crops sank from 9.3 cents per pound to 5 cents by decade's end.[76] The declining prospects of tobacco agriculture coincided with a reduction in the state's manufacturing output. During the 1870s, sales of revenue stamps—an indicator of tobacconists' productivity—declined in Richmond from $10,000 per day to $3,000 per day.[77] Surveying Virginia's tobacco industry in 1879, the grower, booster, and fertilizer proponent Robert Ragland bemoaned the tax's ravages:

> The tax has closed nearly all of the home factories, and driven manufacturing to the cities and into the hands of Northern capitalists—lessening competition for planters' leaf and creating a monopoly. Twenty years ago, thirty or forty factories were operating in some counties ... where not one can be found now. Some of the largest and thriftiest planters then manufactured

their crops, or had it done by the nearest manufacturer, and realized handsome profits thereby. But their occupation ... is gone; and with it went the bright visions of plenteous income."[78]

And as Virginia slipped, new competition emerged elsewhere, from North Carolina to New York to Kentucky.[79] Virginians, however, were convinced that it was not so much competition as public finance that had ruined their fortune. "The mere scratch of an official pen," claimed nearly 700 members of the Hanover County Grange, "deprived [the state] of millions of dollars' worth of her inherited wealth."[80]

White Virginians' hostility toward another federal policy—emancipation—tended to fuel their opposition to the tax. For white critics, the tax and emancipation shared an origin story, when the "wild fanaticism of the Northern mob" overthrew the foundations of Southern political economy and racial hierarchy.[81] One Virginia farmer who compared the tobacco tax to "public robbery" likewise decried "the awful crime ... of placing the negro as a ruler over the white man."[82] White anti-tax sentiment did not preclude Black Virginians' own challenges to the revenue system. In addition to their centrality to the state's agricultural economy, thousands of African Americans worked in Virginia's tobacco factories. Those jobs, however, became less secure as the state's industry faltered, leading a group of African-American factory workers in Lynchburg to denounce the revenue system as a cruel burden upon those "who are poor and have but scant means of livelihood."[83] Prominent African-American Republicans, such as Robert Smalls and Joseph Rainey, encouraged their party to reduce rates because "the heavy tax drives the small dealers from business, and throws out of employment thousands of colored employees in tobacco factories."[84] Nonetheless, as Virginia's tobacco depression wore on, opposition to the tax became a wedge issue for Grangers and Democrats challenging the interracial Readjuster Party and its allies in the national Republican Party. Charles Postel has argued that the National Grange, and not just its Southern affiliates, "turned its back on the equal rights demands of African Americans and leveraged its power to defeat Radical Reconstruction and post-Civil War experiments in racial democracy."[85] In tobacco districts, the animosity to equal rights was always linked with animosity toward the tobacco tax. Moreover, the Democrats' anti-tax position proved attractive to white growers, warehousemen, and manufacturers who increasingly associated Northern tobacco companies, whose tax system thwarted Virginia's historical dominance of the tobacco industry, with freedpeople, whose social and political assertiveness challenged Virginia's historical racial hierarchy.[86]

African-American revenue collectors, appointed to these patronage jobs for their support of the Readjusters, personified this association. "My office looks like Africa," complained Danville's chief collector, "because I have so many colored people in it."[87] The collector's obvious disdain represented that of white manufacturers and growers throughout the region.

The Virginia tobacco industry's decline was especially wrenching, but as the fallout from the Panic worsened, the state's struggles increasingly reflected trends in the national industry. And as prices and sales declined, hard-hit tobacco interests replicated Virginians' strategy of blaming their misfortunes on the tax. Every sector of the industry, even tobacconists, expressed frustration, especially following an 1875 rate hike that the lame-duck Forty-third Congress had enacted in order to protect government income as the Panic caused customs duties to decline.[88] That increase, according to one leading Cincinnati manufacturer, had "been most disastrous to everybody connected with the tobacco trade" and had "resulted in a loss of millions of dollars."[89] Tobacconists, operating on thin margins already, had shifted the increase to both growers and consumers, thereby depressing growers' incomes and reducing rates of consumption. In response, Southern Democrats attempted to rally their bases by seizing on opposition to the tax. Democratic Virginia Representative John Randolph Tucker, who had served as the state's attorney general during the Civil War, quickly became Washington's most fervent tobacco tax opponent. Tucker penned the era's most penetrating analyses of the tax's operation, drawing upon Adam Smith and John Stuart Mill to suggest that the tax's sectionalism violated a key principle of "good government," namely, "to proportion the burdens of its taxation to the capacity of the citizens to bear them, with fair and adequate exemptions of the property and means of the poor."[90] He also convened hearings of tobacco interests before the Ways and Means Committee and led a group of Southern representatives as they proposed dozens of revisions to the tobacco revenue system.[91] Tucker's approach became emblematic of the anti-tax posture assumed by senators and representatives from Southern tobacco states following the Democratic Party's return to national prominence in the mid-seventies. It also suggested a new chapter in the history of the tobacco tax, in which opposition to the revenue system would become a firmly entrenched element of national politics.

As in the 1860s, however, the most aggressive pursuit of tax reform came not from policymakers but from industry associations. Yet unlike the 1860s, when tobacconists had organized to promote the Bureau's regulation of the commodity chain, industry organization now centered on growers' and leaf dealers' calls for abolition, or at least reduction, of the tax. Throughout the late 1870s, organizations of growers and dealers in Virginia, North Carolina, Tennessee, Kentucky, and other tobacco-growing states called for tax reform as a means of providing the grower an "adequate return for his labor."[92] Growers in Powhatan County, Virginia convened a public meeting and signed a petition attacking the tax as "oppressive" because it discriminated against the "crop we look chiefly for support and maintenance, our lands being peculiarly adapted to its growth and our labor to its cultivation."[93] The National Grange, which held its 1878 convention in Richmond, encouraged affiliates in tobacco-growing counties to flood Congress with petitions against the tax. As one such petition suggested, "In free America, it does not comport with the genius of our Government [to] oppress its products with onerous taxation."[94] Building upon the common refrains of corruption, monopolism, and sectionalism, Grangers and other local agricultural movements were harnessing popular anti-tax rhetoric to mount the first significant movement against the tax since its inception during the 1860s.[95] As the movement gained momentum, its supporters imagined a post-tax tobacco economy, in which growers, small dealers, and small manufacturers could "compete successfully with would-be monopolists."[96]

The anti-tax movement's expansion through tobacco country inspired a response from forces within and outside of the industry. A number of Eastern aristocrats, such as Charles Francis Adams, William Backhouse Astor Jr., and Anthony Joseph Drexel, fearing the imposition of an income tax in place of the tobacco tax, reminded Congress, "objects of taxation are more properly sought in the vices and luxuries of the people, such as whisky and tobacco."[97] Green Raum warned that "responsible manufacturers" did not support reduction.[98] Commission merchants, who earned profits as a percentage of sales prices, naturally preferred a higher tax that increased prices; they also enjoyed earnings on interest from small manufacturers who were forced to borrow "constantly for advances to pay this enormous tax."[99] A more concerted defense of the tax came from large manufacturers whose control of the industry depended on the revenue system's regulations. Pierre Lorillard, whose enormous New York factory paid "a larger amount of tax annually than all manufacturers of any one state, excepting only Virginia," and whose firm had come to symbolize the tax's monopolistic tendencies, outlined his support for the tax in an 1878 pamphlet. As Lorillard understood it, the tax was not corrupting, monopolistic, or sectional. Instead, its opponents simply misunderstood how the global tobacco market worked. The "price of Leaf Tobacco," he argued, was "not governed by the Internal Revenue Tax" but foreign markets, to which "60 to 75 percent of our total production is annually shipped." Lorillard likewise asserted, falsely, that the tax could not be monopolistic because there had been "a constant and steady increase in the number of manufacturers since the outbreak of the war." Much more dangerous than the tax, he argued, was public discussion of the tax, which injected uncertainty into the trade and impaired business. As a consequence of the anti-tax movement, "Tobacco Factories are lying still, thousands of operatives are thrown out of employment causing great suffering; trade relations are disorganized, a correspondence which has cost years of labor and vast sums of money to establish, is severed and destroyed."[100] For Lorillard and his allies, the lesson of the anti-tax agitation was clear: public discussion of the tax, and not the tax itself, was the greatest threat to the industry's prosperity. Lorillard's pamphlet illustrated large firms' preference for the BIR's regulatory system as well as the powerful obstacles blocking the anti-tax movement's path.

Tax Politics in the Age of Surplus

As the revenue debate progressed, discussion increasingly focused on tax incidence: who, critics asked, actually paid the tax? Congress's solution to the late-seventies conflict—reducing the rate of tax from twenty-four cents per pound to sixteen cents per pound—had done little to reduce tensions, and in fact ensured that the incidence question would continue into the 1880s. Although tobacconists ostensibly paid the tax when they purchased stamps, the consensus throughout the industry was that they shifted that burden elsewhere. Tobacconists commonly claimed they shifted the burden to consumers, but who were consumers? Were they an undifferentiated mass indulging in a luxurious vice from which they could "abstain," as opponents of tax reform suggested?[101] Or were they poor wageworkers, for whom tobacco represented a rare and thus necessary pleasure? If the latter were the case, then, as Republican leader William Kelley often argued, "You impose upon the toilers in the iron mines a tax of from 2,000 to 4,000 percent when you tax the tobacco in his pipe."[102] For their part, growers contended that tobacconists had shifted tax incidence onto them as well. "I made money in '73 and '74," claimed a Kentucky tobacco farmer in 1878, "but since the increase ... I have not made a dollar. Last year I bought tobacco for less than the cost of producing it." The same farmer described growers in his region in pitiful terms, "so low they can hardly sustain life," living "in rags, and their children in winter are but half clad."[103] By highlighting the tax's punitive, regressive effects, its opponents placed the tobacco tax alongside other emblems of public finance iniquity, such as the tariff and state property taxes. In so doing, they helped provoke the "growing social antagonism" toward contemporary public finance that began seething among labor organizations, socialists, agrarian associations, and legal theorists during the 1880s.[104]

That antagonism intensified as customs receipts rebounded to their pre-Panic highs and both tobacco and alcohol taxes generated unprecedented revenue, a situation that produced a Treasury surplus for the first time since the Civil War. Although policymakers were able to divert some of this surplus into the sinking fund for the national debt, they struggled to spend it off without creating new government programs. By 1884, the surplus had reached nearly $60 million—more than the entire tobacco revenue.[105] The result was an "embarrassment" for Republicans, who depended on the tariff—and its thriving revenue—to satisfy their core constituencies of Eastern and Midwestern industrialists, laborers, and Civil War veterans.[106] Anti-tax tobacco interests, meanwhile, added the tax's apparent uselessness to their list of complaints.

The uproar over the surplus inspired a new wave of political organization within the tobacco industry and increased calls for the tax's abolition. Further, unlike a few years earlier, no major interests, not even Lorillard, mounted a defense of the revenue system. In a passage that captured a growing consensus within the industry, the *United States Tobacco Journal* declared in 1882, "the time has now arrived when the oppressive Federal system of levying taxes upon the tobacco industry can be safely abolished."[107] Building upon the momentum of the 1870s, industry institutions with national clout, such as trade journals and leaf dealers' boards of trade, declared for tobacco interests in "every city, town, village, hamlet and farm, wherever the tobacco trade ramifies," that "the voice, the ballot if need be, should be raised against the 'looters' and plunderers of the public treasury."[108] In response, and in addition to the growers' organizations that had emerged several years earlier, local associations of cigar makers, leaf dealers, growers, and even tobacconists seized upon the demand, "Away with the Internal Revenue System!"[109]

The National Tobacco Association, essentially dormant since its pivotal contributions in the early history of the revenue system, reemerged in response to the industry-wide anti-tax movement. At a major convention in the spring of 1882, "sixty-five representatives of the most influential firms connected with the tobacco industry of the United States were in their seats." Although some members supported reduction of the tax, "most of them" called for abolition. "Uncle Sam," noted one report of the convention, "had bothered them for 19 years, and they wanted to throw him overboard."[110] As the NTA waded into tax politics in the age of surplus, it returned to organizational strategies from the 1860s: it elected an executive committee of representatives from each major tobacco city and state to present the association's views to Congress, and it printed 5,000 copies of the convention's demands for circulation to other trade interests and Congress. The composition of the NTA, however, also reflected the changing face of the tobacco industry.[111] Alongside manufacturers from New York City and Cincinnati now stood representatives from cities such as Durham and Winston, North Carolina, which had grown from tiny crossroads to dominant centers of production under the revenue system.[112] For North Carolina firms such as W.T. Blackwell & Co., made famous by its Durham Smoking Tobacco and the bull it featured in ubiquitous advertisements, and W. Duke & Sons, a growing power in the new cigarette trade, the anti-tax movement presented both opportunities and hazards. On one hand, abolition would be a relief, unencumbering them of their regulatory obligations and even potentially increasing their profits; on the other hand, these firms had thrived under the tax's regulations. Would their position in the trade be secure after abolition if more competitors flooded the market? Following its 1882 convention, the NTA forged an alliance with other industry organizations by demanding "abolition or nothing," but concerns over maintaining their legal advantages clearly weighed on members.[113]

The NTA's wariness illustrated a structural flaw in the industry's tax abolition movement. Because the revenue system's regulations isolated each link of the tobacco commodity chain, interests in each link had developed different positions: growers advocated abolition because it would open their market to a broader field of buyers, including the small tobacconists that had proliferated prior to the internal revenue era and non-licensed entities, thereby enabling them to maximize exchange skills and increase prices. Leaf dealers supported abolition because it would enable more enterprising tobacconists to enter the market, increasing competition and raising prices. Tobacconists supported abolition because the tax was no longer necessary to fund the government and, as the NTA suggested, many felt they had paid their dues long enough. At the same time, however, tobacconists evinced concerns about opening the field of competition. The aspects of abolition that might benefit growers and leaf dealers could threaten tobacconists.

These internal divisions enervated the anti-tax momentum. Discouraged by the chances for total abolition, a number of growers organizations began advocating "free leaf," or the removal of regulations on the sale of leaf tobacco.[114] Tobacconists stridently opposed the "free leaf" movement for the same reasons they had in the 1860s: it granted, as the NTA claimed in 1883, "to one class of citizens"—growers—"privileges denied to other classes"—tobacconists—by enabling growers to sell their tobacco tax-free while tobacconists continued to pay. Put

Figure 9. By the end of the 1870s, Durham, North Carolina's W.T. Blackwell & Co. was publicizing their contributions to the federal revenue in advertisements like this, from Tobacco Leaf. For large tobacconists like Blackwell, the tax proved beneficial, while calls for tax abolition presented threats to their market control. *Tobacco Leaf*, October 11, 1879.

differently, it enabled growers and smaller manufacturers to operate outside of the national tobacco market. The result would be "the utter ruin of manufacturers and dealers in Tobacco," and the destruction of the national market for manufactured tobacco that had emerged under the revenue system.[115] Israel Kimball, head of the Bureau's Tobacco Division and longtime "friend" of tobacconists, reaffirmed this position when he proclaimed that as long as the government taxed tobacco, "you have a right to demand [protection] … from this unjust, unequal and impossible competition with free leaf, with twist tobacco, with cigars made by irresponsible, illegal and unauthorized manufacturers sold in fraud of the revenue."[116] For Kimball and his friends, "responsible" manufacturers were those operating within the Bureau's rules and the commodity chain those rules created. As long as there was a revenue system, they argued, everyone working with tobacco had to participate.

Alongside the industry's structural divisions were widespread concerns that, as Lorillard had suggested several years earlier, the uncertainties surrounding the tax impaired trade. As talk of abolition advanced in 1882, trade became "paralyzed" with "anxiety" in manufacturing nodes such as Chicago, Cincinnati, Louisville, New York, and St. Louis. Tobacconists feared that Congress would abolish the revenue system after they had pre-paid taxes for a large stock, leading most to slow production "to the very minimum" and either lay off thousands of workers or cease operations entirely. In Cincinnati, tobacconists had begun producing for "hand-to-mouth orders" exclusively.[117] The consequences of "agitation" motivated some tobacconists to more firmly support abolition, which would guarantee an end to the tax's influence over productivity; others, however, simply wished to end the agitations at any cost. "We are in favor of abolishment," noted a group of Des Moines tobacconists, "but prefer to still labor under the burden of taxation than to suffer the unjust loss of money we have paid as taxes." "Agitation of the question," they suggested, rather than the tax itself, "is causing us severe stress."[118]

In addition to the tobacco industry's political instability, two external factors hindered the abolition movement. One such factor was the Republican Party's burgeoning dependence on the votes of Civil War veterans, whom the party courted with generous and costly pensions. In the decade and a half after 1865, the system had been quite limited, only compensating grievously injured soldiers and their families or the dependents of those killed in action. With the Arrears Act of 1879, however, Republicans expanded the system to offer "disability, old-age, and survivors' benefits for anyone who could claim minimal service time on the northern side" of the Civil War.[119] As those populations aged, the numbers of pension claimants skyrocketed from 135,000 in 1880 to nearly 250,000 in 1885, and 750,000 by 1895.[120] At the same time, pension expenditures rose from $27 million at the end of the 1870s to roughly $160 million by the 1890s.[121] This growing welfare system served as a patronage tool for Republicans, who depended on veteran support in the competitive national races of the 1880s. Unsurprisingly, veterans' associations, led by the Grand Army of the Republic, were hostile to the idea of tax abolition. According to one G.A.R. newspaper, "it would be supreme nonsense to abolish" the internal revenue system when it was "as certain as any human matter can be that we will need [it] for some extraordinary purpose in the next few years."[122] Proponents of tax abolition, meanwhile, loathed the "soldier element" and the politicians who "hasten to [veterans'] succor."[123] Animosity was especially strong in the South. As one Richmond writer suggested in 1886, the tax on tobacco and the pensions it funded proved that the war had not truly ended. "Long and mighty wars can not be waged for years without entailing many evil consequences," the author noted, "and the tax on Tobacco, which will probably continue as long as there are pensions to pay, is one of those evils."[124]

The other external factor shaping tobacco tax deliberations was the tariff. The tariff was the essential national political question of the post-Reconstruction United States, the one question, as Henry George put it, "upon which party lines must soon be drawn and political discussion must rage."[125] Although those party lines were never perfectly united, the basic outline of each party's position was clear. Republicans supported the tariff on the grounds that it protected domestic industries from foreign competition. Democrats—representing the agrarian West and South—tended to advocate tariff reduction and free trade to open global markets to crops and reduce the costs of manufactured goods for farmers.[126] Those positions, however, distorted each party's historical position on the tobacco tax. As the Democrats' competitiveness threatened the tariff, Republicans, especially those in the industrial Northeast, became some of the staunchest advocates for the abolition of the tobacco tax. Their hope was that eliminating internal sources of revenue would insulate the tariff from serious reduction should the Democrats come to control the government. The *United States Tobacco Journal* detected this development as early as 1883, observing that protectionists were "becoming alarmists as to the effect of any further lowering of the tariff" and were "looking for the removal of the tobacco taxes as a necessity for their salvation."[127] Meanwhile, Democrats, including many Southerners, began trying to preserve the tobacco tax for the very same reasons. In a twist that would have seemed impossible during the 1870s agitation, even representatives from tobacco states, including House Speaker and Kentuckian John Carlisle, declared against abolition.[128] For anti-tax tobacco interests, the tariff's primacy, and its ability to distort party platforms on other issues, revealed the limits of their own political influence.

Despite their internally fractured movement and significant external obstacles, tax abolitionists continued fighting the tax throughout the 1880s. Numerous national developments buoyed their hopes. President Arthur and Treasury Secretary Hugh McCulloch called for abolition of the entire revenue system save for the tax on liquor in 1884, although both departed from office several months later. Tax opponents were confident their time had come when Grover Cleveland assumed office in 1885, but Congress failed to act and, by the end of the year, tax abolitionists' hopes were vanquished again. Indeed, every year of the 1880s witnessed a brief revival of hope for the tax's abolition, followed by a frustrating defeat. In a refrain that could have applied to every legislative session of the decade, the *Western Tobacco Journal* lamented in 1884 that "there was never any intention on the part of those who had it largely in their power to shape the course of Congress to do anything to relieve the Tobacco trade."[129]

The failure of Congress to reform the tax system left many tax opponents, particularly growers and leaf dealers, to rehash the criticisms they had developed during the 1870s. The Oxford, North Carolina Tobacco Board of Trade complained that the revenue system was "protecting the monopolies from competition," and that their section, in which tobacco was "the principal product," was unjustly burdened by the tax. "We have been promised prompt action ... by our representatives on the stump and the Democratic Party in their platform," the farmers complained, but still they labored under the "depression" of low prices. Year after year, petitions for repeal flowed into Congress from more than a dozen tobacco-growing states but elicited little response by the end of the decade.[130] It had come to seem as though the era of low prices and limited competition would be a permanent component, and not simply a phase, of tobacco's political economy. As one agricultural analyst put it, "Tobacco crops" seemed to exist "to make the rich few richer, and leave the poor many, who produce the crops, as poor as before, and often poorer."[131]

As growers grew disenchanted, tobacconists renounced abolition altogether. One Richmond tobacconist called abolition talk "delusion of the rankest kind," while Durham announced its arrival as a major hub when its city paper, the *Tobacco Plant*, announced its support for the internal revenue system.[132] "Durham pays almost, if not altogether, as much internal revenue taxes as the balance of the State," the *Plant*'s editor boasted, echoing Pierre Lorillard from a decade earlier, "and there is no trouble or annoyance here."[133] Others more openly embraced their preference for a system that limited competition. One Philadelphia cigar maker ventured that "abolition would injure the trade—both the employers, by increasing the products of irresponsible parties, who have no reputation at stake, flooding the markets with trash, and thus ruin prices, as well as employees ... by lowering the standard of wages now paid."[134] Even the *United States Tobacco Journal*, which had stridently advocated abolition during the 1870s and early 1880s, had backed off. After years of legislative failures, the *Journal* grew hostile toward tobacco growers who continued to advocate for abolition. Comparing the abolition movement to both the "perverse ... spirit of slave-holding" and to the "Greenback craze," in which rural populists advocated for public control of the monetary system during the 1860s and 1870s, the *Journal* condescended that a "similar illusion seems to have taken hold of our tobacco farmers." The *Journal* disputed the claim that trade was "monopolized," and countered that increased competition would only oversupply the nation's tobacco market and "have the same effect on prices that always results when trade is overdone."[135] For the tax's emboldened defenders, abolition of the system under which they had thrived now seemed an absurd notion.

Although opponents of the revenue system would continue to challenge it in the decades to come, the movement against the tobacco tax effectively died by 1890. In that year, the trend toward "monopolism" reached its pinnacle when James B. Duke, who had risen to prominence under the revenue system, formed the American Tobacco Company. In the years ahead, the ATC, widely derided by competitors, leaf dealers, and growers as "The Trust," would rely on price slashing, horizontal and vertical integration, aggressive advertising, and the internal revenue system's regulations to dominate the global tobacco trade.[136]

It was also in 1890 that Congress' decade-long deliberation of tobacco tax abolition sputtered to its finale. As with each of the preceding legislative sessions, tax deliberations were closely linked to the tariff debate, over which Republicans, in control of Congress and the Presidency, prevailed. The resulting McKinley Tariff expanded protection by raising import duties and adding new items to the protected list, such as tin manufactures and numerous agricultural products.[137] The promise of increased tariff revenue, which would further reduce the need for tobacco revenue, enticed the tobacco tax's opponents through the summer, but in keeping with experience, they were disappointed by fall. Rather than abolish the tax, Congress merely abolished fees for occupational licenses while preserving the occupational license system. The Bureau would continue to require every tobacco business to register with and obtain a license from local collectors; to force growers to sell to limited markets and keep careful records of their sales; and to trace tobacco from the field to the spittoon, cigarette, or cigar.[138] The balance of power instituted by the Internal Revenue System would continue to shape the tobacco industry as it accelerated toward an era of unprecedented wealth, consolidation, and influence.

3

Tobacco's "Imperfect Knowledge"

Governance, Classification, and Conflict in the World Tobacco Market, 1865-1890

During the final third of the nineteenth century, detailed market reports filled the pages of *Tobacco Leaf*, the *Western Tobacco Journal*, and the *United States Tobacco Journal*. These reports traced the flow of tobacco and capital within the world tobacco market, describing *quantity*— how much tobacco was available, and how much demand a given market had for it—but always within overarching, esoteric criteria of *quality*. Reports described the demand for "colory" Virginia tobacco in London and "dry Missouri leaf" in Liverpool, Bremen buyers' anticipation for "Cincinnati leafy lugs of fair color," and the movement of "common leafy lugs to medium grades" in Antwerp. Exporters in the United States relied on similar categories. For example, when Baltimore factors reported their market's prices, they used broad regional categories, such as "Ohios," and richly descriptive subcategories: "greenish and brown," "medium to fine red," "common to medium spangled," and "fine spangled to yellow," none of which applied evenly to tobacco from other regions.[1]

Tobacco's esoteric quality criteria made for a striking contrast with the standards underlying other Gilded Age commodity markets. Reports from the Chicago Board of Trade often included no mention of quality as they tracked the movement of corn, wheat, or hogs, and when they did it was in reference to seemingly objective, intuitive standards, such as "No. 2" corn.[2] During the course of the nineteenth century, technologies—such as the grain elevator—and political institutions—such as the Chicago Board of Trade—had made these commodities interchangeable by joining, or defeating, competing ideas about quality in favor of unified "knowledge infrastructures." As the historian Paul N. Edwards has written, knowledge infrastructures are geographically and culturally extensive networks of trade and governance that grounded a "technical and institutional base supporting everyday work and action."[3] For commodities markets, those bases were shared assumptions about quality. Markets that did not question quality could support increasingly sophisticated means of processing, transportation, and data collection, the combined forces of which produced the turn of the century's globalized, financialized markets in grains, cotton, and other major staples.[4]

But what if a commodity lacked a knowledge infrastructure? What if distant buyers could not reduce it to a numerical abstraction? Such was the case with tobacco.[5] Despite a series of momentous changes that altered global tobacco commerce between the 1860s and 1890s, particularly the emancipation of agrarian labor in the United States and the global reconstruction of states and their tobacco tax systems, no technology or political institution linked tobacco's diverse epistemologies. This meant that buyers in Bremen or brokers in Baltimore could arrive at different opinions about a leaf of tobacco from Ohio while also judging that leaf quite differently from *other* Ohio tobaccos—not to mention those from another state or country. Nonetheless, tobacco remained one of the United States' principal export commodities and a major current of global commerce.[6] Lacking a unified infrastructure, what forces organized tobacco's global trade during the late nineteenth century and promulgated its esoteric quality criteria?[7] What were the consequences of these market conditions?

In place of a knowledge infrastructure, a diverse constellation of import and export institutions governed ideas of quality in the late nineteenth-century world tobacco market. These institutions derived their authority by governing tobacco exchange within bounded territories, and they commonly took one of two forms. *Revenue regimes* were national institutions—states or the contracted partners of states—that exercised sovereignty over geographically circumscribed tobacco economies for the purpose of extracting public revenue. *Junction regimes* were quasi-public agglomerations of merchants and their capital—boards of trade, exchanges, and similar professional associations—that formed at the intersections between tobacco's cultivation and distribution.[8] In the United States, junction regimes stretched their authority from urban junctions to rural hinterlands, drawing tobacco into their warehouses and directing it to buyers around the world, including revenue regimes.

In the exercise of their territorial authority, revenue regimes and junction regimes responded to tobacco's variability with classifications that I call "fictions of standardization." To some extent, these fictions were rooted in each region's climate, soil conditions, and labor routines.[9] Yet tobacco's production was so complex, with growers suckering plants in the field, harvesting at different times, drying and curing for varying periods, and prizing into hogsheads, that the range of outcomes was irreducible to repeatable standards. Fictions of standardization were thus somewhat arbitrary, although even in their arbitrariness they lent order to the world tobacco market. It was for that reason that institutions promoted them, over time making them appear less arbitrary through the disciplines of habituation.[10]

Ideas about quality were regimes' levers of advantage over competitors, subjects, and trade partners. Fictions of standardization enabled revenue regimes to offer tobacco at varying prices, thereby extracting revenue from tobacco consumers at each social rank. In this way, ordering tobacco became a means of ordering society. Junction regimes, on the other hand, relied on fictions of standardization to brand themselves and attract business from local growers and foreign buyers. For instance, when the Louisville Board of Trade presented itself as the leading market for Kentucky's "Burley crop" and "dark and heavy types," it distinguished between itself and markets elsewhere, thereby carving an influential niche in the global trade.[11] In contrast with institutions such as the Chicago Board of Trade, however, tobacco's regimes lacked the political and commercial power to impose their boundaries upon other institutions.[12] The consequence was a tobacco world market defined by multiple, overlapping, and conflicting fictions of standardization.

These conditions produced two outcomes that characterized the Gilded Age tobacco world market. First, middlemen became figures of significant consequence, personifying the powers and limits of tobacco's governing institutions. By claiming special knowledge of tobacco, these figures—brokers, purchasing agents, warehouse inspectors, and tax assessors—thrived upon the contestation and negotiation produced by multiple fictions of standardization. They were the experts of the world tobacco market, interpreting tobacco based on the standards invented by their employers and turning the products of rural nature into legible, saleable goods.[13] Second, coexisting fictions of standardization led to widespread accusations of fraud and deceit. Without a knowledge infrastructure, regimes depended on reputations grounded in porous, negotiable fictions of standardization. When competitors, suppliers, or customers questioned those reputations, as they inevitably did, it was difficult, sometimes impossible, for regimes to defend themselves.[14]

The Global Reconstruction of Revenue Regimes

Emerging states had subjected tobacco to taxation and surveillance since the sixteenth century, when the weed first entered the currents of trans-Atlantic commerce. The Venetians banned the cultivation of tobacco and auctioned rights to a monopoly over its sale. James I assured the productivity of import duties by banning the plant's cultivation in the British Isles and barring imports from colonies other than Virginia. The eighteenth-century Spanish Empire turned tobacco into a prodigious source of revenue by monopolizing its cultivation and sale in Mexico and the Philippines.[15] Prussian authorities in the early nineteenth century taxed growers based on the quantity of tobacco they produced.[16] The French tobacco monopoly, or "Régie," originated under Louis XIV and reemerged—after a brief revolutionary abolition—in 1810, when Napoleon monopolized the purchase and manufacture of leaf tobacco and the sale of finished tobacco products.[17]

The American tobacco tax was an elaboration upon these centuries-long trends as well as an example of the late nineteenth-century global revolution in state making—what Charles Maier has called the "global triumph of the modern state."[18] Between the 1860s and the turn of the century, dozens of states, particularly those undergoing processes of unification or reconstruction, echoed their early-modern predecessors by developing new tobacco revenue regimes or refashioning older ones. In addition to the United States, these governments included Argentina, Austria-Hungary, Brazil, Egypt, Germany, Greece, Italy, Mexico, Portugal, Ottoman Turkey, Romania, and Russia.[19] At the same time, established regimes in France, Great Britain, and Spain extended their influence over new swaths of the tobacco-producing world. For the most part, these tax systems depended on imported American tobacco, and American tobacco interests, who exported roughly fifty percent of the nation's annual crop, depended on the business of foreign fiscal regimes.[20] Some governments, such as Italy, Spain, and Great Britain, were almost entirely reliant on imports from the United States, while others, such as Turkey and Germany, balanced imports with domestic production. National particulars aside, public revenue systems around the globe increasingly depended on the tobacco fields of the American South and Midwest.

Throughout the nineteenth century, states devised a variety of means for extracting tobacco revenue, with each system reflecting the specific historical dynamics by which states distinguished, or appeared to distinguish, between themselves and their economies.[21] Some, modeled on the French and Spanish monopolies, were less concerned with such distinctions and extended state monopoly over the entire domestic commodity chain. French growers applied to a tobacco commission for the right to plant, and the same commission provided seeds and oversaw the destruction of seedbeds after harvest; in between, growers followed "the Government's directions as to the mode of planting, weeding, pruning, etc." Government agents oversaw the purchase and importation of all foreign tobacco and barred private importation. They also operated factories while "old soldiers, or the families of persons who have rendered some service to the state" operated retail establishments.²² Direct monopolies grew increasingly rare toward the century's end, however, as administrative burdens and financial risk led states to contract oversight of their tobacco economies to financiers.²³ In Italy, for instance, a consortium of "native and foreign capitalists" secured monopoly rights through a joint-stock company called *Società Anonima Italiana per la Regia Cointeressata dei Tabacchi* (Italian Limited Company for the Cointerested Direction of Tobacco).²⁴ The Ottoman government, facing a mounting debt crisis during the 1870s and 1880s, had little choice but to sell their monopoly to a consortium of major financial institutions, including the Rothschild-owned Credit-Anstalt and the German financier Gerson Bleichröder.²⁵ The British system functioned similarly to a monopoly, although it was not technically one because it did not fix retail prices. Instead, the state barred all tobacco cultivation—as it had since the sixteenth century—and taxed imported tobacco products at roughly 500 percent of their import value. It also licensed tobacco manufacturers and dealers, who, although technically private enterprises, operated under the supervision of revenue authorities.²⁶

Where tobacco merchant classes maintained political authority, states tended to adopt more liberal revenue regimes. In an approach not unlike that of the United States, tobacco-producing countries such as Belgium and Russia relied on mixed systems by licensing and taxing various points in the commodity chain.²⁷ Germany eventually settled on a similar system, although Bismarck spent years pushing for a French-style monopoly scheme only to be rebuffed by his country's politically influential tobacco interests.²⁸ Likewise, Spanish merchants and Philippine growers successfully pushed for the overthrow of the Philippine monopoly in 1880, while in 1892 the Iranian merchant class orchestrated a successful nationwide revolt against the leasing of the state monopoly to a British investor.²⁹ To be sure, mixed systems were no less "statist" than the French monopoly. Rather, they signified the dual pressures of tobacco-producing states to both extract revenue and produce an exportable tobacco crop. They needed to balance multiple demands, such as incentivizing growers, building partnerships with merchants and manufacturers, limiting smuggling, and administering collection. Mixed systems promised both internal revenue and energized tobacco production, which could make growers more competitive with major tobacco exporters—particularly the United States—for influence in foreign markets.

Despite national particularities, revenue regimes produced comparable consequences around the world. Everywhere it was taxed tobacco became part of state attempts to "civilize" subjects by eliminating other historic uses—for example as an item of ceremonial practice or barter or household independence.[30] An 1874 report from Lebanon, published in *Tobacco Leaf*, illustrates this dynamic:

> The Turkish Government has taken the monopoly of the trade into its own hands, and has imposed conditions upon the tribes of the Lebanon who cultivate this plant, which are found distasteful, and are resented. The surveillance to which they would have to submit in the future cultivation is a source of embarrassment to these shy and half-wild people. They are therefore abandoning the culture, and growing food grains instead.[31]

So-called half-wild tobacco cultivators—those who lived on the peripheries of state power and whose crops were not auditable—existed all over the world in the nineteenth century, from India to the Levant, Russia to the American South. Tobacco held diverse meanings in these cultures: it was a vessel of pleasure, a source of cultural identity, and a means of maintaining relative autonomy from states and markets. This was why revenue regimes, no matter the specifics of their tax systems, devised strict regulations for the agricultural production of tobacco. As long as unsupervised tobacco cultivation continued, the state would lose revenue and struggle to draw its subjects into its influence. In the age of the modern state, it was thus increasingly difficult to remain "half-wild" and continue cultivating tobacco.[32]

As states pulled tobacco growers into their revenue apparatuses, they also drew thousands of agrarians, especially women, into tobacco factories. The Spanish monopoly's Seville factory, "one of the 'sights' to be seen by foreigners visiting that city," employed 2,000 women and girls.[33] The Regie Company of the United Principalities of Moldavia and Walachia, a private contractor financed by English capital, relied on female labor to produce "all the tobacco of the country," while 22,000 of the 36,000 employees of the Austrian monopoly were women.[34] This process played out in the United States as well, where major tobacco firms relied on agrarian women who were often, especially in the South, members of tobacco-growing families. Allen and Ginter, one of the leading cigarette manufacturers of the Gilded Age, employed 800 women and 100 men in its Richmond plant in 1886; by 1900, more women than men worked as industrial tobacco workers in Virginia.[35] This feminization of industrial tobacco production was part of the broader agro-political shift inherent in tobacco taxation, by which authorities compelled tobacco growers to depend on state-sanctioned markets. By drawing female labor into tobacco factories, authorities could depress wages while subsidizing the low pay with the unpaid subsistence labor of men on the farm. Under such a system, tobacco would ideally flow into carefully regulated channels and workers would scrape by with their low wages and reduced subsistence production.[36] As the Turkish example suggests, however, growers resisted such systems and would only produce tobacco if incentivized—or, more likely, compelled—to do so.

Procuring Tobacco, Producing the State Effect: Revenue Regimes

Global taxation made tobacco perhaps the most policed commodity of the late nineteenth century. Anxious to collect revenue, states directed their police powers both inward—onto farms, factories, and shops—and outward, onto the borders and ports where untaxed foreign tobacco could enter. In a particularly evocative example of such outward authority, Spain banned incoming vessels from landing if they held any tobacco not consigned to the government—even if it was consigned to another government. So strictly was the regulation observed that in 1880, the U.S. Navy had to delay a tobacco-laden vessel bound for France via Valencia until, after more than a week, the Spanish Treasury granted permission to dock. Several years earlier, a private American vessel, unaware of the law, was fined half a million dollars for carrying Italian-bound tobacco into the port of Cartagena. These were glaring examples, but they illustrated a trend that played out in far more mundane ways at ports and borders around the world, as customs inspectors, weighers, appraisers, and other treasury officials inspected vessels and people for signs of illicit tobacco.[37]

Along with policing, revenue regimes managed their tobacco economies through data collection. Hence the French monopoly could confidently identify the nation's total number of smokers (5,671,000), mean annual consumption (4.98 kilos, or just over ten pounds), and the number of cigarettes consumed per day (805 million) and per second (9,323).[38] Likewise, faced with Bismarck's monopolization scheme, the German Parliament ordered a comprehensive statistical report on Germany's total agricultural and manufacturing output—an effort similar to those compiled by the U.S. Department of Agriculture's Bureau of Statistics and Census Bureau.[39] Liberal tax regimes drew on the data collection of merchants, and those in the tobacco economy's core cities—Antwerp, Bremen, Liverpool, and New York—produced reams of statistics on the volume, quality, and sources of trade within the global tobacco economy.

But official statistics did not tell the whole story. Despite extensive policing and surveillance efforts, smuggling persisted. Cigars slipped past customs officers, leaf tobacco passed over borders, and exporters and importers manipulated scales and other measures. "The severe fiscal regulations to which the trade is everywhere subjected," claimed an editor of Cincinnati's *Western Tobacco Journal*, "have given rise to all kinds of extra-legal devises for supplying smokers with their beloved weed." Such was the extent of the black market, the editor continued, that "the official statistics which are periodically published in connection with Tobacco can never be accepted as a truthful, or even moderately truthful, reflex of its real history."[40] The "real history" was never completely knowable, but its existence—or even popular discussion of its existence in trade journals—exposed a gulf between states' performances of power and their actual management of the tobacco economies. As the editor implied, there was something delusional about the production of so-called official tobacco statistics.

Policing and statistics were only delusional, however, if their intention was complete elimination of illicit tobacco trades. In fact, these techniques of governance had purposes that extended beyond revenue collection. When states hunted down tobacco products at their borders or enumerated their citizens' taste for cigarettes, they manufactured the very idea of the state—an entity at once incorporeal and seemingly autonomous, embodied by physical manifestations such as ports of entry, tobacco tax stamps, and uniformed customs officers. They constituted themselves through external discipline—confiscation, imprisonment, and fines—but did so even more effectively through internal, habituated discipline: the exporter studying a given port's regulations, for example, or the nervous sailor stashing smuggled cigars under his cap. States required actual revenue, but the discovery of smuggled tobacco and the precision of statistics were less significant than the internal disciplines tobacco taxes produced. This entire process, what Timothy Mitchell has called the "state effect," gave the appearance of a world made simple, a "binary order" of individual life on one hand and the state on the other, an "inert 'structure' that somehow stands apart from individuals, precedes them, and contains them and gives a framework to their lives." In the age of the modern state, tobacco, even if it was illicit, inculcated this "binary order." It always signified that other side of life, that of the "inert structure" apart from society.[41]

The state effect was particularly evident in the ways government monopolies, known by U.S. tobacco interests as "*régies*" or "regies," procured American tobacco. Although procurement processes varied between governments, they always depended on elaborate, state-designed fictions of standardization. The French procurement process exemplified this tendency. Each year, the government publicly posted its tobacco demands in Paris, New York, and New Orleans and called for bids to fill the contract. The state structured its demands around a gross total subdivided into highly specific subcategories. The 1877 contract, for example, called for 5.1 million kilos from Kentucky, 2 million from Virginia, and 2.2 million each from Maryland and Ohio. Sub-classes divided these categories further: "MS," for example, for "Maryland Selections," supposedly the finest Maryland tobacco, which comprised five percent of the order. "MA," "MB," and "MC" made up the rest of the order and signified, respectively, medium quality, common quality, and "lugs." The Spanish government specified further: "Selections" were "of body, ripe, fresh, juicy, of good color, spread and flavor, and perfectly sound," while "Medium Leaf," although ripe, fresh, and "of good color," was not "perfectly sound." "Lugs" were merely ripe, fresh, and sound.[42] At times, contracts specified region more particularly, such as the Italian Regie's demand for "heavy Clarksville (Tennessee) wrappers, 26 inches long" and "Paducah (Kentucky) style, 24 inches long."[43] Wary that their demands be misunderstood, regies presented samples in their New York and New Orleans consulates. Exactitude adorned the entire process: selections were "perfectly sound," a supply must be "precisely of Virginia or Kentucky," and the contracted amounts—5.1 million pounds here, 2.2 million there—exuded precision. Yet subjectivity shot through these demands, too. After all, there was no universal definition of "fresh," no final arbiter of "good color."

Within their borders, effective state monopolies imposed standards with minimal contestation.[44] In so doing, they extrapolated from tobacco a broader ordering of society, such as the elite stratum of smokers who consumed "Selections" or the masses who got by on "lugs." The world tobacco market was a collection of these taxonomies, each offering a slightly different ordering of leaf quality and social class.

States maintained fictions of standardization with the support of international networks of middlemen who procured tobacco for them.[45] At the top of these networks were contractors who bid to supply a regie with American tobacco. Although they were ultimately responsible for filling regies' orders, contractors did not usually obtain tobacco themselves. For that task, they financed U.S.-based correspondents, many of whom were well known in American tobacco circles, such as New York's George Reusens, Max Abenheim, and Toel, Rose & Company. Because American tobacco markets were geographically diffuse, correspondents oversaw staffs of buyers, or "agents," who fanned out into the tobacco districts of the South and West. Through this network of contractors, correspondents, and agents, foreign states extended their fictions of standardization into the export-tobacco regions of Maryland, Virginia, Ohio, Kentucky, and Tennessee.

Theoretically, regie agents entered markets at a disadvantage. Because regies very publicly stated their demands, sellers knew what agents wanted, how much they could afford to pay, and by which date they had to deliver. Sellers could use this information to extort maximum prices from agents by "cornering" tobacco that matched the contractors' needs and holding onto it as the deadline approached. This was only a theoretical problem, however, as sellers could only do this if they knew, first, how much progress contractors had made toward filling their lot in other markets and, second, which agents represented regie contractors. For these reasons, agents obscured their identities, slowly eroding sellers' advantages as the clock ticked toward the regie deadline. "These gentlemen are among the brightest, most astute and close-mouthed dealers in American tobacco," noted *Tobacco Leaf* in 1887. "They do much when to the ordinary observer they seem to be doing little."[46]

Sellers likewise held a theoretical advantage based on the fictions of standardization that accompanied their region and the quality of their crop. Such was the case, for example, for producers of "Clarksville" tobacco. For dealers in that region, awareness that the Italian buyer needed 100 hogsheads of Clarksville selections would be extremely valuable. But that advantage shifted to regie agents if they were willing to misrepresent the tobacco they purchased. This was not difficult because regie standards were, as *Tobacco Leaf* put it, merely an "approximation" of regie demands.[47]

Under these circumstances, agents became masters at matching the diffuse, subjective qualities of a given tobacco crop with regies' precise but fictitious demands. Their task was not necessarily to find exactly what regies had asked for, but to estimate what regies would actually accept. "I tell you the displaying of types by these governments is only a formality," asserted one prominent buyer. "What we sell to them suits them, and that's nobody else's business."[48] Of course, this practice eliminated sellers' knowledge of their own goods, and with it their ability to bargain with agents. Under these circumstances, growers and dealers might sell tobacco under the impression it fit within one category—"Medium Leaf," for instance—and middlemen could subsequently declare it "Selections" when delivering to regies.

According to one whistleblower, swindling of this sort was the only way middlemen could earn a profit. Writing in 1879, J.S. Moore, an employee of the New York Custom House and prominent free trade advocate, argued that middlemen, "in connivance with European officials, palm off to their respective governments the refuse of our Kentucky, Virginia, Maryland, and Ohio tobaccos as a first-class article." In a detailed analysis published in the *New York Evening Post* and *Tobacco Leaf,* Moore suggested the procurement process had distorted prices and diminished American tobacco's "good name for its excellent quality." Although critics challenged the accuracy of Moore's conclusions, the debate that followed suggested his argument was sound. Writing in *Tobacco Leaf*, a journal with close ties to middlemen, Edward Burke bounced between blaming growers for raising poor tobacco and defending middlemen. Taxonomies of standards, Burke argued, merely symbolized "the ultimate extreme ... of the Regie's desires, but in nowise indicate what the Regie will accept if it will be impracticable to secure exactly what they want."[49] Nor did middlemen necessarily disagree. "Who can tell the difference in what the European governments want?" asked George Reusens, perhaps the most prominent regie buyer of the era. "They display their samples or types, according to which they want their tobacco. I try and come up to their demands to the best of my knowledge and ability." It was, he continued, "ridiculous" to expect that anyone could "procure ... exactly what they really want."[50]

The gulf between regie demands and supply realities illustrated the dissonance of the Gilded Age world tobacco market. On one hand, states and private buyers regimented the market with ornate fictions of standardization that, at least on paper, seemed to eliminate subjectivity and uncertainty. Beyond these standards, impressive representations of state power—police, statistics, and tax revenues—appeared to verify this framework, and American sellers ostensibly intended to verify it further by meeting its demands. But the actual experiences of sellers and buyers evinced something more opaque, a market in which ideas about type or quality were much more fluid than regie demands suggested. In this context, middlemen were the only authority that really mattered—it was up to them to determine what "selections" or "lugs" were, and they kept how they did that to themselves.

The global market's opacity incensed American sellers. Growers, dealers, and their representatives in government regularly denounced regie procurement networks. "The Regie system," insisted one critic in Chicago's *National Tobacco Review*, "is a tacit complex government syndicate, to control the Tobacco trade of the world; to make all the revenue possible for themselves. It is based on the old feudal parental principal of the Kings—the people are our children and our slaves, and our will is law."[51] At times, American interests responded by attempting to play the middlemen's game. Such was the case in 1885 when a Louisville firm named Sawyer, Wallace & Co. attempted to corner a grade needed—"or supposed to be needed"—by the Spanish regie's agents. Others, notably local boards of trade, turned to the federal state for support, and at various points in the postbellum era institutions such as the House Committee on Foreign Affairs and the State and Agriculture departments attempted to mitigate foreign buyers' power.[52] In the end, perhaps for lack of political will or leverage, little came of these strategies. Throughout the late nineteenth century, American tobacco producers made the case that they were bound to the unfair conditions of the global market, "a prey to the organized operators of foreign contractors."[53]

Controlling the Traffic of World Tobacco Commerce: Junction Regimes

Amid the global reconstruction of tobacco revenue regimes, dozens of junction regimes took shape in the United States. Junction regimes were governing institutions in the form of trade associations. Established primarily by warehousemen but often in partnership with buyers, brokers, and manufacturers, they emerged in response to postbellum upheavals in the tobacco economy.[54] Although some junction regimes organized in the antebellum period, their widespread development was part of the broader political surge sparked by internal taxation, as business interests formalized their relations in order to influence revenue policy. The growing significance of western tobacco culture, particularly in Ohio and Kentucky, likewise encouraged institutional development around railroad junctions where business interests could concentrate political and commercial power. As such, junction regimes reflected tobacco's postbellum commercial concentration into several major cities—New York, Baltimore, Richmond, Cincinnati, and Louisville—and many smaller hubs. "Concentration is the thing," pronounced a booster in Clarksville, Tennessee, indicating the central function of every junction regime: to draw together hinterland growers and distant, often foreign buyers, connecting each American node to the world tobacco market. The annual reports of the Richmond Tobacco Exchange illustrated the importance of concentration, enumerating the millions of pounds of tobacco drawn into the exchange and the cities to which Richmond buyers exported it: Bordeaux, Bremen, Fiume, Genoa, Glasgow, Le Havre, Liverpool, London, and Trieste.

Once tobacco entered a junction, the dominant local regime determined its quality through the perpetually controversial practice of inspection. Ideally, inspectors mitigated the inherent risks of purchasing half-ton barrels of tobacco with only "imperfect knowledge" of their contents by providing information about what was inside of them.[55] Some regimes merely assured buyers that hogsheads had not been falsely packed, while others offered more thorough analysis of the "true inwardness of the thing," including selecting a batch of tobacco, or "sample," that represented the tobacco's quality.[56] Although the process differed from city to city, an Arkansas traveler's 1887 description of inspection in Louisville captured the labor routines and racial exploitation common to tobacco inspection:

Let me first explain that there are a number of official inspectors, one of whom, on the morning this or that hogshead is to be "put up," comes along with his big strapping negro bucks, who lift the staves clean off the big yellow cylinder of prized leaf inside, and thrust great sharp iron cleavers, big as crowbars, into the bulk at various places, and thus the mass is riven apart so that samples may be drawn. This breaking of the hogsheads has caused the sales to be called "breaks." The inspector takes a number of "hands," as the bunches of leaf are termed, and putting them together, ties them in a new and larger bunch, to which he attaches a label showing the number of the hogshead, and which, after his official seal in wax has been affixed, becomes a "sample."[57]

Inspection originated in colonial Virginia and Maryland and generally fell under the purview of states until the Civil War era. Virginia's inspection system, the archetype of state oversight, traced its origins to the Inspection Act of 1730. Under the law, growers of export tobacco marketed their crops at public warehouses, where public officials inspected it and, if it failed inspection, destroyed the crop. Growers and buyers paid fees associated with the storage, the inspectors' wages, and state taxes. During the antebellum period, the power to appoint inspectors shifted from county courts to the governor's office and inspectors became salaried

Figure 10. The work of a junction regime. In the tobacco warehouses of Danville, Virginia, buyers sampled hogsheads of tobacco to judge their quality. In Danville's factories, as in tobacco factories around the world, women did much of the work to prepare tobacco for consumption. In Southern junction regimes, African American women were essential to the tobacco manufacturing economy. From *The New South: Supplement to Harper's Weekly*, January 29, 1887.

state officials.⁵⁸ The system had invited accusations of corruption since its inception, which only intensified amid the wrenching changes and sense of decline within Virginia's tobacco political economy. In response, elite growers and their political allies defended the system as a bulwark of international confidence in Virginia tobacco, with James Kemper, the Conservative Reconstruction-era governor, describing inspectors as the "impartial" interpreters of tobacco's "numerous grades in respect of character and value."⁵⁹

Virginia's ascendant junction regimes, particularly the powerful Richmond Tobacco Association (RTA), did not agree. In a lengthy petition decrying state inspection, Association members reminded Kemper and the General Assembly "that there are as many qualities of tobacco nearly as there are wines," and that the affixing of a state inspection brand "can in no way affect the standard of tobacco." Tobacco's criteria of quality were simply too varied, too esoteric for a single standard—"passed"—to affect buyers' trust. Moreover, Association members believed fraudulent inspections had degraded international confidence in Virginia tobacco, thereby contributing to the industry's postbellum decline.⁶⁰ Maryland's junction regimes proclaimed that the crisis was equally severe there. "Nearly every shipping merchant who has seen Maryland tobacco samples abroad," argued the Baltimore Tobacco Board of Trade, "has encountered numerous instances of the grossest carelessness in a failure to fairly indicate the character, quality, and condition of the tobacco which such samples are intended to represent."⁶¹

According to junction regimes in Virginia, Maryland, and Missouri—all states that employed some form of state inspection—eliminating export inspections would preclude these abuses.⁶² They embedded this demand within broader theories of social, commercial, and state development. State inspection was appropriate for earlier eras, argued members of the Tobacco Association of St. Louis, when it "fostered and developed" tobacco commerce and ensured that "justice might be done to both owners and buyers of leaf tobacco."⁶³ The RTA's secretary, a commission merchant named Peyton Wise, claimed the "police power of society, protecting all against dishonesty, as well as against their own incapacity to take care of themselves, was only tolerated during those periods when the principles of civil liberty and political economy were unknown." Wise was a former Confederate general and ardent promoter of the Lost Cause, but he could let go of the past when it suited him.⁶⁴ The age of state-directed market regulation had passed, he suggested, and with it passed the need for public tobacco inspection. Drawing on the abolition of inspection laws for other commodities, junction regimes demanded like treatment so the "laws of trade," and not laws of the state, could direct the movement of tobacco into global markets.⁶⁵

Anti-inspection campaigns formed against the backdrop of emancipation and, particularly in Virginia, the parceling of erstwhile plantations into freeholder and sharecropping plots.[66] With the system's demise, urban warehousemen could advance capitalist social relations over the thousands of growers now farming former plantation land. This process had begun several decades earlier elsewhere in Virginia and North Carolina, where a newer form of marketing—the loose-leaf auction system—sidestepped inspection laws by selling tobacco in bare piles, rather than in hogsheads.[67] Although loose-leaf auctions supplied domestic buyers, their logic—buyers and growers interacting directly as independent agents, rather than through state intermediaries—informed the laissez-faire philosophies of export-focused junction regimes elsewhere in the South.

Under pressure from the state's junction regimes, the Virginia General Assembly abolished state inspection in 1878.[68] Scholars have described this as a signal event in the "unstoppable emergence of the laissez-faire market," but that is not quite accurate.[69] Rather, the end of state inspection merely shifted governance of tobacco's quality from the state to junction regimes.

This became clear by 1881, just three years after the abolition of state inspection. Abolition had not eased RTA's concerns about the international reputation of Richmond tobacco and, in a hedge against their earlier laissez-faire faith, they formed a "Committee on the General Interests of the Market" to develop a strategy to "vivify" the tobacco trade. The strategy they landed on, apparently without irony, was a law of inspection for all leaf tobacco traded in the city. For the first inspector under the new law, RTA selected Peyton Wise, the leader of Richmond's anti-inspection campaign several years earlier. Under the new rules he faced annual reelection by his peers, hired deputies approved by the RTA's Board of Managers, executed a bond to insure "faithful performance of his duties," and assumed responsibility for accurate sampling of all hogsheads inspected under his watch. "He shall also act as a reporter," the new law stated, "and furnish daily, weekly, monthly, and annual reports of the market, with statistics." The city's tobacco market would be more assiduously governed than it had been in the days of state inspection.[70]

Federal tax law facilitated junction regimes' exercise of power. As indicated in chapter 2, the Bureau of Internal Revenue forbade the sale of tobacco in open markets, instead compelling growers to sell only to licensed dealers or manufacturers. As those buyers congregated in warehouses controlled by junction regimes, the boundaries of the tobacco market narrowed, limiting growers' competitive advantages while giving them no voice in the inspection process. Growers protested vigorously, particularly the elite planters who held sway under the earlier state inspection systems and had decried their abolition. "The planters want fair play and equal justice," argued the tobacco-growing members of Nottoway County, Virginia's Bellefonte Grange. As "farmers and planters," they suggested, "[we] have rights as well as the Tobacco Exchange at Richmond."[71] Their protests had little effect. The junction regimes, comprised of warehousemen and manufacturers, exercised complete authority over inspection.[72]

By the 1880s, junction regimes dominated the U.S. export tobacco trade. They included the Association of the Tobacco Trade of Cincinnati (ATTC), which had proved so influential during the era's internal revenue debates and served as a model of market governance for regimes elsewhere. Other prominent junction regimes were the tobacco boards of trade in cities from New York to Louisville to Paducah, as well as the tobacco associations of Richmond and Lynchburg. Looking outward from the United States, these institutions were portals to global markets, facilitating the movement of leaf tobacco from rural hinterlands into foreign revenue regimes and exerting impressive authority over its purchase and distribution. They adjudicated disputes, appointed officials, extracted fees, and set the hours tobacco sales could take place and the procedures for protest and reclamation. They tracked the credit of the sellers and buyers who used their market, making it a condition of entry.[73] Critically, junction regimes established tobacco's valuation by generating essential information about each hogshead. They controlled the scales that were so essential for long-distance trade. To create criteria of quality, they studied tobacco's colors, textures, and size. The New York Tobacco Board of Trade, for example, appointed a committee to "ascertain monthly the natural shrinkage on tobacco grown in the different parts of the United States."[74] In the public pronouncements, junction regimes positioned themselves as the disinterested, rational sentinels of the free tobacco market, "actuated," in the words of one booster, "by honorable motives in determining questions for the guidance of the Tobacco market."[75]

Most fundamentally, junction regimes controlled warehouses, and through them they directed the traffic of world tobacco commerce. Urban warehouses, especially those lacking open-floor auctions, are often overshadowed in tobacco's mythology by more romantic (or menacing) spaces, such as rolling tobacco fields, sturdy curing barns, and smoke-filled boardrooms. Warehouses seem banal in comparison, "the equivalent of a waiting room," as one scholar has suggested. But even in their banality, warehouses were "the threshold of the national economy," a place where the demands of revenue regimes, the stored values of manufacturing and agriculture, and the logistics of global trade overlapped.[76] In the case of Gilded Age tobacco, warehouses were thresholds of many national

Figure 11. Evaluating tobacco's quality in the junction city of Louisville, Kentucky, circa 1890. Library of Congress, Prints & Photographs Division, Detroit Publishing Company Collection.

economies, receiving, storing, and sorting tobacco that would fuel revenue regimes around the world.

It was impossible to overlook warehouses' centrality to the tobacco economy when visiting junction cities such as Louisville, Durham, or Cincinnati. Laid out one after the other, blocks of warehouses spread over neighborhoods and in some cases entire cities. One visitor to Manhattan described the "tobacco warehouses and dealers' offices" that covered "[w]hole blocks in the lower portion of the city"; across the river, the German-American Stores, the nation's largest tobacco warehousing facility, took up ten acres in Brooklyn, capable of storing twenty thousand hogsheads at a time.[77]

As uniformed customs officers did for revenue regimes, warehouses projected the state effects of junction regimes. That is, they produced the sense of a binary order, with buyers and sellers on one side and the junction regime on the other, organizing and regulating tobacco commerce. Spread out over city blocks, their omnipresence naturalized the junction regimes' authority. Within warehouses, inspectors furthered the state effect by subjecting thousands of hogsheads to repetitive disciplines of breaking, sampling, and classifying. As with revenue regimes, this last task was of utmost significance, a way of both organizing an unwieldy commodity and projecting power over the market. It was, according to one ATTC member, "upon [an inspector's] decision that the classification of all tobacco is made."[78] At the New York Naval Stores and Tobacco Exchange, one of several competing junction regimes in that city, a committee of three carried these responsibilities, issuing "a certificate of classification" for "the grade assigned to the respective hogsheads."[79] To further the legitimacy of these processes, junction regimes subjected inspectors to regular elections, had them register bonds, and devised elaborate checks on their work. The embodiment of the junction regime's authority, the inspector had to be a "man whose honesty is unquestioned," whose accurate classifications drove swindlers "for shelter to other markets, less careful of their reputations."[80]

The twin processes of warehousing and inspection transformed tobacco from the product of thousands of growers into the product of unitary junction regimes. The twin processes made tobacco both accessible and legible for distant buyers while justifying urban control over the export market. At the same time, these processes protected the global flow of tobacco from the political claims of those, particularly growers, who might interrupt that flow and demand more equitable distributions of power and wealth. When growers complained, junction regimes responded by decrying growers' ignorance, the poor quality of their tobacco, and their lack of appreciation for warehouse proprietors' risks. "While all tobacco growers have their ideas with regard to the leaf tobacco trade," contended one critic, "unfortunately there are few, comparatively, who understand the amount of business done in this industry or the manner of doing it."[81] Growers would not understand the inner workings of the warehouses, however, because junction regimes had worked since the Civil War to prevent grower influence on the conditions of the export economy.[82]

For junction regimes to influence tobacco's flow and prices they had to produce something even more imposing than warehouses: confidence.[83] If buyers expressed confidence in a node's fictions of standardization, they legitimized the junction regime's authority. "The effects of this system," wrote one booster of RTA's inspection revival in 1882, "are already observable in the better and more reliable packing of the Tobaccos which come to this market, and in the greater confidence with which the samples taken in this market, when exported, are bought."[84] Yet maintaining confidence could be difficult amid many overlapping and porous fictions of standardization, which created temptations for various agents—brokers, inspectors, packers, and sellers—to falsely weigh and intentionally misclassify tobacco.

Although American interests complained about inconsistencies in regie contracting, many foreign buyers argued that it was actually the American frauds that destabilized the world tobacco market. Buyers throughout Europe and Africa routinely complained of hogsheads that were "dishonestly packed, dishonestly inspected, or both."[85] One Scottish firm claimed to find "an average deficiency of 20 pounds pr. hogshead," while Bremen's buyers instituted mandatory "reinspection" of all American tobacco.[86] In Liverpool, one of the leading tobacco markets of Europe, buyers formed the Central Association of Tobacco Manufacturers for the express purpose of combatting American speculators who drove up prices by concealing data about the amount of tobacco available at a given time.[87] Under the light of this evidence, regie buyers' manipulations seemed less like outright frauds than necessary security measures, a buffer that buyers in freer markets lacked.

Most, if not all, junction regimes faced accusations of fraud, although some were more frequent targets. By the mid-1880s, charges against Maryland tobacco—the only node still operating under a state inspection regime—had become commonplace, with buyers claiming inspection samples were "nearly always greatly superior to the true contents of hogsheads."[88] New York's reputation drew close to Maryland's. Buyers in Antwerp claimed they held "not the slightest faith" in any hogsheads from New York, while their counterparts in Marseilles believed New York exporters simply ignored inspection altogether.[89] Although Maryland and New York garnered particularly damning reputations, similar accusations found their way to tobacco from Louisville, Richmond, and other important nodes.

Such accusations signified the possibility, and perhaps prevalence, of intentional wrongdoing within junction regimes. Yet accusations against junction regimes, like those against revenue regime's fictions of standardization, evinced more than the mere presence of malfeasance in the world tobacco market. They also suggested that the world tobacco market, with its diverse constellation of governing institutions and conflicting fictions of standardization, was particularly fertile ground for accusation and suspicion. Confidence was difficult to build, it seemed, and even more difficult to keep.

The United States Consular Service and the Search for Trade Standards

During the 1880s, the proliferation of doubt in the world tobacco market attracted the attention of American consuls. Embedded within the State Department, the consular service had represented U.S. legal and commercial interests around the world since the nation's founding. Consuls' daily labors included authenticating foreign documents for U.S. customs agents, producing official documents for Americans abroad, and producing information about their assigned regions' trade opportunities, obstacles, and rules. Their purpose, in other words, was to facilitate the movement of Americans and their goods through the world.[90]

During the Gilded Age, dozens of consuls took special interest in tobacco, producing detailed reports of the tax laws, local demand, and competition American exporters might encounter. Often, this meant translating official state publications and circulating them in the U.S. tobacco press. Thanks to consuls, readers of *Tobacco Leaf*, the *United States Tobacco Journal*, and the *Western Tobacco Journal* could access otherwise inaccessible information, from German studies of tobacco agriculture to the Italian government's statistics of manufacturing productivity. They even provided accounts of the weather. E.M. Smith, Consul at Mannheim, Germany in 1881, reported that expectations for "a large crop" had been dashed by "several weeks" of drought—an outcome that helped junction regimes prepare for higher demands on U.S. cigar tobacco in the upcoming year.[91] Along similar lines, consuls prepared junction regimes for changes in foreign tax systems, which could dramatically alter export opportunities. In one such instance, Consul John F. Winter of Rotterdam allayed exporters' fears about increasing Dutch import duties by divulging rumors "that such a law will never come into effect."[92] In any case, consuls saw it as their duty to make the conditions of global commerce transparent, thereby promoting the transnational flow of American tobacco.

Accusations of fraud made this mission more challenging. Consular reports regularly relayed buyers' complaints about inspection samples that were "far superior" to hogsheads' true contents. "I beg leave to inform you," reported an importer in Sierra Leone to Consul Judson Lewis, "that two-thirds at least of the hogsheads of tobacco we have received ... from America were not according to the samples." Lewis visited local importers, studying American hogsheads and documenting their evasive practices. In a number of cases, packers had constructed cavities within hogsheads, filling them "with short leaves, scraps, and refuse tobacco generally."[93] Evan Jones, Consul at Newcastle-upon-Tyne, noted that tobacco manufacturers in his city were distressed by exporters' inattention to quality criteria. "It is maintained," he argued, "that at most of the plantations 'long,' 'medium,' and 'short' leaf are promiscuously put up together." The result, according to both Lewis and Jones, was distrust and speculation, as importers could never predict the character of a hogshead.

The most vocal consular critic of junction regimes was William F. Grinnell who, from his post in Bremen, launched several inquiries into the inspections, packing procedures, and business relations of U.S. exporters. Prior to his promotion, Grinnell had been a commercial agent in the St. Etienne, France consular office, and later he would serve as consul in Bradford and Manchester, England.[94] His post in Bremen came at a critical time for the city's tobacco trade, as Bismarck's monopolization scheme loomed.[95] Grinnell believed if junction regimes dealt "honorably," they could capitalize in any political environment because Germany "must import very largely of our Tobacco to mix and render salable her own weak and flavorless plant." The path to cementing trade relations would go through Bremen, a crucial hub for central Europe where tobacco was, in Grinnell's estimation, the most significant import, "considering the number of people employed and maintained in the handling and care, its sale, delivery, and manufacture."[96] It was for these reasons that Grinnell grew dismayed when Bremen importers approached him with complaints. Exports from New York, he found, were routinely different than their samples would suggest, the latter being "clipped, trimmed, and pressed" to make them seem like a different quality than they actually were.[97] He surmised that inspectors from Baltimore "scarcely knew what a hogshead of tobacco was," for no explanation could merit the poor quality of Maryland tobacco crowding Bremen's docks. Through interviews with Bremen's "oldest and wealthiest firms" and the city's chamber of commerce, as well as his personal inspections of hogsheads, Grinnell concluded that several junction regimes had enabled "dead beats" to flourish.[98]

Grinnell's letters sparked unrest among junction regimes. In addition to filing his report with the State Department, he had reached out to the New York Chamber of Commerce and published his analysis in *The New York Journal of Commerce*. In response, the city's Tobacco Board of Trade convened a mass meeting to discuss the findings, reconsider their inspection practices, and formulate a reply to their Bremen counterparts.[99] The Baltimore tobacco trade, limited by the state's control of inspections, nonetheless recommended changes to "represent the hogshead faithfully," including developing a court of arbitration composed of buyers, sellers, and inspectors to handle similar complaints in the future.[100] In the years ahead, even after Grinnell had left Bremen for England, junction regimes drew upon Grinnell's letters when they sought to influence a change in local practices, as if to suggest that unless they got their way, their trade would be open to "dead beats." When the Virginia Assembly considered reestablishing state inspection in 1882, for example, the Richmond Tobacco Association drew upon Grinnell's findings to support its successful campaign against the plan.[101]

Although the extent of consuls' influence could be difficult to measure, Grinnell's reports suggested their ability to shape the broader discourse of governance and quality. For a market that needed information, particularly because it lacked a knowledge infrastructure, they produced it. They clarified, in other words, the conditions of global trade in ways revenue regimes and junction regimes did not.

As the editors of trade journals recognized, consular reports could be immensely valuable even beyond the issue of quality. Throughout the 1880s, consular reports of foreign tobacco industries became a prominent feature in the trades. At times, editors serialized lengthy reports over the course of weeks and even months, providing readers a detailed history and analysis of a given tobacco market. By the end of the decade, editors were demanding regular content from consuls. "Last December," reported the *United States Tobacco Journal* in 1889, "we called the attention of our State Department at Washington to the fact that the Consular Reports published by its authority were 'shamefully neglectful of any information regarding the weed, its culture and manufacture, and totally deficient of any benefit to our domestic tobacco producers.'"[102] In the months that followed, the journal included extensive studies of the expansion of tobacco culture in India, the Dutch East Indies, South Africa, and throughout Latin America.

If they had not already realized it, readers quickly learned that global tobacco agriculture was undergoing a momentous shift. While revenue regimes and junction regimes struggled over the meanings of quality, tobacco frontiers were spreading rapidly, drawing vast landscapes into the world tobacco market. Everywhere tobacco cultivation expanded, it drew agrarian people more fully into the influence of tax systems and markets, which sought to achieve quality ideals through the disciplining of agricultural labor. Consular reports routinely relayed officials' frustrations with growers who resisted their demands in favor of traditional practices. "Tobacco raisers here are, as a rule, ignore of the proper method of curing," wrote one consul in Guatemala.[103] "The native method of curing," noted a consul in Madras, "is defective in many ways."[104] Benjamin Bonham, Consul-General of India, wrote that "the cultivation and curing of tobacco are ... in a very primitive and undeveloped state, owing to the fact that they are mostly conducted by the poorer classes of natives."[105]

These reports reflected a growing sense among those forces driving the tobacco frontier's expansion—revenue regimes, agricultural scientists, manufacturing firms, and so on—that quality could be more than a means of promoting one regime's self-interest against its competitors. Rather, quality could also be a wellspring of discipline, a means of coercing agrarian people to produce tobacco for global commercial consumption. As the chapter 4 suggests, this realization was as relevant to agricultural interests in the United States as those in Asia, Africa, or Latin America.

4

"The Road to Prosperity"

Power and the Politics of Quality on the Bright Tobacco Frontier, 1865-1900

Amid the turmoil of Reconstruction, a fertilizer manufacturer named John Ott positioned himself as one of the nation's foremost analysts of tobacco agriculture. Ott was secretary of Richmond's Southern Fertilizing Company, and his many employer-published pamphlets evinced a sense of dread about the state of Virginia tobacco, which, he argued, had been mortally threatened by emancipation. "Since the negroes have been freed," Ott argued in 1876, "too many of them refuse to work as laborers," and, consequently, the market was "bound to be demoralized." At the same time, tobacco taxes had "shifted the burden of sustaining the government almost entirely to the shoulders of the West and the Tobacco-growing States of the South." Emergent junction regimes and new growing hinterlands, particularly west of Appalachia, challenged Virginia's "fortress" of tobacco supremacy, while revenue regimes from British India to Australia intensified production and "shamed" American growers with their "energy and enterprise." Reviewing the situation, he surmised, it was no wonder Virginia in the 1870s seemed "but little ahead of the kingdom of Powhatan when Capt. John Smith made its acquaintance."[1]

But Ott was a businessman and a booster, and he could not indulge his desperation without giving readers some encouragement. There was an alternative to decline, one available to white tobacco growers throughout the South. "Taking a general view of the situation," Ott concluded, "no product for sale in this country has the same promise of remunerative returns ... as tobacco." The key to those profits, however, was "handsome," or high-quality, tobacco. "With so much of our crop now in the hands of negroes," Ott complained, "the market is bound to show a very considerable quantity of indifferent Tobacco, but the white men, whether large or small farmers, having the requisite intelligence and skill, have it in their power ... to bring a handsome result."[2]

Ott's racism reflected widespread assumptions about tobacco quality—that it came from white growers' fields, and that it reflected its producers' innate "intelligence and skill." But Ott's claim raised questions about what else he meant by "handsome," or quality, tobacco. Besides the race of its cultivators, did anything differentiate "handsome" from "indifferent" tobacco? What constituted white growers' "power" to produce quality tobacco? Why was a fertilizer manufacturer so invested in these issues?

The answers to these questions became clear by the turn of the century as "tobacco capitalists"—Ott and his colleagues in the fertilizer industry, along with ancillary interests in the banking, warehouse, and railroad sectors—reconstructed the conditions of Southern tobacco agriculture. The core of the political economy they built was a twin-purposed ideological formulation I call the "quality principle." One of the quality principle's purposes was to scale up production by building upon the fictions of standardization deployed by revenue regimes and junction regimes. In their drive for standardization, however, tobacco capitalists also used the quality principle to exert control over the tobacco frontier. In this role, the quality principle served as a prescription for growers' labor practices, an inducement for investing in expensive fertilizers, and, for warehouse buyers, a justification for low prices at the end of the season.

In the age of the quality principle, fertilizer, credit, and a growing infrastructure of trade and distribution made an unprecedented scale of tobacco culture possible. This expanding "tobacco frontier," which emanated out from Ott's Virginia to North Carolina, South Carolina, and even as far south as Florida, drew thousands of new grower households into the tobacco economy. As households devoted small plots to tobacco and invested in fertilizers, they struggled to achieve adequate prices. Although these hardships were widespread, the quality principle deflected criticism. As a member of Durham, North Carolina's Board of Trade blithely advised growers in North Carolina, "make your tobacco better … and you will soon be on the road to prosperity."[3] Yet the definition of "better" could shift rapidly, as buyers attempted to bargain down sellers. Writing in 1883, a journalist with the Lancaster, Pennsylvania *Intelligencer*, illustrated this process as he described his travels with a tobacco buyer. Although the exchanges he documented occurred outside of the tobacco South, they illustrated the price-deflating dynamic of the quality principle. The buyer, "John," had attempted to purchase a crop from a grower named Abe, but found it difficult to bargain Abe down after the unnamed reporter described Abe's crop as "mighty nice." As they pulled away from the field, John angrily explained how he preferred such exchanges proceed:

> John was moody and silent for some distance, when he breaks out vehemently, "Some d—d Jew will buy that crop for less money than I have offered; mind,

if they don't; and see here, young man, if you make any more such remarks as you did in that cellar you can hoof it back." To which I meekly answered that I thought it was fine. John assented, saying: "If you must talk, always talk down the crop," of which I took a note.[4]

The essence of the quality principle was thus for buyers to demand consistent leaf characteristics across widespread growing regions while also "talking down" whatever crop came before them. Unlike Abe, who could keep his crop in his field and wait for another buyer to come along, Southern growers had to transport their crops to centralized warehouses and sell amid a crowd of buyers, each of whom "talked down" their crops while demanding they produce higher quality in the future. They had no choice but to try doing just that. Through attempts to make their tobacco "better," growers altered and extended their routines of cultivation, marketing, and relations of credit and debt, which increased the amount of labor they dedicated to each acre of their crops. By 1910, an acre of tobacco required 356 labor hours per acre, compared with 116 for cotton, 35 for corn, and merely 15 for wheat.[5] At the same time, tobacco capitalists concentrated the power of judging "better" from "worse" within the overlapping authority of fertilizer manufacturers, warehouses, railroads, banks, and tobacco manufacturers. Under the new system, the quality principle not only mediated commercial relations, but also came to justify decreasing returns and increasingly regimented work regimes.

The quality principle and the intellectual, financial, and cultural coercion that made it possible were governmental acts, influencing the disciplines, fortunes, and despair of hundreds of thousands of people in the tobacco South.[6] This was especially clear in the rapidly expanding "bright" tobacco frontier, which became one of the world's largest tobacco-producing territories during this period. For that reason, much of this chapter focuses on the culture of bright tobacco, the fine, yellow leaf that dominated cigarette production. In the next chapter, I will consider how the patterns of governance described below, particularly the quality principle, shaped state development through the U.S. Department of Agriculture's (USDA) Office of Tobacco Investigations. That office, and the USDA's tobacco work more generally, emerged only at the turn of the century, roughly three decades after the creation of the federal tobacco tax. As I will suggest, the USDA's concerns and methods did not "fall from the sky or emerge ready formed."[7] Instead, they grew out of the new tobacco capitalism of the postbellum South and from the ideals of men like John Ott.

Household Tobacco Culture in the Age of Emancipation

Households of Black, white, Sapponny, and Lumbee farmers dominated bright tobacco production in the generations following the Civil War. Although their histories were different, for each group small plots of tobacco symbolized the rapid postbellum advance of capitalist socioeconomic relations.[8] Many were tenants, forced to grow tobacco as a condition of their tenancy and ensnared by the financial and social control of landlords or furnishing merchants.[9] Yet tenancy was not as widespread in tobacco country as it was among other Southern cultivators, and a surprising degree of land ownership prevailed among tobacco growers. Smallholders were especially common in the Piedmont of Virginia and North Carolina, where the postbellum breakup of large plantations and declining land values provided growers access to their own farms. By the early twentieth century, nearly half of the region's Black tobacco growers owned their own land. For example, in Louisa County, Virginia, the number of Black landowners soared from 22 in 1870 to 1,314 in 1900—the equivalent of 39% of all landowners in the county. Again, these plots were small: although Louisa's Black tobacco growers represented 39% of the county's owners, they held only 11% of the county's land.[10] As W.E.B. Du Bois noted of Prince Edward County, Virginia, in the "economic center" of the state's tobacco region, a "considerable number" of Black farmers owned their land, although their holdings amounted to less than one-tenth of the county's land and land value despite Black inhabitants outnumbering whites nearly two to one.[11] Despite extreme inequality, Black ownership and the broader pervasiveness of smallholding were points of contrast between tobacco growers and farmers elsewhere in the South.

The prevalence of small farmers indicated the centrality of household labor, a second characteristic of postbellum tobacco cultivation. For this reason, it makes sense to think of tobacco growers not as atomized individuals but as family collectives. A male farmer and his sons may have stood beside a crop in the auction warehouse or signed off on their family's debt, but as tobacco was the product of household labor, the households' female members were "co-owners" of crop returns.[12] For white patriarchs such as Abram Moye of Pitt County, North Carolina, these shared circumstances could be a source of distress. At the end of one particularly difficult season, he advised growers to abandon tobacco because of its apparently degrading labor demands. "Everything must be neglected for [tobacco crops]," he lamented. "If you have two hundred acres of land and a fine house, your wife and girls for at least two months must labor in the field—just the same as a disfranchised free negro."[13]

A third defining characteristic of postbellum tobacco culture was the rapid expansion of tobacco's growing frontier.[14] This "tobacco frontier" included regions that knew little or no tobacco farming prior to the 1870s and 1880s but by the twentieth century were either dominated by tobacco culture or were the sites of state experimentation in developing it. As one historian has argued, tobacco in the postbellum era, and particularly bright tobacco, became a "southeastern crop," rather than the highly regional specialty of a few counties in Virginia or North Carolina.[15] In South Carolina, for example, tobacco production rose from 45,000 pounds annually in 1880 to 20 million pounds in 1900. In North Carolina, places such as Pitt and Wilson counties shifted from producing a few hundred pounds annually in 1880 to being among the world's most important tobacco regions twenty years later. Pitt County, for example, produced only 580 pounds of tobacco in 1880 but 11 million by 1900.[16]

The expansion of the tobacco frontier brought with it the sorts of ecological crises endemic to monocropping. Throughout the postbellum period, waves of insect infestations descended on tobacco fields. Growers waged nearly endless "wars" against their "arch enemies," the tobacco flea beetle, horn worm, and bud worm.[17] In some years, infestations destroyed as much as half of a region's crop.[18] The consequences of infestation were not always adverse, as reduced production for some farmers could increase prices for others. Nonetheless, for growers whose crop suffered, the results of infestation could be devastating. "I sowed fourteen beds," recounted one grower in the Clarksville district of Tennessee, "they have eaten the plants clean from thirteen. I have one small bed they have not finished yet, and I don't care a d—."[19] In time, growers, state experiment stations, and private industry developed remedies, such as pesticides and cloth covers for plant beds. Yet insect repellants also enabled growers to continue pushing ecological limits. As Nannie Mae Tilley argued, "as fast as the farmer learned one lesson, another demanded mastery."[20] Threats such as root knot, an infection caused by microscopic soil-dwelling worms called nematodes, and the "Granville" wilt, named for the county in North Carolina where it first appeared, could spoil tobacco fields for years. Reliant on the income their crops generated, growers often continued to plant tobacco in these soils, producing smaller and more damaged crops each year while exacerbating the affliction.[21]

Tobacco growers were deeply susceptible to cycles of boom and bust, although the latter were more common for the postbellum and turn-of-the-century generations. It was a grim truth that as a source of income, tobacco's most consistent characteristic was its price fluctuation. A year or two of good prices would encourage new growers to enter the market and old growers to stay with it, even as prices cratered with the inflation of supply. Following the boom year of 1874, in which average prices in the Danville, Virginia market reached 20.45 cents per pound, they crashed to 8.8 cents by 1876. A similar pattern emerged after the relatively strong years of 1883 and 1884. The 1890s were less forgiving, as the good years became leaner and the bad years piled up. In Danville, prices never rose above nine cents between 1891 and 1899, typically hovering between six and seven cents.[22] These were poverty prices. One USDA analyst summed up growers' tribulations in 1877, writing "there is no other crop more languishing, or one from which the producer has ... derived so little profit."[23] Ironically, economic insecurity itself precipitated the spread of tobacco culture and its attendant low prices. Locked into agreements with landlords or furnishing merchants, indebted growers needed cash, but other common cash crops either lacked viable markets or, like cotton, had become even more precarious than tobacco.[24]

Growers blamed a range of interests and circumstances for low prices, with the most common targets being the combination of warehouses and other buyers, the consolidating market power of manufacturers in the 1890s, and the "agitation" surrounding tax questions. In turn, warehousemen and manufacturers, as well as analysts from the USDA, blamed the growers themselves. During the price decline of the 1870s, one USDA critic concluded, "it is no less certain that the greater share of that depression is traceable to the door of the planter himself."[25] Some growers accepted these diagnoses—particularly when they referred to producers outside their own towns or districts—but they also recognized that forces beyond simple supply and demand were determining prices. One such critic in Winston, North Carolina, attacked the capricious practices of warehousemen in the 1890s, claiming he "saw Bright Wrappers bid off at 20 cts. lb., 28 cts., 30, 33, 34, and 36 cts. lb, all the same grade of goods as evidenced by the buyers putting it all together on the warehouse floor as one and the same class."[26] Whether his observation identified the nefarious operations of warehouses or simply the caprices of buyers, the critic illustrated what for many growers was the maddeningly opaque nature of the tobacco market.

Even in the rare boom year, the conditions of tobacco culture produced frustration among growers; in most years, they produced despair. A grower-landlord named U.B. Gwynn—writing in 1889, before conditions truly spiraled in the 1890s—claimed that tobacco culture had become "a struggle for existence," all but promising perpetual debt and "utter ruin." Drawing from the cultural lexicon of Social Darwinism, Gwynn depicted tobacco culture as an undoing of civilization, a "survival of the fittest." "Our fix," he fretted, "if it don't get any better, will be so desperate that there will be no help for it than to relapse back into a state of savagery, become troglodytes over again, and live on varmints."[27] More than a decade later, the same despair permeated the agricultural and tobacco trade journals. "What will become of us?" wondered a North Carolina grower in 1901. "We are confronted with poverty."[28]

According to critics, including some farmers in the tobacco belts, the solutions to these problems were obvious. If returns from the tobacco crop could not cover growers' expenses, then they should plant something else. "Don't be deceived into the ruinous idea of the one crop policy," warned D. Reid Parker, a Durham-area grower. "Make your own supplies and be self-sustaining and independent—plant what you may."[29] Critics repeated refrains like this throughout the postbellum age. They argued that growers would ensure their own welfare by preserving household economies, practicing commercial agriculture only when market conditions seemed most favorable. Better to "live at home" by raising their own corn, wheat, and meat, then to rely on minimal tobacco profits—or debt—to buy such essentials.[30]

Moreover, critics argued that asserting greater control over Black labor, including tenants and smallholders, would improve quality and prices. Joseph Killebrew, a renowned tobacco analyst and federal census investigator, argued that the decline of Virginia's tobacco prices was largely due to Black smallholders and tenants who refused to labor for white masters. "Tenants, the majority of whom are negroes," he claimed, "raise as a rule, an inferior grade, which is forced into the market through local dealers in an unfit condition." Killebrew's accusation gained a broad audience because of its inclusion in the federal census of 1880, but it reflected a general belief among white tobacco interests in the post-emancipation South: freedpeople could not produce "quality" tobacco, because they paid "but little attention to the management of their tobacco."[31]

These critics—usually planters with ties to the emerging capitalist networks of warehouses, railroads, manufacturers, and fertilizer producers whom growers blamed for their poverty—proposed an idyllic compromise between capitalism and subsistence. They imagined that capitalist agriculture's "open system" of commercial fertilizers and cash crops could merely supplement subsistence agriculture—a "closed system," in which nutrients were produced from local recycling or fallow fields and farmers sustained themselves with gardens.[32] With such a reasonable compromise available, it was growers' own fault if they found themselves drowning in debts. Others suggested that growers simply expand their markets by raising saleable livestock, poultry, and truck crops. After suggesting that tobacco-growing households also raise turkeys, potatoes, beans, and asparagus, one critic groused that it was growers' greed that produced poverty.

"Small industries," he insisted, "are looked on with contempt by many a tobacco farmer, who loves to gaze on his broad acres of yellowing tobacco with visions of greenbacks dancing in his head."[33] The elite criticism of growers' market dependence echoed North Carolina slaveholders' antebellum critiques of yeoman turpentine producers. Non-slaveholding whites, complained one planter in 1848, "placed too much emphasis on turpentining and not enough on agriculture. Because the strongest hands were used in turpentine production ... farms had fallen into disrepair and producers had to buy corn and pork because they no longer supplied their own food staples."[34] These critiques evinced their authors' judgment of rural people's profligacy and irrationality, as well as implying a faith in the inherent rationality of commodities markets. They also exposed tobacco boosters' hope that household production would subsidize the spread of tobacco culture, an arrangement that would shift the costs and risks of production onto producers while landlords, middlemen, and buyers enjoyed tobacco revenue without responsibility for households' fortunes.[35]

Elite critics failed to recognize that despite hardships, many tobacco farmers were maintaining their household economies. In Granville County, North Carolina, one of the most important tobacco-producing regions in the South, between thirty and sixty percent of renters and smallholders maintained gardens, harvested cord wood, and produced their own eggs, meat, or butter during the late 1870s and early 1880s. Small growers strategically adopted capitalist agriculture in order to generate discretionary income that buttressed both households and communal institutions, such as schools, churches, and civic associations.[36] In other words, for most households the entire purpose of tobacco culture was to preserve autonomy—not escape it. Yet in the final decades of the nineteenth century, the costs of attaining discretionary income increased, making it more difficult for small growers to maintain household economies. Landlords imposed more stringent terms in order to limit tenants' work outside of cash-crop cultivation. State legislatures passed fish, game, and stock laws that precluded farmers' subsistence practices as well as their reliance on raising livestock commercially.[37] More specific to the tobacco regions was the emergence of a new political economy that encircled Southern farmers, coercing them into tobacco culture even when they knew its risks.

Tobacco Capitalists and the Politics of Quality

Directing tobacco's reconstructed political economy was a cast of "tobacco capitalists"—manufacturers, middlemen, financiers, and elite growers—who encouraged farmers across the southeast to adopt tobacco culture. Although their efforts revolutionized the economic fortunes and physical rhythms of growers' lives—in short, the very culture of tobacco—these figures were not necessarily allied with one another. When it suited them, for example, manufacturers and warehouse operators could publicly blame each other for growers' poor returns.[38] But it was the combined effects of tobacco capitalists' work, and not their antagonisms, that kept farmers in the punishing tobacco economy. The irony of this new political economy was that before it became the problem, tobacco was very often the solution to growers' economic and ecological woes. In the decades following emancipation, in countrysides plagued by falling cotton prices, soil infertility, and expensive credit, tobacco capitalists seemed to offer a better option.

At the center of tobacco's political economy was the emergent Southern fertilizer industry. Since the antebellum period, manufacturers in Baltimore, New York, and other industrial centers had been producing fertilizers from Peruvian guano and "superphosphates"—bones dissolved by acid. The industry flourished after the war, stimulated by the widespread agricultural demand for Peruvian guano, Chilean sodium nitrate, potash from Germany, and phosphorous extracted from the Bahamas and South Carolina.[39] Development was especially rapid in the post-emancipation South, where fertilizer provided a financial outlet for investors seeking to shift investment capital from enslaved people to the debts of small farmers who relied on guano. Richmond's Cat Island Guano Company exemplified this trend. Cat Island was a subsidiary of Branch & Company, a prominent investment firm that had built its antebellum fortune as a brokerage house dealing in slaves.[40] Following emancipation, the firm established Cat Island with the goal of creating a specialty tobacco fertilizer from high-phosphate guano mined in the Bahamas. While some of its agents cataloged the guano content Bahamian caves or oversaw mining operations, dozens more traveled through the tobacco districts of Maryland, Virginia, and North Carolina, convincing small farmers and local merchants that Cat Island's special mixture could produce "quality" tobacco and wring prosperity from their fields. Branch & Company dissolved Cat Island by 1880, trading its mining, manufacture, and sales operations for strictly financial speculations in stocks, bonds, and leaf tobacco. Cat Island's competitors may not have noticed, however, because by that point the fertilizer market had become astoundingly crowded.

Manufacturers of tobacco fertilizer emerged from Baltimore to Atlanta, but Richmond was the industry's epicenter. As a major Southern industrial center, Richmond was home to a significant population of skilled and unskilled wageworkers, including thousands of formerly enslaved people. It was also both a figurative, intellectual hub of Southern agriculture (the influential *Southern Planter and Farmer* was published in the city) and a literal hub of Southern railways (including the Southern, Chesapeake & Ohio, and, in nearby Petersburg, Norfolk & Western).[41] Seizing on these assets, fertilizer manufacturers quickly came to exemplify the city's economic influence over its agricultural hinterland. These manufacturers included the leading producers of tobacco fertilizer, such as the Southern Fertilizing Company, Allison & Addison, and, by the 1890s, the monopolistic Virginia-Carolina Chemical Company. The companies aggressively peddled their products from Maryland to Georgia with the intent, according to John Ott, secretary of the Southern Fertilizing Company, of making their products "the resort" of tobacco growers throughout the South.[42]

The essence of fertilizer companies' sales strategy was to mask the subjectivity of the quality principle, suggesting instead that "quality" tobacco could be judged objectively: if growers used, for example, the Southern Fertilizing Company's Anchor Brand or Allison & Addison's Star Brand, the tobacco was "quality"; if they did not, it was not. As one fertilizer advertisement claimed, "The use of low grade, and consequently low-priced fertilizers is, to a considerable extent, the cause of the production of the large quantity of low grade, nondescript tobacco, which has done more than any one thing to depress prices."[43] SFC's John Ott illustrated this approach in an 1874 pamphlet, writing that no matter the variety, "our Tobacco Fertilizer alone" would achieve the finest results.[44] According to this logic, the difference between tobacco's real prices and growers' (inevitably higher) ideal prices was due to the growers' failure to follow fertilizer companies' suggestions.

Aware that factors besides fertilizer shaped tobacco crops' character, fertilizer companies positioned themselves as an indispensable resource for knowing how to identify and address those factors. They published pamphlets, books, and scores of newspaper and journal articles about every relevant topic, including the best soils for various tobacco types, the choice of seeds, and the ideal designs for curing barns.[45] Through the 1880s, Ott was the most influential such publisher. His many pamphlets and books illustrated his overlapping commitments as a critic of emancipation, defender of Virginia's tobacco heritage, and aggressive promoter of SFC's Anchor Brand Tobacco Fertilizer. He produced statistics on the global and domestic tobacco trades, arguing that white Virginians would recover high prices through vigilant cultivation and generous fertilization.[46] If white growers relied on Anchor Brand and prices continued to fall, he claimed, they should blame freedpeople and the warehouses that purchased their tobacco. It was emancipated growers' produce, he declared, that "had … the effect of throwing on the market innumerable small crops; and nothing but the most careful and faithful assortment by warehousemen will keep the general range on a basis of reasonable uniformity."[47] By shifting responsibility toward freedpeople and warehouses, Ott played into white Virginians' mix of redemption-era racial resentment and populist suspicion of middlemen. Yet he also associated white tobacco culture with the use of SFC's Anchor Brand and, therefore, quality crops.[48]

In addition to commercial demagoguery, fertilizer manufacturers adopted a range of tactics to forge associations between their products and quality, high-priced tobacco. They hosted competitions for growers who used their products, offering "premiums" for the best crops. The Raleigh Oil Mill and Fertilizer Company, manufacturers of "Raleigh Standard Guano," offered "FIFTY DOLLARS IN GOLD" for the "best" sample of "Yellow Leaf Tobacco made where Raleigh Standard Guano is used."[49] Fertilizer manufacturers encouraged, and often hired, grower-boosters to promote their brands. In a typical advertisement for Allison & Addison's Star Brand, a North Carolina grower named J.A. Jones claimed he had "been using your 'Star Brand' Special Tobacco Manure for the past eight years in company with other high grade fertilizers, and have this to say: As far as my experience is concerned, I consider it the best fertilizer offered to the public for producing fine, yellow, leafy tobacco, with good body."[50] Cat Island's records include numerous similar testimonials, claiming the fertilizer had produced "much better than average" tobacco.[51] Grower-boosters from throughout the tobacco South submitted these testimonials, suggesting that fertilizer companies turned to local elites to bolster their reputations among planter-landlords and furnishing merchants. As boosters, these elites benefited from a growing fertilizer business that could create a greater supply of tobacco and, subsequently, new or expanded local manufacturers and warehouses.[52] For grower-boosters near established tobacco towns such as Danville and, by the 1880s, Durham, the expansion of the tobacco frontier promised to transform their cities into significant industrial centers in the heart of a rapidly growing agricultural hinterland.

Fertilizer manufacturers also associated their products with quality by popularizing the vernacular and disciplines of "scientific agriculture" in the tobacco South. Scientific agriculture was a cultural, political, and economic phenomenon of the postbellum period. With its origins in antebellum agricultural reform movements, scientific agriculture held an "incantatory quality" for postbellum agriculturists, boosters, and politicians who believed the insights of chemistry, botany, biology, and soil and veterinary science would unleash the productive powers of state and economy.[53] In other parts of the United States, a range of institutions led that movement, including the ascendant USDA. But the USDA remained ambivalent about tobacco culture until the 1890s, which enabled fertilizer companies to significantly influence the development of tobacco's scientific agriculture. The Southern Fertilizing Company published geological studies of tobacco soils and the chemical analyses of leaves grown in SFC-treated fields and published chemical analyses of their tobacco. "It would be a shame," commented one SFC publication, "if our people refused to avail themselves of the researches, bearing on soils and plants, now in progress so generally throughout the thickly peopled portions of the earth."[54] Allison & Addison claimed that their Star Brand tobacco fertilizer was "the result of thirteen years' study of the requirements of the plant, aided by careful and thorough experiments, and the best chemical ability in the country."

> It is composed of the best grades of the different materials known to the trade, in such physical condition as we have in such proportions as to give the plant an early and healthy start, sustain it in a thrifty and growing condition throughout the season, resist the injurious effects of both wet and dry seasons, and make a crop whenever and wherever it is possible to do so; making rich, leathery tobacco of fine texture on soils adapted to the growth of shipping and manufacturing grades, and fine, silky bright wrappers on lighter lands, suitable for "brights."[55]

Such advertisements depicted fertilizer science as an emancipatory force. Star Brand could free growers from the constraints of weather and soil, achieving finished crops of whatever quality growers desired. Similarly, Robert Ragland, a tobacco booster and spokesman for the Southern Fertilizing Company, published widely circulated treatises about the "science of tobacco culture"—a discipline, he often suggested, that required both skill and the best formulated chemical amendments.[56] "The man who thinks he has compassed the whole subject of tobacco planting and management of the crop is egregiously mistaken," Ragland famously argued, "for there is yet much to be learned, which will, when known, revolutionize this industry and benefit all engaged therein."[57] Yet Ragland, like his other colleagues in the fertilizer industry, was adamant that growers could not "revolutionize" the industry on their own. For that, they would have to turn to outside sources of expertise, which the industry was happy to supply.

State governments supported fertilizer companies' intellectual and financial control over tobacco culture. In some cases, this support was blatant, such as the Southern Fertilizing Company's hire of Virginia state chemist W.H. Taylor while Taylor retained his position with the state.[58] Later in the decade, Thomas Pollard, the state's Commissioner of Agriculture, published an instructional manual for new growers by SFC spokesman Robert Ragland called "Cultivation and curing of fine yellow and shipping tobacco."[59] In North Carolina, state support was less deliberate but more consequential. Unlike other tobacco states, the populist North Carolina Board of Agriculture competed with fertilizer companies for scientific hegemony. In 1879, North Carolina became the second state to establish an experiment station; that institution's primary task was to analyze all fertilizers sold in the state for irregularities. This was part of the state's broader framework of regulated entry for fertilizer companies, inspired by the hundreds of "comparatively worthless" fertilizers that emerged during the 1870s.[60] State law forced all manufacturers to submit their products for analysis, obtain a license to manufacture and sell fertilizer, and label all products with "the name, location, and trade-mark of the manufacturer."[61] Unfortunately, North Carolina's chemists and soil scientists could not say how a given fertilizer would actually affect tobacco culture from one region to another—their studies would not advance that far until the turn of the century. Consequently, the state's regulated entry eliminated small and obviously fraudulent competition, thereby strengthening the market power of Richmond's large manufacturers by implicitly endorsing their products with licenses.[62]

Fertilizer manufacturers' exhortations influenced the daily labors of smallholders and tenants, but not necessarily because their advertisements were terribly convincing. In all likelihood, many growers never read these advertisements. Illiteracy rates among adult males in the tobacco-growing South were high—rarely lower than sixteen percent of adult males, and often higher than twenty-five percent.[63] Fertilizer manufacturers were not directing their appeals to small growers themselves, but to planter-landlords, furnishing merchants, and warehousemen—figures who controlled household debts and determined the shifting meanings of "quality" in day-to-day interactions on farms and warehouse floors. And, as the only sources of fertilizer for many growers, landlords and furnishing merchants could effectively turn all tobacco farmers in their region into consumers of a given fertilizer brand and practitioners of that brand's recommended labor disciplines.

The conditions of tobacco agriculture, including growers' dependence on fertilizer and lack of economic alternatives, encouraged consolidation among leading fertilizer manufacturers. Allison & Addison acquired the Southern Fertilizing Company in 1889; six years later, Allison & Addison was one of nine firms in Virginia and North Carolina to form the Virginia-Carolina Chemical Company (VCC). By the early twentieth century, VCC controlled more than thirty brands and fifty factories, a capital stock of nearly $50,000,000, and as much as eighty percent of the tobacco fertilizer business. The company claimed to sell more than one million tons of its fertilizers annually.[64] VCC also depended on close relationships with tobacco manufacturers, including the American Tobacco Company, itself a monopolistic power at the turn of the century. George Watts, president of the Durham Fertilizer Company, a "nucleus" firm of the VCC, was also a partner in the ATC and one of its forerunners, W. Duke, Sons & Co.[65] Like fertilizer companies before it, VCC energetically promoted the disciplinary rhetoric of scientific agriculture and boosterism. The company distributed, without charge, almanacs and pamphlets that instructed growers in the practices of tobacco culture. A 1905 pamphlet, titled "Money in Tobacco," depicted tobacco plants with "Uncle Sam's greenbacks protruding from underneath."[66] In addition to associating their product with "quality" tobacco, VCC's publications also made the accurate but novel claim that the "dead and dying soils" of the tobacco South—a product of decades of monocropping—now necessitated intensive chemical treatment.[67] Throughout the postbellum decades, the fertilizer industry had boasted of its indispensability to tobacco culture. Ironically, widespread adoption of their products had made that boast a reality.

Fertilizer manufacturers were the scientific, intellectual, and financial engines of this changing political economy, but they were not the only entities shaping life in the tobacco frontier. In cities and towns throughout the tobacco South, commercial powers constructed new institutions that drew, and kept, more growers in tobacco. Charles Dudley Warner chronicled this process in an 1887 *Harper's* profile of Danville, Virginia—a city synonymous with the new political economy of tobacco. Danville's "local development and prosperity," asserted Warner, "are due to co-operation, to associated effort to foster individual interests, and to advertise to the world the advantages of Danville." Warner continued:

> The city has a vigorous and wide-awake organization in its Chamber of Commerce, a Tobacco Association, a Tobacco Manufacturer's Board, and a Tobacco Warehouse Board. These organizations work together for increasing the business facilities of the place and for enlarging its trade, inducing the inflow of capital and population, and making it a desirable place of residence.[68]

Warner's profile detailed the ways Danville's tobacco capitalists had constructed commercial relations, directed growers toward their auction and manufacturing markets, and distributed the products of their markets toward consumers beyond the tobacco South. Similar efforts were underway throughout Virginia, the Carolinas, Kentucky, and Tennessee, representing a wholesale transformation

Figures 12 and 13. The offices of the Virginia-Carolina Chemical company and the Allison & Addison fertilizer plant, a major source of tobacco fertilizer during the postbellum period. From the VCC's undated book *Where Guano Is Made: Some of the Plants of Virginia-Carolina Chemical Company*, which depicted the firm's 23 factories along with the number of tons manufactured and men employed at each. The factories spread VCC's presence throughout the tobacco frontier. They were in Baltimore, Maryland; Richmond, Norfolk, Petersburg, and Alexandria, Virginia; Wilmington and Durham, North Carolina; and Charleston, Port Royal, and Pon Pon, South Carolina. From the South Caroliniana Library, University of South Carolina, Columbia, S.C.

of the region's agricultural political economy. Nor were the institutions Warner identified, such as the Warehouse Board, Chamber of Commerce, and Manufacturer's Board, independent from one another. The career of Jesse Willis Grainger exemplified the deep associations between such institutions. In addition to owning his Kinston, North Carolina warehouse, Grainger was president of the local Chamber of Commerce, an executive at three area banks, president of the Atlantic and North Carolina Railroad, and a leading member of the state Democratic Party.[69] Men like Grainger were well positioned to profit from the expansion of the tobacco frontier, and it was their control over warehouses that enabled them to shape growing practices in the countryside.

Figure 13.

Like fertilizer manufacturers, auction warehouses assumed significance in the postbellum decades.[70] Often organized by consortiums of investors, warehouses operated at the intersection of tobacco agriculture and manufacture—a formidable position under the new internal revenue system, which barred growers from "dealing" their tobacco without a license. It was in and around warehouses where growers gathered their crops and displayed them on the warehouse floor. There they would wait anxiously as buyers judged their year's work while an auctioneer bid up the price. Warehouses enjoyed revenue during high-price periods from commissions, auction charges for weighing and organizing tobacco piles, and the flurry of trade that accompanied such periods.[71] Yet as nodes of commerce in the rural South, they were interested in promoting tobacco culture even when low prices prevailed. To attract growers, they advertised "premiums," such as cash prizes or, in one instance, tickets to Grover Cleveland's second inauguration in 1893; offered to prepare farmers' tax documents for free; and borrowed fertilizer manufacturers' approach of publishing instruction manuals to teach growers how to produce quality tobacco.[72] In New Bern, North Carolina, a warehouseman named E.M. Pace distributed a guide to cotton planters and other farmers called *Tobacco: How to Grow It! And Better Still—Make it Pay*. During the 1890s, the grower K.H. Watson founded a warehouse in North Carolina's coastal plain and drummed up business through a series of advice columns in the Wilson, North Carolina *Times*.[73] The effect of this promotional activity was twofold. First, it could generate enthusiasm among new tobacco growers, attracting business to the warehouse towns while transforming their hinterlands into tobacco country. This was the case for both Pace and Watson, who helped shift the coastal plain of North Carolina from cotton to tobacco culture at the end of the nineteenth century. Second, instruction manuals advanced the disciplinary regimes propagated by fertilizer manufacturers—when to plant, how much to plant, fertilize, and cultivate, and a string of other suggestions that would, perhaps, produce an ideal leaf and fetch a high price, but also regiment the annual labors of thousands of farm families.

In addition to their own publication of advice literature, warehouses and fertilizer manufacturers relied on local newspapers to drum up interest in tobacco culture. As fertilizer and warehouses proliferated, papers such as North Carolina's *Henderson Gold Leaf*, *Durham Globe*, and *Oxford Public Ledger* boosted the

Figure 14. A "tobacco street" in the model town of tobacco's reconstructed economy: Danville, Virginia. From *The New South: Supplement to Harper's Weekly*, January 29, 1887.

possibilities of tobacco culture. Critics, such as an editorialist in Durham's *Daily Tobacco Plant*, highlighted the dangers of newspapers' boosterism. Writing in 1889, he argued that "a great many men have been deceived by flaming advertisements, and publishing fancy prices that did not represent five per cent of the crop. There are a great many men in the business today that regret that they ever went into the tobacco growing business. Newspapers do a great deal of good, but sometimes they do harm."[74] Yet it was not only "flaming advertisements" that enticed new growers. As newspapers amplified the advice of fertilizer manufacturers and warehouses, they also constructed a sense of economic and cultural consistency between warehouse towns and the countryside. For example, when a paper such as the *Gold Leaf* published daily warehouse prices or reports from growers in the countryside, it created a sense of Henderson and its environs as a tobacco region, thereby naturalizing farmers' cultivation practices and indebtedness.[75] It also produced a regionally coherent rendering of the interaction between growers' daily labors, their soils, and the product they sent into global markets. This was the refashioning of Southern tobacco's *terroir* identity, a tool with which boosters and entities further down the commodity chain, particularly tobacco manufacturers, could naturalize tobacco production and broadcast ideas of quality and value to consumers around the world.[76]

Transformations in southeastern banking and railroads likewise shaped the emergent political economy of tobacco. The proprietors or board members of warehouses and tobacco manufacturing firms regularly amplified their commercial power through banks. Benjamin Duke, brother of James Buchanan Duke and business partner in the American Tobacco Company, was also the president of Durham's Fidelity Bank; across town, Julian Carr, a rival of the Dukes and partner in W.T. Blackwell's & Co., founded the First National Bank; and in Danville, nine tobacco warehousemen and manufacturers jointly directed the People's Savings Bank.[77] Many of these figures likewise held stakes in railroads. William T. Sutherlin, a prominent Virginia planter, manufacturer, and warehouseman, was an early partner in Danville's Border Grange Bank, which financed tobacco planting throughout the region.[78] Sutherlin was also instrumental in railroad magnate Tom Scott's acquisition of Virginia's state-owned railway stock, a maneuver that enabled Scott to consolidate his control over the state's transportation system. By the mid-1870s, Scott's holding company, the Southern Railway Security Company (SRSC), controlled crop distribution from Baltimore to Atlanta, enabling it to promote tobacco culture by dramatically slashing shipping rates for the weed while increasing rates on other crops. Under the SRSC, growers and other distributers could ship tobacco without pre-payment of their freight, a benefit that enabled them to avoid outlays or interest on transport loans. Such policies subsidized tobacco (and cotton) against the raising of other cash crops or livestock. They also enabled railroads to shift their rates for tobacco or cotton depending on market trends.[79] For example, when the cotton market cratered in 1894, the Atlantic Coast Line Railroad joined warehousemen into coaxing eastern North Carolina cotton farmers into tobacco culture with twenty thousand free copies of an instructional pamphlet on the disciplines of tobacco culture, which the railroad published in coordination with the warehouse-friendly *Southern Tobacco Journal*.[80]

The postbellum political economy of tobacco did not merely traffic in fertilizer and the "golden weed." It was also premised on the creation and perpetuation of indebtedness. For postbellum Southern agrarians, everything could be tied up in debt: land, clothing, tools, even food. State governments created the legal foundations of agrarian debt throughout the South, but the racial, class, and commodity specificities of different regions shaped the mechanisms of borrowing. In the tobacco South, as soils exhausted, cotton prices plunged, and railroads discouraged the growth of other cash crops, fertilizer dependence was an incredibly reliable producer of debts. Between the Civil War and 1880, southeastern farmers expended more than $14,000,000 on fertilizers, and in North Carolina credit financed ninety percent of that consumption.[81] Fertilizer companies worked through furnishing merchants as well as loaning directly to farmers, on whose land and crops they placed surety liens.[82] So central were fertilizer bills to the daily operations of tobacco farms that smallholders who hired out shifted parts of their debts to workers. Virginia grower Sampson White claimed he compensated workers with "1/2 the crop," but only on the condition that they paid "1/2 the fertilizer bill."[83] The result of was a shifting of risk from fertilizer manufacturers to the growers who used their products, a condition that deepened growers' need for cash. Following the circuitous logic of agrarian debt, that need for cash meant growers needed to sell more tobacco, and to grow tobacco they needed to borrow more fertilizer.[84]

Although they fueled farmers' indebtedness, fertilizer manufacturers promoted the claim that growers could compromise between subsistence and capitalist agriculture if they devoted more labor to their gardens. As one of the most influential manufacturers of the period, Allison & Addison also produced an annual "Hand Book of the Garden, Seed Catalogue, and Almanac," based on their contention that "our Farmers and Planters pay too little attention to their gardens."[85] But for most growers, the need to generate cash prevented such a compromise. The tobacco frontier was therefore also a debt frontier, a rapidly expanding region unified by the crop it produced and the indebtedness of its producers.[86]

Their control of growers' debts enabled tobacco capitalists, particularly fertilizer manufacturers, to impose universal measures of tobacco's quality. In the process, they effectively reconstructed tobacco's disciplinary economy—the insights, practices, and habits that defined its valuation but also its cultivation. Tobacco capitalists accomplished this reconstruction through indebtedness, stock laws, fertilizer dependence, and other attacks on Southern agrarian livelihoods. Their embrace of scientific agriculture, aggressive publication of pamphlets and books, and relations with elite growers were all part of this conquest.

Fertilizer manufacturers therefore benefited from the Reconstruction-era overthrow of the colonial and early national export inspection systems that had judged tobacco's quality for over a century. These systems had emerged in the eighteenth century, when colonial and state governments sought to police standards of quality for export tobacco. By the antebellum period, inspection warehouses from New Orleans to Richmond analyzed tobacco destined for overseas markets in an effort to preserve their regions' commercial reputations abroad. Nor were inspectors the only mediating figures in the tobacco economy. Growers producing for domestic markets likewise faced the discriminating tastes of urban manufacturers or merchants. Despite such barriers, however, antebellum growers operated within a commodity "web," which gave them options. They could sell a portion of their crop to foreign buyers, twisting or pressing lower-quality leaf for sale at a local market or for trade with neighbors.[87] The emergence of the federal internal revenue system foreclosed these options by legally segregating growers from leaf dealers and manufacturers, forcing growers into a narrower market and making possible the further circumscription of marketable "quality." At the same time, as private auction warehouses extended their authority over the tobacco economy in the 1870s, states abolished public inspections. Although some members of the fertilizer industry opposed abolition, including the Southern Fertilizing Company's spokesman Robert Ragland, tobacco capitalists generally profited from the emerging power of private auction warehouses.[88] Under the new system, judgment of quality was thrown open, creating a void into which new forces—fertilizer manufacturers and warehouses—could situate themselves as the new arbiters of excellence.

Grower Protests

Tobacco growers did not passively accept these new arrangements, and agrarian protests defined tobacco politics in the decades between the creation of the internal revenue system and the early twentieth century. Freedpeople launched the first such protests, although white observers derided their resistance as obstinacy, as opposed to a self-conscious attempt to preserve household economies. The tobacco analyst B.W. Arnold captured this perspective in his 1897 history of tobacco in the United States, arguing that freedpeople "were in a position to force their claims, and the negro share-owner became a new factor in the production of [Virginia]. As he took many holidays, being a faithful attendant upon all camp-meetings, political gatherings and church festivals, he did not add much to the sum-total of the State's production."[89] Common throughout the postbellum decades, criticisms like Arnold's failed to recognize that freedpeople's resistance to monocropping was a carefully orchestrated attempt to balance subsistence and capitalist agriculture—the same balance that tobacco capitalists and elite growers often criticized impoverished growers for failing to maintain.[90]

Between the 1870s and 1890s, the Grange and the Farmers' Alliance focused their attention on tobacco growers' struggles. While they criticized the internal revenue system, the political influence of manufacturers, and the cycle of debt underlying tobacco culture, these agrarian protests tended to challenge the organized capitalists of warehouse towns. Where Charles Dudley Warner saw Danville's "co-operation" and "associated effort to foster individual interests" as evidence of city leaders' business acumen, hinterland growers saw the same efforts as a plot to suppress prices. During the 1870s, the Virginia Grange launched the first challenge against organized warehouses and established the course for future growers' protests. Echoing the Grangers' complaints from a decade earlier, a member of the Vance County, North Carolina Farmers' Alliance lamented that his crops had "to pass ... into the hands of one of the most perfect, thorough, and powerful organizations of the country, not all together the local 'Board of Trade.'" By "not all together," this grower suggested that tobacco capitalists were not the local boosters they often claimed to be, but "only a branch of the great combined tobacco interest of the United States."[91] The latter point was crucial: although they targeted warehouses, which were the most visible manifestation of tobacco's new economy, agrarian protesters recognized that more systematic changes were underway.

The most visible venue for tobacco growers' protests was *The Progressive Farmer*, a North Carolina-based populist agricultural newspaper founded by Leonidas Lafayette Polk. Polk was among the Farmers' Alliance's most influential national leaders. An agricultural modernizer, president of the Southern Alliance, and North Carolina's first Commissioner of Agriculture, Polk promoted many of the era's cutting-edge positions: the regulation of fertilizer manufacturers, the replacement of Black smallholders with European immigrants, and the creation of a state experiment station. Founded in 1886, *The Progressive Farmer* was a critical tool for Polk's advocacy that helped him project his vision beyond North Carolina. Through *The Progressive Farmer*, Polk helped organize dozens of "Farmers' Clubs," which organized white growers and their allies to discuss agricultural concerns among their neighbors—an accomplishment that served Polk's broader goal of organizing white agriculturists against finance and industrial capitalists.[92] Following Polk's death and the decline of the Alliance, *The Progressive Farmer* continued this mission. Under Polk's successor Clarence Poe, the paper supported a series of related white growers' protests into the early-twentieth century, such as the North Carolina Farmers' Protective Association, the Tobacco Growers' Protective Association, and the Interstate Tobacco Growers' Protective Association.[93]

The alternative political economy promoted by *The Progressive Farmer* and the groups it supported rested on several ideological principles. They were staunchly antimonopolist, although not anti-capitalist. As critics of the internal revenue system had maintained throughout the 1870s and 1880s, monopolies distorted market relations and degraded farmers' ability to, among other things, preserve household economies. In the case of tobacco growers, the most commonly targeted monopolies were the warehouses and boards of trade that governed local commerce and, beginning in the 1890s, the increasingly consolidated American Tobacco Company. While growers' associations challenged specific concentrations of capital, they defended "cooperative" capitalism that, they imagined, could sustain household economies and bring prosperity to tobacco country. This principle was apparent in the statements of movement leaders, such as J. Bryan Grimes, the president of the North Carolina Tobacco Growers' Protective Association, who proclaimed in 1900 that growers wanted "capital to come into our territory and assist in developing our latent resources and manufacturing our raw material."[94] More than a decade earlier, the North Carolina Farmers' Alliance projected a similar position when it welcomed the support of W. Duke & Sons, who provided chairs for a statewide Alliance gathering in Durham just one year before incorporating the monopolistic American Tobacco Company. The same Alliance meeting enjoyed the support of Durham's Fidelity Bank, operated by future ATC operative Benjamin Duke.[95] Grower households themselves lived this cooperative principle when they sent children, some as young as eight years old, to earn discretionary income in tobacco warehouses and factories.[96]

Most notably, however, proponents of alternatives illustrated their commitment to cooperation not by aligning with already existing capitalist institutions, but instead by attempting to create their own to control the tobacco market.

These efforts signified a second principle of the growers' alternative political economy: white agrarian control of the means of production and distribution. At the height of its influence, the Farmers' Alliance founded nine tobacco warehouses in Virginia and North Carolina as well as several manufacturing enterprises, whose products would not "be sold on the markets in such a manner as to cut or underbid each other."[97] By 1890, they had formed the Farmers' Alliance Cooperative Plug and Smoking Tobacco Company and purchased a Raleigh factory once owned by the Knights of Labor.[98] At the same time, North Carolina Alliance members also began producing their own fertilizers.[99] None of these schemes succeeded, which growers attributed to the rapidly expanding market power of the American Tobacco Company. By the turn of the century, the ideal of white growers' market control had shifted from organizing warehouses and factories to the creation of cartels with the goals of reducing production and "pooling" tobacco, or holding it off the market until manufacturers offered an acceptable price. The most infamous examples of this ideal were in Tennessee and Kentucky, where night-riding growers violently attacked neighbors who refused to pool their crops, but growers in every tobacco district considered crop pooling.[100] The growers of Person County, North Carolina, for example, formed committees of "influential men" to coerce growers into pledging a fifty percent reduction in their crop production.[101] Each of these strategies—founding their own warehouses and factories, manufacturing fertilizer, and pooling crops—accepted the structural norms of tobacco's postbellum commodity chain and focused on controlling points of distribution and sale as well as the quantity of tobacco marketed by growers.

Yet growers also recognized that perceptions of quality, not only quantity, influenced their daily labors, the prices their crops fetched, and the perpetuation of their indebtedness. For the white leaders of the Alliance and its turn-of-the-century successors, the principle of quality constructed by fertilizer manufacturers could be a profitable tool that helped them distinguish their tobacco from the competition of their neighbors as well as growers around the world. Throughout the postbellum decades, growers echoed the argument of the Southern Fertilizing Company's John Ott that "low grade Tobacco" could be produced by "too many people in the world … and with whom we cannot compete on equal terms."[102] Yet the quality principle's advantages were not merely economic. Quality was a standard upon which white agrarians could ascribe ideals of masculinity, racial superiority, land management, morality, and class. J. Bryan Grimes reflected these priorities in a speech before the North Carolina Tobacco Growers' Protective Association, arguing that quality was a way for white growers to distinguish their crops, and thus themselves, from non-white producers at home and abroad. According to Grimes, quality tobacco, and a political economy that protected its producers, represented "manhood and rugged individuality" and could not be produced by "the peasant of Europe," "the half breeds of the Antilles," or "millions of Mongolian coolies."[103] When figures like Grimes repeated these assertions, they joined fertilizer manufacturers and warehouses in the construction of quality ideals while simultaneously constructing the gendered and racial caste system of the tobacco frontier.[104]

Not all growers accepted the quality principle. For more radical agrarians, the threats facing household economies and the proliferation of rural poverty were not the results of overproduction, low-grade tobacco, or even monopoly. The problem instead was tobacco itself, a commodity too tied to the capricious fortunes of global capitalism to sustain agrarian communities. From this perspective, "quality" was an elusive promise that captured growers in an economy that could not sustain them. "We impoverish ourselves to buy guano to go under our tobacco," wrote a grower named W.H. Schoolfield, of Reidsville, North Carolina, "and then when the stuff comes to market, the buyers say the reason it sells so low is because it is a 'sorry crop and it ain't no account.'"[105] Nor was supply and demand a reliable metric for understanding prices, as years of price fluctuations, particularly in the bleak 1890s, refuted that supposedly ironclad law. Comparing tobacco with cotton, one grower reported to his colleagues in 1896 that while cotton's prices had increased with declining production, that was "not so with tobacco." "There," he continued, "the market has been so throttled that a decline of 20 per cent in production is marked by a 43 per cent. decline in value."[106] Several years later, as the crisis continued, another North Carolina grower reminded his audience of the coercive reality of tobacco's reconstructed political economy. Writing from Pitt County, where the annual production of tobacco had increased from 580 pounds in 1880 to 11 million in 1900, Abram Moye chided his neighbors: "[M]y brethren, if you wish to spend your year in severe toil for the especial benefit of two of these gigantic aggregations of capital called ... trusts, then by all means plant tobacco and plant largely. The Virginia-Carolina Chemical Company and the American Tobacco Company will take exquisite pleasure in gathering in the cash whether you prosper or not."[107]

Throughout the 1890s, these different strands of agrarian protest returned to the question of the state. Where was the government, in particular the federal government and its most rapidly expanding agency, the Department of Agriculture? What role did that agency have in the protection of tobacco growers' livelihoods? Could it ease the despair wrought by tobacco's reconstructed political economy? W.H. Schoolfield, the Reidsville farmer who despised tobacco culture, hoped the USDA would lead his neighbors away from tobacco. "Suppose," he suggested to his neighbors, "we petition the Agricultural Department not to send us any more tobacco seed, but to send us some pigs." The commercial and political power of tobacco capitalists had disillusioned Schoolfield, however, and he did not believe the state could promote viable agrarian livelihoods. Encouraging hog raising, for example, "would take away from the tobacco trust from this one county alone a half million pounds of its yearly supplies," as well as "from the railroads the freight on that tobacco, wherever it goes," and "that one hundred and fifty tons [of guano] at an average cost of $25 per ton."[108] The federal state, he lamented, would never betray its capitalist allies. Schoolfield composed his analysis in 1892, thirty years after the founding of the Department of Agriculture but on the eve of the agency's first serious foray into tobacco. In the years ahead, the USDA would provide enough evidence for him to check his hypothesis.

5

The Health of the State

The USDA, Agricultural Hegemony, and the Federal Improvement of Tobacco Quality, 1890-1933

The records of the U.S. Department of Agriculture's Office of Tobacco Investigations (OTI) contain hundreds of experiment reports produced during the first third of the twentieth century. These large, gridded forms documented the annual tobacco field work at experiment stations in Virginia, North Carolina, and South Carolina, offering a glimpse into the priorities of federal tobacco agronomists, men whose professional discipline was itself a product of the interwoven forces of scientific agriculture, industrial capitalism, and imperialism (see fig. 15). The forms explore hyper-specialized questions, such as the price—as determined by auction house buyers—of a crop grown from "Warner" tobacco seed in a field fertilized with a mixture of dried blood and acid phosphate, hand-hoed twice, suckered twice, and replanted three times. The sheer volume of the records, the seeming minutiae of their data, and the amount of physical and analytical labor necessary to produce them illustrate a tenacious governmental effort to *know* tobacco—its physiology, its responses to climate and soil, and the origins of its marketable characteristics, such as its color, oiliness, malleability, and burning rate.[1]

OTI's research agenda exemplified the turn-of-the-century federal effort to secure American hegemony over the world tobacco market. The Department of Agriculture (USDA) created the office during an era of both plenty and insecurity for U.S. growers, when annual production neared one billion pounds annually, far outpacing other nations, but prices were low and quality inconsistent. If unaddressed, USDA officials feared, these problems might discourage growers and drive away foreign buyers. Amid booming production, agricultural observers saw a crisis of potentially existential proportions. Between the 1890s and 1920s, these concerns kept the state focused on tobacco, with agricultural officials associating tobacco's biology and cultivation with issues of considerable national interest, including the competitiveness of American agriculture in global markets and the protection of domestic markets from foreign economic interests.

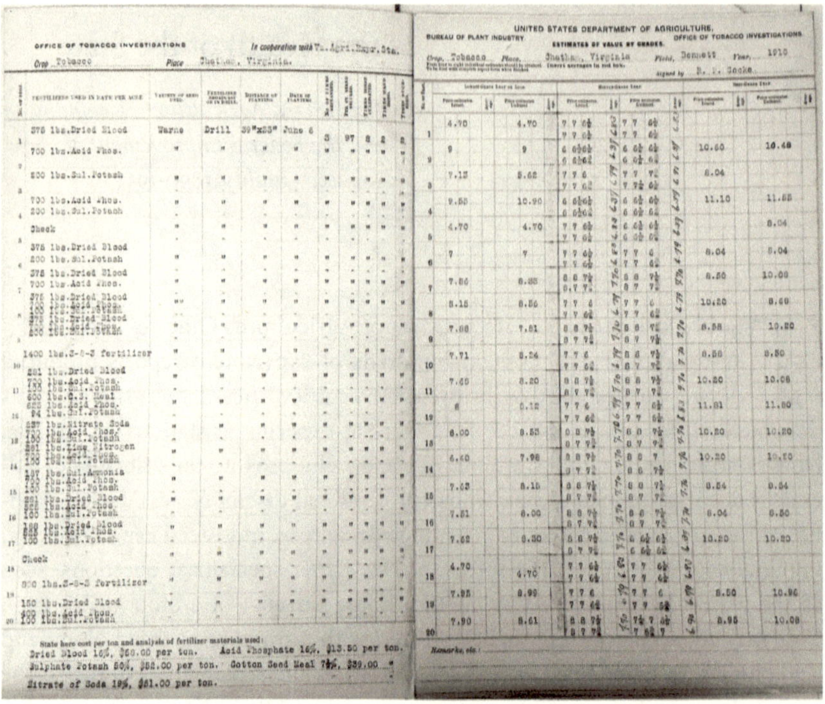

Figure 15. The USDA's Office of Tobacco Investigations carried out hundreds of experiments during the early twentieth century as part of a tremendous federal effort to make tobacco culture more predictable and assert American power over the world tobacco market. Records of the Division of Tobacco and Plant Nutrition, National Archives Building, College Park, Maryland.

With its global outlook and hegemonic ambitions, the Office of Tobacco Investigations turned the demands of the American "commodifying empire" inward.[2] "Empire" generally connotes processes directed outward—the penetration of foreign markets or the conquest of resource-rich territories—but the federal government's tobacco experiments suggest the ways outward-oriented concerns determined domestic policy. The USDA's intervention in tobacco culture and its ecological contexts was both an offensive strategy to promote American tobacco and expand foreign consumption, and a defensive strategy concerned with protecting hegemony from competitor states attempting to develop their own tobacco cultures.

As it turned the commodifying empire inward, OTI bureaucratized the quality principle—the liberal belief that objective qualities determined tobacco's value and that undisciplined growers, rather than deeper structural inequities, caused the tobacco economy's hardships. Although OTI officials shared this belief with tobacco capitalists, they aspired to more than the capitalists' rhetorical justifications for low prices. Rather, OTI agronomists believed that whatever inequities and inefficiencies plagued tobacco culture could be solved by transforming the physiology and agro-ecology of the commodity itself.[3]

In pursuit of this goal, the USDA and OTI deployed a mode of governance best described as "bureaucratic commodification." A central feature of "high modernist" states, bureaucratic commodification derived from the overlapping demands of imperialism and capitalist agriculture. It was self-consciously rational, striving for order and commensurability in commodity production. It was liberal and scientific, in that it evinced a commitment to markets through the biological optimization of nature. Finally, it claimed to be apolitical, carefully operating through existing relations of production while avoiding sociopolitical analysis of these relations and their histories. In sum, bureaucratic commodification strove to advance national economic power through commodities, imagining that commodity chains would reform themselves in the process.

But commodification is about more than the physical properties of a given commodity; it is also about the politics of the commodity chain. As OTI officials realized by the 1920s, the economic and political order of American tobacco culture—codified in the regulations of the Bureau of Internal Revenue and exploited by tobacco capitalists during the Gilded Age—precluded genuine, long-lasting improvement in growers' fortunes. Moreover, the OTI's hybridization, plant pathology, and soil studies were beginning to produce unprecedented increases in the nation's annual tobacco crop. As long as the market's character depended on grower discipline and education, and not some more radical regulatory reform, low prices would prevail and inexperienced growers, hopeful for any kind of payday, would continue to flood markets with poor tobacco.

The USDA and the Expansionist Aspirations of Postbellum Scientific Agriculture

By the turn of the century, the USDA would become a cabinet-level executive agency wielding extensive political, scientific, and cultural influence in rural America. But in its earliest decades, particularly prior to the 1880s, scientifically minded USDA officials were often frustrated in their aspirations. This was, at least in part, because the Department was chronically underfunded and understaffed. A decade and a half after its founding, USDA officials complained that their agency was the most poorly funded in the federal bureaucracy, working with just $174,000 total in 1877 (compared with $14 million for the Treasury Department, $5.1 million for Indian Affairs, and $385,876 for Justice).[4] Fuming over the 1877 appropriation, Agriculture Commissioner William Le Duc protested to Congress, "When it is remembered that the last census established the fact that one-half the population of the United States is either directly engaged in agricultural pursuits, or wholly dependent on them for support, this sum becomes still more insignificant."[5] Under these conditions, the agency's studies of agricultural forces of production, from soils and fertilizer to crops and insects, remained limited. What operations the USDA did oversee, moreover, were largely subordinated to the patronage relationships of farmers and their congressional representatives. The most conspicuous such program was seed distribution, which consumed roughly half of the USDA's budget by providing free seeds to members of Congress, who distributed them to "curry favor" with constituents. If those constituents wanted more extensive political support or business advice, they were likely to turn to local agricultural societies or state boards of agriculture.[6] Under these circumstances, the USDA struggled to retain staff, with administrative and scientific leaders "fluidly" passing through its ranks throughout the 1860s and 1870s.[7]

Despite its limited appropriations and political submission to seed distribution, the Department aspired to significant influence, and its core ideologies remained consistent throughout the postbellum period. The Department's ideology reflected a vision of political economy popularized by Henry Carey, including his belief in the symbiosis of nutrient-producing agricultural hinterlands (which required energy-rich waste to fuel crop growth and human capital to improve cultivation) and nutrient-consuming industrial metropoles (which produced energy-rich waste byproducts and technologically sophisticated human capital). Likewise, the Department shared the Republican Party's postbellum goal of extending federal authority across North America through the creation of market-oriented agriculturist citizens.[8] When USDA officials such as Le Duc proclaimed that agriculture was "at the foundation of national prosperity," they were expressing a truth held deeply by the Department's agents: that the perpetuation of American state sovereignty depended on agroecological development. The United States, insisted Le Duc in 1877, could "not hope to take that rank among the producers of the world until we have exhausted all efforts to produce within our own borders ... everything now imported from other nations, which can be obtained from careful cultivation of our productive soil."⁹ This was an ideology of possibility, one that viewed the continental web of life as holding extensive, previously unimaginable agro-economic possibilities, and the role of the state was to make those possibilities imaginable.

Early USDA officials envisaged North America as a vast but beguiling garden, capable of producing commodities, or "economic plants," that Americans had historically imported, such as coffee, sugar, citrus trees, wine grapes, tea, and jute.¹⁰ In order to nurture these industries, the USDA adopted a range of schemes. In 1879, officials attempted to establish coffee culture in Florida by sending several trees to an experimental planter near Bradenton named Julia Atzeroth.¹¹ Other projects were more systematic and retained Department interest for much of the late nineteenth century. The USDA sent envoys to France to study viticulture and distributed findings to growers in California. It also claimed responsibility for the early emergence of the California citrus industry, which, according an 1883 report, began "from the progeny of plants originally imported by the Department from Brazil, and subsequently disseminated in [California] and other States."¹² It collected plant life from across North America, which frontier-roaming military officers sent to Washington for study. These studies, officials imagined, would yield new industries that would exist in harmony with their ecological settings and promote the prosperity of white settlers across the continent. Le Duc's dreams for the American tea industry exemplified this Department-wide faith in experimental, imperial agriculture more generally: "American tea," he pronounced in 1880, "grown and manufactured by ourselves, is destined at no late day to supply the demand of our own people and to enter the world's market in favorable competition."¹³

USDA administrators likewise sought to rationalize commercial agriculture around a coherent "system," and to serve that goal they prioritized the collection and analysis of crop data.¹⁴ Earlier in the nineteenth century, elite agricultural societies had begun quantitatively analyzing farm production, and several influential antebellum newspapers, such as Orange Judd's *American Agriculturist*, published regular crop reports from their readers.¹⁵ Beginning in 1863, with the Department's creation of a crop reporting network, USDA data collection and analysis became the most significant effort of its kind in the nineteenth century, "more extensive, regular, and prompt in communication, more systematic and thorough in detail, and more intelligent and practical in the material of its returns" than any previous endeavor.¹⁶ By the turn of the century, the crop-reporting network relied on roughly 40,000 correspondents whose data the USDA compiled into nearly twenty reports annually, of which it published more than 1.5 million copies.[17] In contrast to the American agricultural past, which USDA officials often assumed to have been atomized and haphazard, data collection revealed a national aggregate of commodity production that could be ordered, measured, and analyzed for improvement. Officials believed that as the system improved individual growers would better understand how their production fit within national and global markets, and with that knowledge they could master the law of supply and demand and avoid the instabilities that had long plagued cash-crop producers.

According to USDA statistician J.R. Dodge, data collection offered distinct promise for tobacco growers. During the 1870s, Dodge argued that the ideal U.S. tobacco output could be produced "on twenty townships of land yielding 800 pounds per acre," a reality that left tobacco growers spread across eastern North America vulnerable to "great fluctuations in the breadth of production," glutted markets, and low prices.[18] With regular reports and forecasts, however, tobacco growers could rationalize production and reduce uncertainty. Further, USDA officials claimed that in taming supply and demand, crop reporting would starve the speculators, middlemen, and frauds who fed on information asymmetries in global crop markets.[19] Tobacco manufacturers, even those outside of the United States, agreed with this point and relied on Department reports for accurate predictions of the supply and price of leaf tobacco. For example, Liverpool's Central Association of Tobacco Manufacturers, which formed in response to the "fictitious" prices of speculative American leaf dealers, recommended its members obtain "the monthly reports of the United States Agricultural Bureau, in which full and reliable information is given from month to month as to the condition of the tobacco crop."[20] Like the Liverpool manufacturers, early USDA officials believed the problems facing American farmers and their markets were informational. Moreover, they believed that with precise data they could not only measure the nation's progress and prosperity, but also achieve them in perpetuity.

As the USDA publicized the data it extracted from the countryside, it slowly positioned itself as a hub of all information relating to agriculture. In so doing, it worked through the influential networks of editors, agricultural society officers, and elite farmers who controlled rural newspapers. At times, this meant recirculating notable articles and studies that had appeared in the agricultural press, even if they were from decades earlier. The Department's 1867 Annual Report, for instance, included W.W.W. Bowie's 1849 essay "Culture and Management of Tobacco," which had first appeared in *American Agriculturist*.[21] The Department also joined other government institutions and figures, such as state boards of agriculture or college faculty, in circulating its original work to newspapers, which kept farmers abreast of the Department's activities.

These strategies altered the power dynamics at play in the agricultural press. Since their proliferation in the antebellum period, agricultural newspapers had relied on an "open policy," inviting contributions from thousands of farmers under the belief that the accumulation of experience would promote more consistent and systematic farming practices.[22] By intervening in these pages, the Department of Agriculture offered a more authoritative perspective than any single farmer could muster, implicitly suggesting that the concentration of experimental and analytical power under a government agency—as opposed to its diffusion amongst thousands of farmers—would produce a higher order of scientific knowledge.[23]

USDA officials and their backers in Congress spent the final decades of the nineteenth century building upon early programs and steadily amassing bureaucratic authority. Most visibly, the Department achieved cabinet status in 1889, a landmark that reflected growing national recognition for the USDA's regulatory and scientific significance. The former was apparent following Congress's creation, in 1884, of the USDA's Bureau of Animal Industry (BAI) in response to outbreaks of Texas fever and contagious bovine pleuropneumonia (CBPP) that threatened national dairy and beef commerce. Organized three years before the Interstate Commerce Commission, the BAI wielded extensive, even unprecedented, regulatory power from Washington. Its agents worked with state governments to establish quarantines and destroy private property, from cattle to barns to railcars, which could transmit the diseases. By 1892, the BAI had eradicated CBPP across the United States—the first disease eradication "on a continental scale" in history.[24] Another milestone came in 1887 when Congress passed the Hatch Act, which realized the USDA's long-held ambition of creating a national system of experiment stations that linked the networking capacity of the national Department with the entrenched expertise of land grant colleges.[25] By the early 1890s, each station was publishing "inexpensive popular bulletins" for local farmers—a precedent that anticipated the founding of the USDA's annual *Yearbook* in 1895, which by 1900 was the single largest annual publication of the federal government.[26] Station bulletins and the *Yearbook* provided a prominent pedestal for Department officials to promote their findings in crop science, making possible the planting of non-native "economic plants" on a scale only imagined by USDA officials in the 1870s. By the turn of the century, American growers were planting USDA-introduced Egyptian cotton in New Mexico, Bavarian hops in the Pacific Northwest, and Russian winter wheat in the Great Plains, the latter of which farmers produced 20 million bushels only five years after the USDA introduced it in 1898.[27]

Amid these expansions in authority and landmark accomplishments, the USDA underwent personnel reorganizations that relieved the agency's dependence on Congress. Whereas USDA employment had once required a legislator's patronage support, by the 1890s the agency demanded more meritocratic credentials, such as land-grant college training. This shift created more stable professional tracks that helped the USDA retain scientists who had long been tempted by more lucrative work with private industry or foreign governments, while also helping scientists deepen their specialized expertise over time.

As the USDA exercised unprecedented regulatory authority over private property, flooded markets with information, and distanced itself from party and patronage alignments, it evinced a broader realignment of the boundaries between state and economy. Essential to this realignment was the federal state's burgeoning power to promote and direct the systems by which things became commodities.[28] To meet domestic demand and extend American influence abroad, the USDA sought to draw new things—plants, animals, landscapes—into the market. For the same reasons, it relied on its ever-increasing pool of data to determine strategies through which old, unwieldy commodities—like tobacco—could be remade.

Economic Imperialism and the Making of Federal Tobacco Science

In the midst of the USDA's maturation, Department officials regarded tobacco suspiciously, particularly if it came from the South. To USDA modernizers, Southern tobacco seemed like a wasteful relic of plantation agriculture, a crop that had exhausted both the enslaved laborers who cultivated it and the soils on which it grew. Those who continued to cultivate tobacco after emancipation, many of whom were formerly enslaved or yeoman household growers, conflicted with the Department's ideal of scientific, business-minded farmers. "The planters of our Southern States," noted one 1873 report, "undertake to cultivate too much land with too little diversity of crop, thereby disabling themselves from obtaining that rotation so essential to successful farming."[29] Throughout Reconstruction, Department officials complained about a flood of "inferior" tobacco from American fields despite the era's market contractions. "We say," noted an 1878 USDA report, "that overproduction (which means ... the production of poor tobacco) is the controlling cause of the unhappy condition in which the tobacco-planters of the United States now find themselves."[30] If growers could address overproduction, officials believed tobacco could fit within the nation's agricultural future. It was, after all, a staple of the federal revenue system, although by the late 1870s the USDA was embarrassed to report that federal tobacco tax revenue greatly exceeded the combined earnings of the nation's tobacco growers. But many expressed doubt that Southern farmers were equipped to address overproduction. In the same 1878 report bemoaning "inferior" tobacco, the author charged that growers' backwardness threatened national welfare: "In [the tobacco grower's] neglect—whether from overcropping or otherwise—of the crop in the field, or his equally fatal neglect or ignorance in handling it after being housed, may be found the 'direful source of woes unnumbered,' not to him only, but to the trade and to the country."[31] A decade later, the USDA's position had barely changed, with the 1888 Annual Report blaming growers for the prevalence of "inferior and low grades of tobacco."[32] As USDA officials constructed a coherent vision of the agricultural state during the Department's first twenty-five years, tobacco, particularly Southern tobacco, remained in this liminal phase, a prominent but problematic crop without a clear stake in the future of agricultural state development.

Nonetheless, changes in the Department's tobacco position appeared by the late 1880s, albeit outside historical growing regions. In 1886, the Department contracted one grower per county in South Carolina to attempt tobacco cultivation, and then hired Danville's E.M. Pace, a well-known booster and warehouse proprietor, to judge the samples and determine "the availability of South Carolina as a tobacco-growing State."[33] Other early experiments occurred even further from tobacco's traditional regions, at experiment stations in Arkansas, Mississippi, Oregon, and Washington. After one successful planting season, even crop scientists at the Utah experiment station claimed that tobacco could be "one of the leading, if not the best agricultural product of the territory."[34] The first ever USDA publication dealing specifically with tobacco came not from agronomists in Virginia or Connecticut but from the Colorado Experiment Station.[35] This new direction represented an extension of the USDA's long-held interest in establishing "economic plants" where they had not previously grown.

It also grew out of an older fascination within the tobacco industry of producing types and qualities associated with foreign growing regions, such as Cuban "Vuelta Abajo" or Sumatran cigar leaf. These were the world's finest tobaccos, and postbellum trade journals regularly filled their pages with proprietors' claims to have unlocked their secrets. During the 1870s, New York's Appleby Cigar

Machine Company advertised "Remsen Appleby's Pure Havana Flavoring," which, its producer claimed, would give tobacco "that sweetness and aroma" often associated with Cuban cigars.[36] Another proprietor, James Chaskel, peddled his "de la Vuelta Abajo" flavor extract to cigar makers with the reassurance that it would "never be discovered" that their cigars were "artificially flavored."[37] As absurd as such products seem, they evinced a late-century obsession with challenging the market power of foreign tobacco producers, an obsession echoed by the USDA when its scientists produced thousands of pounds of Cuban tobacco in the Pacific Northwest.

Beyond an extension of earlier industry interests, the USDA's tobacco experiments symbolized an emerging global outlook within the Department. This outlook prioritized the conquest of foreign markets, in contrast to earlier USDA officials' ideological commitments to the virtuous cycles of hinterland supply and urban demand. In 1894, the USDA declared an official policy of "extending the demands of foreign markets for the agricultural products of the United States," and several years later Agriculture Secretary James Wilson proclaimed his agency would promote "every particle of information bearing upon the natural resources of the country which will in any way tend to increase the production of our present crops or to develop new methods or build up new industries."[38] Anxious to push American tobacco into the world's markets, the Department intensified its study of tobacco during the 1890s.

Further motivating USDA officials were competing governments' attempts to expand their own tobacco frontiers, thereby reducing the dependence of their overlapping consumer markets and internal revenue systems on American tobacco. During the final third of the nineteenth century, European states regularly hired agricultural scientists to analyze their domestic tobacco crops and experiment in new modes of production.[39] Many of those same states also oversaw colonial tobacco experiments throughout the Global South. British officials in India had experimented with tobacco for much of the nineteenth century, and between the 1870s and the turn of the century they intensified their work in the Ganges Valley and greater Bombay.[40] Their colleagues in Burma embarked on similar experiments and boasted in 1883 that the colony would "in a few years time ... supply, in part at least, the wants of European nations."[41] In the Dutch East Indies, a consortium of government officials and corporate investors established cigar leaf culture by dispossessing natives, felling the forest, maligning peasants' "insufficient modes of husbandry," imposing commercial agriculture, and importing migrant laborers from China.[42] Together these schemes illustrated an imperialist urge to liberate markets from the dominance of American tobacco. Not even American consumers were immune from these forces. Although they had imported approximately 11 million pounds of tobacco annually between 1877 and 1886, by 1900 that total had jumped to 26 million pounds, worth roughly $12,000,000. In the world's preeminent tobacco-producing country, tobacco was the sixth most valuable imported crop.[43] The American tobacco hegemony, as USDA officials came to realize by the 1890s, was drifting uneasily into the new era of imperialist agriculture.

The global outlook illuminated two challenges facing the USDA. The first was to reduce American consumers' demand for foreign tobacco. According to Archibald Shamel, a tobacco specialist and plant breeder with the USDA's Bureau of Plant Industry, displacing foreign producers would distribute "money now expended for the imported article ... among the American growers."[44] Although USDA officials rarely spoke of it, reducing import demand would also secure consumer spending on internal tobacco taxes, thereby curtailing government dependence on foreign commerce. The second challenge, essentially the inverse of the first, was to entrench American tobacco in foreign markets. If the USDA could help American growers produce tobacco of such quality and consistency that foreign growers could not replicate it, the agency would significantly bolster U.S. influence over foreign consumers and revenue systems. Yet the merchantability of American tobacco was often inconsistent, so by the 1890s USDA officials turned to the same concept that had shaped the political economy of the tobacco South since the 1870s: the quality principle.

The USDA's approach to the quality principle was more ambitious than anything offered by fertilizer manufacturers, warehouse proprietors, or other tobacco capitalists. While the latter were concerned with controlling quality through labor discipline and chemical treatment of soils, they were also willing to jeopardize quality by expanding tobacco's growing frontier—a choice that improved fertilizer sales and warehouse business but attracted more inexperienced growers. For these interests, quality was most valuable as a justification for low prices. The Department of Agriculture offered an approach that challenged tobacco capitalists' boosterism as well as the industrial, yield-increasing priorities of USDA programs in other parts of the United States.[45] Instead of simply producing more tobacco, the USDA sought to turn the ideals of the quality principle into a repeatable organic reality by unlocking the plant's physiology.

The Department took halting steps toward this ambitious goal. For much of the 1890s the USDA's primary tobacco intervention was the distribution of manuals, such as John Estes' "Tobacco: Instructions for Its Cultivation and Curing," of which the USDA claimed to have circulated 46,000 copies after its publication in 1893.[46] Such tactics were "fragmentary" and "incidental," according to A.C. True, the USDA's Director of Experiment Stations. True suggested a more thorough and groundbreaking approach, one that would tackle problems that bore directly on "the style or character of the leaf" as it related to "market demands," such as "the chemical composition of the leaf, the chemical substances produced in the leaf, the relation of nicotine to the flavor and aroma, the changes in the curing and fermentation, the influence of soil, of seed, of climatic conditions, of cultivation and of handling." Put more simply, going forward the USDA would prioritize the "improvement of the leaf." It would also "improve" the grower through mastery of "the economic details of tobacco culture," including the careful selection of seed and soil and the creation of regimented work routines. Guided by True's vision, the federal government entered the field of tobacco science.[47]

The foundational insight of federal tobacco science was that leaf quality depended on "climactic and soil conditions."[48] Generations of growers and buyers had intuited this insight, and postbellum manufacturers had even begun advertising products by touting the soils that produced their tobacco. R.J. Reynolds proclaimed to the readers of the *Southern Tobacco Journal* that their factory was located in "the only section of country yet discovered that produces Chewing Tobacco which is palatable without the use of drugs."[49] Despite Reynolds' boast, however, the emergence of the fertilizer industry and the increasing number of farmers looking for viable cash crops had destabilized the boundaries of commercial tobacco agriculture.[50] Facilitating that process was the tobacco plant itself, which was incredibly adaptable and could be grown essentially anywhere in the continental United States. Its adaptability, however, led to significant fluctuations in the quality of tobacco entering markets during the late nineteenth century. By analyzing and ordering the soils of major tobacco-producing regions, the USDA could begin to answer basic questions about these fluctuations. Why, for example, did "the poorer soils of the Clarksville district" of Tennessee and Kentucky produce the "coarse, dark, heavy type of tobacco" desired in Italian and German markets? What features made the sandy "pine barrens" of the Piedmont ideal for cigarette tobacco?[51]

Seeking to answer these questions and deploying the same "managerial relationship with nature" that had guided contemporary federal irrigation surveys, the USDA established the Division of Agricultural Soils in 1894.[52] Soil science, which identified the composite elements of a given soil and analyzed how they affected various crops, was essential to the Department's concern with rationalizing agriculture by ensuring the highest "return per unit of land."[53] The division's first chief, Milton Whitney, had launched his career studying tobacco soils at the Connecticut Experiment Station in the 1880s and later continued that work at the North Carolina Experiment Station.[54] With Whitney in charge, the USDA's soil science program was almost entirely focused on tobacco culture. As one team of soil surveyors put it, the purpose of their work was to provide "the basis of a very extensive and systematic investigation into the physiology of the tobacco, and into the possibilities of changing the type and character of the tobacco through cultural methods and fermentation."[55] Whitney's work attracted attention, and in 1899 the Department created a tobacco-specific department within the Division of Soils and placed Whitney in charge of the American tobacco exhibit at the 1900 Paris Exposition.[56] In the same year, Congress authorized the division to map all of the tobacco soils in the United States with the intent of establishing tobacco "districts"—a term that intentionally evoked the USDA's increasing belief in the classification and management of tobacco agriculture.[57] Soon thereafter the Department elevated the division to "bureau" status, which increased its annual appropriation from $31,300 to $109,140 and ensured tobacco lands from New England to the South would be the most carefully analyzed agricultural soils in the country.[58]

As the Bureau of Soils classified tobacco districts, other USDA scientists interrogated the tobacco plant's physiology. Leading this work was the Division of Vegetable Physiology and Pathology, an office initially organized in 1887 as the Section of Plant Pathology.[59] Building on the disease-control successes of the Bureau of Animal Industry, the Division initially focused on the management of blights that endangered cotton, fruit trees, potatoes, and cereals. As division chief Beverly Galloway argued, however, the study of plant pathology necessarily encompassed "the fundamental principles underlying plant growth," including climate, cultural practices, and plant physiology, and these insights led the division to expand its operations throughout the 1890s.[60] At the same time, Galloway recruited—with the help of private donors, such as the industrialist Barbour Lathrop—a number of plant scientists to scour the planet in search of improved seeds.[61] Like the Bureau of Soils, the division was part of Secretary James Wilson's reorganization of the USDA along "scientific lines" by elevating divisions to bureau status, and in 1901 it became the Bureau of Plant Industry (BPI).[62] Throughout this process, the USDA's plant scientists gradually turned their attention to tobacco. In 1898, Galloway displayed an interest in introducing "a new variety of tobacco ... through scientific breeding and hybridization."[63] Two years later, the division launched studies of the microbial and chemical origins of tobacco's "peculiar flavor and aroma."[64] BPI also hired a plant-breeding specialist named Archibald Shamel who believed the U.S. could produce "more profitable" tobacco by establishing "uniform types" through breeding and seed selection.[65] By 1906, Shamel's "Committee on Tobacco Breeding" claimed to have produced three new "varieties" of tobacco and had launched experiments in ten states, working through state experiment stations or directly with individual growers.[66]

The bureaus of Soils and Plant Industry were advancing the science of tobacco culture, with the ultimate goal of redefining the nature—literally—of commodifiable tobacco. Both bureaus hoped to reduce tobacco to its most commodifiable form, emphasizing leaf characteristics that were legible to buyers around the world while also eliminating the production of tobacco that lacked a clearly defined market. As Whitney put it in 1898, "nondescript tobacco is not worth growing, and should not be grown, as it lowers the price of really good types of tobacco, to the detriment alike of growers and consumers."[67] To that end, USDA officials fanned out into tobacco-growing districts "to train people as to the methods of cultivation and curing."[68] Tobacco growers, wrote the USDA agronomist Ernest Mathewson, had "not kept up with the agricultural progress of the last quarter century," and it was the USDA's mission to catch them up quickly.[69] The intention of these efforts was to expand the quality principle from a measure of a given crop's value to a precondition of a crop's very existence.

The USDA's drive to create organic manifestations of the quality principle transformed tobacco fields into "state spaces."[70] To some extent, tobacco fields in North America had always been state spaces, from the crop's initial commodification in the colonial Chesapeake to the Bureau of Internal Revenue's surveillance of leaf tobacco sales since the Civil War era. Yet by classifying soil districts, analyzing diseases, and tinkering with plant genetics, the federal government tied not only the plant's commerce but also its physiology to national sovereignty and economic power. The tobacco crop stretching from Connecticut to Florida to Missouri was not simply a mass of disaggregated investments made by small growers; it was instead a collective investment of national resources which, when ordered and overseen by the Soils and Plant Industry bureaus, could contribute significantly to the national "balance sheets" of agriculture the USDA began producing in the early twentieth century.[71] Nor was their work a secret: lest Department officials forget the global stakes of the tobacco program, they spent the turn of the century attempting to convince tobacco specialists to stay with the USDA despite "the efforts of foreign countries" and corporations "to induce our experts to leave and transfer their work."[72] Following the Japanese government's hiring of a key soils scientist, Oscar Loew, the Department offered "much higher salaries" to retain its tobacco specialists.[73] Like the USDA, these governments saw tobacco science as an integral component of state building and, as one historian has put it, "exercising hegemony through trade."[74]

In pursuit of a national tobacco program, USDA officials encountered limits to their belief in a harmonious American tobacco economy squared off against global competitors. Although they regularly spoke of "the farmer" and the "tobacco industry" as monolithic economic entities, in reality the nation's farmers, warehouses, manufacturers, and dealers coexisted in volatile tension. In many cases it was competition from other Americans, not producers abroad, that concerned interested parties. For example, as the Bureau of Soils began mapping tobacco soils, congressional representatives from tobacco districts reported constituent pressure to withhold appropriations for the study of soils in other, potentially competitive, districts. Of equal concern was the increasingly global reach of U.S. tobacco manufacturers, in particular the American Tobacco Company, which threatened to shift its supply chain away from U.S. producers toward cheaper foreign tobacco plantations. As one protectionist tobacco booster in Connecticut argued in response to the prospect of duty-free Philippine tobacco during the early twentieth century, "The moment that you open up free trade with the Philippines the American Tobacco Company and those large concerns will go there and build factories, employ 13-cents-a-day labor, and send the manufactured products here." From this perspective, the USDA's tobacco program was a nationalizing project meant to instill—not protect—harmony, consistency, and order where it had not previously existed.[75]

The first major success of the USDA's tobacco program came in the Connecticut River Valley of western New England. There, in the half decade following 1900, the Bureau of Soils introduced shade-grown "Sumatra type" cigar leaf. Grown beneath sun-filtering cotton cloth pitched over entire fields like "a countryside of snow," as one observer put it, the Sumatran seed produced thin leaves that burned evenly and stretched uniformly around cigars.[76] Those qualities had made it among the world's most desirable and expensive tobaccos since its infiltration of world markets in the last third of the nineteenth century. Sumatran leaf was the primary East Indies staple crop of the Dutch colonial government and the Deli Company, a limited liability company form by European planters in 1869 that served as a partner to the colonial administration. Sumatran tobacco culture was centralized on the island's plantations and depended on the importation of thousands of unfree migrant "coolies" from Java and China. Further, similar to American tobacco culture in the South, the Deli Company also relied on the labor of native peasant households, over whom it exercised control by steadily limiting access to subsistence crops and forest rights.[77] Thirteen plantations produced Sumatran tobacco in 1873, but by 1891 the number had grown to 169.[78] Plantation lords imported thousands—perhaps hundreds of thousands—of migrant workers to the island and production boomed. American producers in Connecticut, Pennsylvania, and Ohio—major cigar leaf regions—lobbied for tariff protections from the new style, but USDA officials envisioned a different form of protection, one more in line with their promotion of "economic plants." If American growers established even a modest Sumatran leaf operation, they would create a domestic source for a crop Americans clearly desired; they would also advance the nation's tobacco hegemony by diminishing the Dutch competitive advantage.

When an 1899 soil survey of western New England suggested Sumatran seed might succeed there, the Bureau of Soils allied with the New York Tobacco Board of Trade, the National Tobacco Board of Trade (headquartered in Philadelphia), and tobacco interests in the Connecticut Valley to successfully lobby Congress for an appropriation to expand experiments in the region.[79] Soon thereafter, the Bureau contracted thirteen growers working on 41 acres to experiment with shade-grown Sumatran.[80] Overseeing the growers' operations throughout the year, the Bureau eventually transported the finished leaf to a Hartford auction house where "a very handsome financial transaction" concluded the first successful tobacco experiment in USDA history. In 1902, the Bureau expanded its effort by contracting nearly forty growers and cultivating 645 acres, and by that point there was little doubt that Sumatran tobacco could flourish in New England.[81] By 1903 the operation had expanded to 1,000 acres divided into five "growing districts," each overseen by an assistant director answering to a permanent "expert."[82] Sumatran tobacco in the Connecticut Valley seemed to prove that federal tobacco science could not only optimize the economic productivity of American soils, but also enable American producers to challenge foreign institutions for influence over consumer markets and tobacco tax systems. "We have demonstrated our ability to produce a leaf which is desired by our people," wrote Whitney, "and for which about $6,000,000 have annually been expended in foreign countries."[83]

The New England experiments also suggested how the USDA would operate through seemingly "non-state" entities, from the growers it contracted to the auction houses who verified the quality of its work. Moreover, the Sumatran experiments offered a glimpse into the generative potential of tobacco science, as a range of corporations, such as the Connecticut Tobacco and Trading Company and the Connecticut Leaf Tobacco Corporation, organized rapidly once the Bureau of Soils made public the "handsome" results of its first experiments.[84]

In an explicit example of this dynamic, Marcus Floyd, the director of the Sumatra experiment, left the USDA to become general manager of the Connecticut Leaf Tobacco Corporation.[85] Milton Whitney offered a more capacious analysis of these outcomes, arguing that the Bureau's work had not only encouraged the formation of corporations and provided employment "to large numbers of men and women," but even "brought about the production of millions of square yards of cloth by the cloth manufacturers" and "furnished a market for thousands of chestnut posts" to support the cloth.[86] Inspired by the promise of its New England program, the USDA launched experiments in the culture of Cuban cigar filler tobacco in Alabama, Ohio, Pennsylvania, South Carolina, and Texas, and sent a team of experts to "give object lessons in the production of Sumatra tobacco" to growers in North Carolina.[87]

The Office of Tobacco Investigations and the USDA's "Discovery" of Southern Tobacco

Suggesting Sumatran cultivation in the South was curious, considering that North Carolina was already home to thousands of tobacco growers annually producing millions of pounds of "bright" leaf—the main ingredient in cigarettes. Moreover, those growers had struggled against low prices for years, a struggle that intensified following the emergence of the British-American Tobacco Trust in 1903. "Farmers in this county are in bad shape," wrote one such grower in 1905. "Cause: low price tobacco."[88]

The USDA believed that the answer to these problems was, at least in part, the adoption of higher-quality tobacco, such as shade-grown Sumatran. It was for this reason that the USDA's initial activities in the tobacco South emphasized optimization, as scientists at the Virginia Experiment Station, near Chatham, investigated tobacco physiology and Milton Whitney prioritized mapping Southern tobacco soils.[89] But the agency's long-held suspicions of Southern agriculturists, which had limited its investigations of tobacco science until the 1890s, continued to shape its tobacco program into the twentieth century. Wilbur Fisk Massey, a horticulturist with the North Carolina State Experiment Station, captured this suspicion when he imagined the perspective of a Northern witness to the tobacco-growing South's "great area of washed and wasted lands, red gullied hillsides and old fields abandoned for nature to restore."[90]

As they sought explanations for the region's poverty and economic degradation, USDA analysts resorted to Lost Cause mythology. One such analyst was Seaman Knapp, who, as the USDA's "Special Agent for the Promotion of Agriculture in the South," was the Department's most visible face from the Carolinas to Texas. During the "period of greatest disaster," wrote Knapp, referring to the Civil War era, "all that was excellent in the old civilization was swept away and little of value was substituted." That "excellence" referred to the antebellum South's racial and labor hierarchies that had, unlike Reconstruction governments, prevented Black agriculturists—the "subordinate race"—from "the possession of lands." According to Knapp, if Black growers were to sustain themselves, they would have to "supplant the one-crop system" with "diversified agriculture"—that is, they must produce for the market but sustain themselves outside the market.[91] This was the same logic that undergirded tobacco capitalists' justifications of low prices during the postbellum decades. It demanded that growers produce high-quality cash crops without depending on cash—that they maintain subsistence lifestyles while supplying the capitalist world economy. This logic overlooked the legal and economic dynamics that drove growers to cultivate tobacco in the first place, and, despite its myopia, it suffused the USDA as the agency embraced tobacco science.

Despite agencywide suspicion, three developments attracted the USDA's tobacco scientists to Southern tobacco districts in the early twentieth century. The first was the persistence of poor prices, an old problem that agronomists were beginning to explain not merely as a failure of grower discipline—although that diagnosis certainly continued—but also as scientific problem worthy of study. In 1904, the Bureau of Plant Industry established an experiment farm in Appomattox County, Virginia, where a team of plant physiologists compared fertilizers and "methods of culture" in order to "ascertain which will give the best financial results to the grower." From there, BPI set up similar programs in Kentucky and North Carolina.[92]

The second development was the proliferation in North Carolina of "wilt," an infection of tobacco soils that threatened "the complete destruction of the large tobacco industry in North Carolina."[93] Wilt spread slowly—it was more or less confined to a single county twenty years after it first appeared during the 1880s—but its effects were drastic. Stricken fields lost their entire crops and could not sustain tobacco again until the infection died, which could take as long as a decade. Concerns about wilt reached BPI by 1903, following the publication of F.L. Stevens' "The History of Tobacco Wilt." Stevens, a plant biologist at the North Carolina Experiment Station, argued that if wilt spread more quickly, it could eradicate huge tobacco-producing swaths of the South, as the boll weevil was doing to cotton. In 1905, BPI began attempting to control the wilt, which it would continue to do until 1944 when it bred a wilt-resistant strain.[94]

The third development was the agencywide recognition that it had overlooked the South for nearly forty years, a failure that had created a void between the Department and thousands of cultivators whose crops—tobacco as well as cotton, rice, potatoes, corn, and cattle—were critical to the national "balance sheet" of agriculture. Secretary James Wilson appointed Knapp to address this void. With financial backing from the General Education Board—a philanthropic outlet for John D. Rockefeller's fortune—and the BPI's congressional appropriation, Knapp developed programs that became the foundation of cooperative extension—the blend of demonstration and advising work that, by the 1920s, would be the largest employer in the USDA.[95] Pressured by these developments in economics, ecology, and bureaucratic momentum, the USDA was finally encountering the tobacco South.

Amid these developments, the Department consolidated its tobacco work into the Office of Tobacco Investigations (OTI) in 1907. OTI's mission was to introduce "more profitable and permanent systems of farming with tobacco as the central money crop," a vision that rejected the USDA's earlier ambivalence about tobacco.[96] A job description for the OTI's North Carolina tobacco expert outlined the tasks the office associated with creating a "profitable and permanent" tobacco culture:

> To carry on tobacco investigations ... including the improvement of native strains of tobacco by seed selection, determination by experiment of the best use of fertilizers for improving the yield and quality of tobacco, the development of a better rotation system with tobacco as the leading crop, and means of controlling wilt and other diseases of tobacco by the breeding of resistant strains, and to study the relation of nutrition of the plant to these diseases.[97]

OTI did not carry out these responsibilities alone. Like Knapp's cooperative extension work, which relied on philanthropic funding and worked through already existing institutions such as public schools and county-based farmers' institutes, OTI depended on various forms of local support. In 1908, BPI and the North Carolina Board of Agriculture entered into a memorandum of understanding, guaranteeing shared financial responsibility for tobacco investigations in the state, and by 1910 Virginia and Maryland were considering similar arrangements. At times, these partnerships presented challenges for OTI, as even a threat of reduced state appropriations could alter experiment plans. A 1911 power struggle within the North Carolina Board of Agriculture nearly shut down OTI operations in the state, leaving the office's field director, Eugene Moss, to fret that his supervisor in Washington would "be a better financier than I am if you can figure out how we are going to keep going on such a small am't."[98] Such crises were personally disconcerting for Moss because North Carolina paid twenty percent of his salary.[99] Nor were conflicts strictly financial. When a North Carolina agronomist planned to use OTI data in an article about tobacco diseases, Moss's supervisor, W.W. Garner, blocked him. "As a matter of fact," Garner wrote, "the Memorandum of Understanding under which we are working provides definitely that nothing shall be published by either party without the consent of both parties."[100] OTI owed its existence to grand visions of economic expansion and global competitiveness, but the office was not autonomous. Rather, it was embedded in pluralistic patterns of governance that preceded its creation. To preserve its mission and advance its interests, OTI had to be flexible and recognize boundaries between various nodes of power.

The federal-state partnership brought benefits that might have eluded a more centralized operation. The partnership enabled federal scientists to leverage relationships between growers and their states that had been developing for decades prior to the USDA's interest in the tobacco South. This was especially critical in OTI's early years, when the fledgling office consisted of small groups of young and newly hired scientists at stations—often just plots rented from local farmers—in the rural South. Soon after the formation of OTI, for example, North Carolina field director E.G. Moss and another tobacco scientist, Ernest Mathewson, relied on a local official, the North Carolina state agronomist, to schedule meetings with growers so they could promote scientific tobacco culture and introduce farmers to the federal agricultural state.[101] "The great National Department of Agriculture sends me here," noted Mathewson to one such audience in 1907, "for the purpose of putting before you tobacco-growers in a specific way some of the information which has been accumulated, at no little expense, for the improvement and increased profit of your industry."[102] At other times, OTI officials worked through boards of trade and chambers of commerce.[103] Moss's ingratiation into these networks became so central to OTI's operations that it justified his draft deferment in 1918.[104] Eventually he became a frequent contributor to *The Progressive Farmer* and, along with various officials in the North Carolina government, a leader in the growers' cooperative movements of the 1920s.[105] In other words, through Moss the Office of Tobacco Investigations became entrenched in the political and cultural worlds of bright tobacco.

OTI was likewise enmeshed in the racialized culture of bright tobacco. Moss, himself a native of North Carolina, shared tobacco capitalists' belief that the quality of a tobacco crop depended on the race of its cultivators. When an experimental plot in South Carolina failed, Moss accepted the white plot manager's claim that a stubborn Black sharecropper was to blame. "Mr. Evans," recounted Moss, referring to the plot manager, "says the negro has been promising and promising, and he can not get him started to cultivate." Moss visited the sharecropper himself "and told him he had broken his part of the contract and unless he got all his force in the crop ... we would consider the contract at an end, which would mean he would lose all the work he had done up to the present as the contract was not binding if he broke his part of it willfully, so I think I got him stirred up and at the same time kept him in good humor and made him think it was all his fault." With blame safely shifted away from the white plot manager, Moss sent samples from the field to the BPI laboratory in Washington. The samples confirmed what W.W. Garner, OTI's chief in Washington, had suspected: the field was infected with nematodes. "Under the circumstances," Garner wrote to Moss, "it is perhaps not surprising that the laborer was unwilling to cultivate the crop properly."[106]

By improperly blaming a Black sharecropper, Moss provided OTI with a socially acceptable excuse for its own failure to sustain a tobacco crop. He also preserved the association between race and tobacco quality that tobacco capitalists had promoted during the age of emancipation and other USDA officials, such as Seaman Knapp, had publicized through Lost Cause mythology. Despite these associations, OTI continually turned to Black labor for help with painstaking tasks such as curing and grading. Like white growers throughout the tobacco South, then, OTI officials exploited Black labor as both an excuse for their own shortcomings and a source of highly skilled labor.

Beyond its labor practices, OTI's principles complemented the emergent Jim Crow order in tobacco states such as North Carolina. There, the reactionary Democratic Party had aggressively, often violently seized control of the state government.[107] As it did so, its county-level backers advanced stock laws that banned open grazing and deepened poor growers' dependence on tobacco production. Corporate partners, particularly railroads, shared the Democratic elite's support for stock laws, as fences limited their liability for accidents with cattle. As one scholar has suggested, the "widespread adoption" of stock laws "marked the triumph of elites in the South who sought the change in order to preserve their control over laborers and to find new ways to make money."[108] This process complemented the proliferation of scientific tobacco culture because it advanced the capitalist social relations that underlay all USDA programs. Rather than subsistence cattle raising, in which small farmers' herds roamed the countryside until they could be consumed or sold, commercial cattle raising depended on large, concentrated operations producing uniform, disease-free herds that would enter, as one state publication it, "all markets of the world."[109] That end goal echoed the ideals of tobacco scientists at the bureaus of Soils and Plant Industry, suggesting an agencywide concern with directing U.S. agricultural production away from domestic subsistence. The USDA indirectly promoted commercial stock-raising in the South as early as 1892, when it quarantined cattle in response to a Texas fever outbreak. By 1899, the year the Division of Soils began mapping North Carolina's tobacco soils, USDA agents joined with the state Department of Agriculture to advocate for stock laws—a practice that extension agents would continue until the legislature passed a statewide stock law in 1921.[110] Yet OTI's relationship to stock laws was not only coincidental. Tobacco scientists, like elite farmers and New South boosters, saw tobacco culture as the province of trained, white experts, not subsistence growers, and they advanced that vision by advocating for the elimination of subsistence practices.

As it established itself, the OTI maintained an ambitious scientific agenda. At the test farms OTI shared with state departments of agriculture, such as the Oxford, North Carolina Tobacco Experiment Station, figures like Moss and Mathewson measured crop responses to a vast range of variables, including the chemical composition of fertilizer, seed varieties, dates of planting and harvesting, climate, curing methods ("air, flue, or open fire"), crop rotation cycles, and various cultivation routines, such as "the times hand hoed" or "times suckered."[111] These were not the first tobacco experiments of the era—the famous bright tobacco booster Robert Ragland bred new strains and analyzed soil types throughout the postbellum period—but OTI was able to sustain continuity and geographical breadth of operations that private figures like Ragland, and even state departments of agriculture, could not.[112]

Despite their efforts to establish objective quality, OTI officials recognized that external forces beyond their control, or the control of any grower, could dramatically affect the crop. Experiments failed when heavy rains in the spring delayed planting and in the fall delayed harvesting. In 1914 it was too dry and "tobacco never did anything as it should have."[113] When they left their experimental plots and toured tobacco country, OTI officials encountered a range of other challenges: soils infected by wilt or nematodes and plants stricken by bacterial leaf spot, insect infestations that spread across entire counties, growers selling untested disease remedies to their neighbors, and reports of fertilizers contaminated with poison.[114]

These crises revealed what was perhaps OTI's most significant task: the preservation of relations of production. This market preservation depended in part on

OTI's experimental work, and the goal for figures like Moss and Mathewson was to "improve" tobacco growers' conditions not by restructuring the market but by better understanding the physiological secrets—the forces of production—of the quality principle. W.W. Garner who, as "Physiologist in Charge," managed both experimental and public relations tasks, urged his staff to strike this balance. Conflicts within the trade, or "problems of marketing," contended Garner, "belong outside of this Bureau, consequently it would be only a short time [after OTI intervened] before conflict of interests would develop."[115]

But the early twentieth-century tobacco trade was nothing if not contentious. Frustrated by the low prices offered by monopolistic buyers, growers responded by aligning with a host of cooperative organizations, which succeeded one another almost seamlessly after the turn of the century: the Inter-State Tobacco Growers' Protective Association, the Farmers Union, the North Carolina Tobacco Growers' Association, and, by the mid-twenties, the Tri-State Tobacco Growers' Cooperative Association.[116] These political upheavals pulled OTI toward a more political form of market preservation, which meant engaging with institutions—industry interests and growers associations—who sought to alter the terms of market relations. As with its partnerships with state governments, OTI's interactions with industry and growers could empower the office to publicize its work and extend its influence. Yet these interactions also posed threats to OTI, as competing factions challenged the office's effort to retain an appearance of scientific objectivity and political ambivalence.

Since their emergence in the 1890s, USDA tobacco programs had applied their findings to key institutions within the tobacco industry. It was leaf dealers, after all, who declared the success of the Connecticut Sumatran experiments that had preceded OTI's formation. OTI continued this trend, working through both the tobacco industry and the fertilizer industry. In order to determine the quality of a given experimental crop, OTI scientists hauled tobacco to auction houses, just like every other Southern grower.[117] It also coordinated experiments with manufacturers, which became particularly significant as the cigarette industry gained momentum during the second decade of the twentieth century. The mass-produced cigarette, perhaps more than any manufactured tobacco product, required specific qualities in its leaf supply, such as an even rate of burn and mildness, on account of its acidity, so it could be easily inhaled.[118] As OTI targeted these outcomes, E.G. Moss gauged his progress by sending experimental crops to cigarette manufacturers such as Liggett & Myers. After harvest, he gathered up the seeds and sent them to leaf buyers, such as the Export Leaf Tobacco Company, a subsidiary of British-American.[119] Despite his reticence about conflicts of interest, Garner shared his research findings before meetings of the Tobacco Merchants Association, a corporate lobby formed in 1915 to represent the largest tobacco manufacturers in the country.[120] OTI offered similar services to fertilizer manufacturers, corresponding with representatives from Swift & Co. and Virginia-Carolina Chemical about their chemical research as well as providing lectures to the "Fertilizer Salesmen School" in Richmond.[121] In 1917, when reports tied commercial fertilizer to the spread of bacterial leafspot, also known as "wildfire," the industry became "stirred up" and worked with OTI to alleviate concerns among growers.[122] Speaking to a group of growers with stricken fields, Moss avoided mention of the potential fertilizer contamination, "as the growers are always too anxious to blame the fertilizer anyway."[123] Mathewson, meanwhile, worked closely with a major leaf dealers' association, the Tobacco Association of the United States. For several years he maintained a regular correspondence with the association's president, Tazewell Carrington, and in 1910 traveled with the group's members across eastern North Carolina and South Carolina to meet with growers and "look into the question of how tobacco can be improved as to smoking quality by intelligent farming."[124] OTI certainly served tobacco capitalists as it developed these networks, but it would be reductive to suggest that was the office's only purpose. Rather, OTI's industry relations represented one aspect of the office's effort to develop influence—to build the agricultural state—through associationalism. This was an agencywide priority in the USDA, and associationalism supported OTI's broader effort to expand the market reach of American-produced tobacco.[125]

In a similar fashion, OTI adopted advisory and associational roles in an attempt to regulate growers' practices. Moss and Mathewson frequently traveled tobacco counties from Virginia to South Carolina studying crop diseases or advising growers in the selection of seed and fertilizer. They hosted county extension agents and agricultural educators at experiment stations, where they discussed findings in everything from plant biology to labor practices. Much of this work reflected a core philosophy of OTI: that it was their duty to encourage or discourage certain practices but to avoid direct intervention whenever possible. For example, when Moss visited growers in Hoke County, North Carolina, where soil conditions seemed promising for tobacco, he confined his talk to "methods of growing and handling the tobacco, carefully avoiding anything in the matter of urging ... farmers to take up the culture of tobacco leaving this matter in their own hands."[126] The office was similarly oblique even when requests came from outside—often far outside—traditional tobacco districts. Thousands of farmers in the Progressive Era viewed tobacco as a quick and steady source of income and wrote to OTI for advice about everything from crop rotations to marketing to tax laws. Because OTI officials concluded that the American tobacco hegemony was best served by quality, and not quantity, they dissuaded eager farmers outside of established growing regions. For example, Garner intervened when an ambitious Mississippi farmer named Walter D. Griffing encouraged his neighbors to turn their county into a producer of "merchantable tobacco." The neighbors wrote Garner for suggestions, and his responses thwarted Griffing's scheme: "We do not think," he demurred, "that there would be a market demand for large quantities of tobacco of any established type grown in your section or in any section not growing tobacco at the present time."[127]

During the decade after its founding, then, OTI's relations with growers developed a market preservationist purpose: to restrain, gently, the spread of the tobacco frontier by encouraging established—and white—growers and discouraging everyone else. As such, OTI was building upon the founding ideals of the Bureau of Soils by attempting to create borders of tobacco culture. Such work, wrote Moss, was "in justice to ... men who are [already] growing tob." because, at least theoretically, it limited the supply of tobacco and stabilized prices.[128] This was market intervention, albeit subtle, and as OTI developed its methods it relied on the support of USDA colleagues in the extension service, who, especially after the Smith-Lever Act of 1914 formalized their roles, became the face of the USDA, even the entire federal government, in much of the South.[129] OTI developed new disciplines of tobacco culture and then relied on extension agents to promote those disciplines while discouraging new entrants into the market. Beyond shaping the market, these roles established the "internal distinctions" between state, society, and economy in the tobacco South. The role of the grower was to tend the crops, the role of the warehouses and leaf dealers was to connect those crops to buyers; the agricultural state, or least the bureaucratic pocket known as the Office of Tobacco Investigations, developed in between and carefully guarded its prerogatives of promotion, encouragement, and discouragement.[130]

The Decline of the Quality Principle

Those distinctions began to collapse between the First World War and the 1930s, an era of tremendous upheaval in the global tobacco economy. The initial signs of disruption came in 1916 when Congress passed the Warehouse Act, which directed the USDA to establish standard grades for the valuation of commodities, provided for the creation of government inspection services to implement the grades, and opened the door to the creation of federal warehouses where growers could store tobacco prior to sale. If fully implemented, the Warehouse Act would benefit growers by providing universally recognized tobacco grades, thereby obviating the opaque and subjective quality principle. That process was slow, and it was not until the Depression era that the act was fully implemented. Nonetheless, its passage presaged the decline of the quality principle.

Since its emergence in the postbellum period, the quality principle had always justified tobacco growers' inequality and poverty with shifting and opaque ideals of quality. Moreover, auction warehouses preyed on growers' desperation, which stemmed from, among other causes, the impossibility of moving a crop from warehouse to warehouse in search of the best price. With federal warehouses, growers could store their crops for long periods before sale, use receipts as collateral for loans, and evaluate prices before hauling their crop to market. Federal grading would similarly upset manufacturers' status quo. Firms such as American Tobacco and R.J. Reynolds had long used internally produced grades to direct their buyers' warehouse purchases, but they kept those grades secret, thereby leaving growers ignorant of the market demands they intended to supply.[131] "As a rule," concluded Garner and Moss in 1922, "the buyers for the large companies are governed in their bids entirely by their private grades, so it becomes largely a matter on the auction floors for the buyer first to determine to which of his grades, if any, a certain lot of tobacco belongs." By shifting grades from the proprietary system of the auction house to an open system, the Warehouse Act made possible a "rival or antagonistic principle" to the warehouse-manufacturer syndicate. As such, the act also disturbed the ability of tobacco capitalists to govern without seeming to govern, to appear, under the logic of the market, as the only possible order.[132] It was unsurprising, then, that warehousemen spent much of the 1920s contesting grade standardization and federal warehousing.[133]

For OTI, which had established cordial relations with auction warehouses and manufacturers, the Warehouse Act presented an opportunity and a challenge. The USDA had founded the office under the liberal promise of the quality principle: that growers' competitive advantage lay in the quality and consistency of their tobacco, and that improving both would improve growers' fortunes. But the opacity and asymmetries of tobacco marketing had largely hobbled OTI's ability to accomplish its goals. Federal grading would organize the market along new terms, which meant that producers of the better tobacco might actually earn higher prices. Without transparent grades, quality remained elusive and, as Moss put it, "arbitrary." His own definition—that quality related to "Color, aroma, elasticity, texture, body and burn"—was admittedly vague, but, lacking universal grades, it was all he had "to clear up in our minds what we are trying to discuss."[134] Federal grades would obviate the vagueness of the quality principle and give OTI clearer standards with which to align experiments and advise growers.

The problem was that OTI had long practiced restraint over issues of marketing. By taking up the grading question, which it did in 1920, OTI was confronting warehouses and manufacturers—albeit delicately—and suggesting that its programs of biological investigation and grower encouragement were not enough, that supply and demand did not govern the tobacco economy.[135] This was the first blow to the internal distinctions of state and economy that OTI had cultivated since its founding.

The second blow resulted from conflicts over prices, competition, and monopolization—the issues that had largely defined tobacco's political economy since the populist uprisings of the 1890s. Ironically, they reignited in the years following the federal breakup of the American Tobacco Company in 1911—"a golden decade for bright leaf growers," as Pete Daniel has argued, one made brighter still by the spiking cigarette demands and declining foreign competition of the First World War.[136] Between 1915 and 1920, bright tobacco prices jumped from ten cents per pound to forty-five.[137] In response to the boom, thousands of growers rushed to plant tobacco, with the total national output closing in on 1.5 *billion* pounds in 1919—an increase of nearly five hundred million pounds from annual average output between 1909 and 1913.[138] The surging output necessitated a dramatic expansion of the tobacco frontier by roughly 800,000 acres, precisely the outcome OTI had feared since its inception. The bright tobacco region, once confined to the Piedmont of Virginia and North Carolina, now reached into Florida. This expansion forced OTI to recognize the feebleness of its discouragement strategy. Adding to the severity, the war's end flooded global markets with foreign-produced tobacco. The combination glutted global markets and contributed to a massive agricultural collapse. Between the summer of 1920 and 1921, prices for ten major U.S. crops declined by two-thirds, dipping below the cost of production and leaving tobacco growers reeling.[139]

The onset of depression in the tobacco belt highlighted the opacity and inequity of tobacco auction warehouses and the quality principle under which they operated. In response, tobacco growers in the North Carolina Piedmont—those closest to OTI's experiment station in Oxford—began organizing a cooperative growers' association in 1920.[140] Under the leadership of *The Progressive Farmer* editor Clarence Poe and North Carolina Commissioner of Agriculture

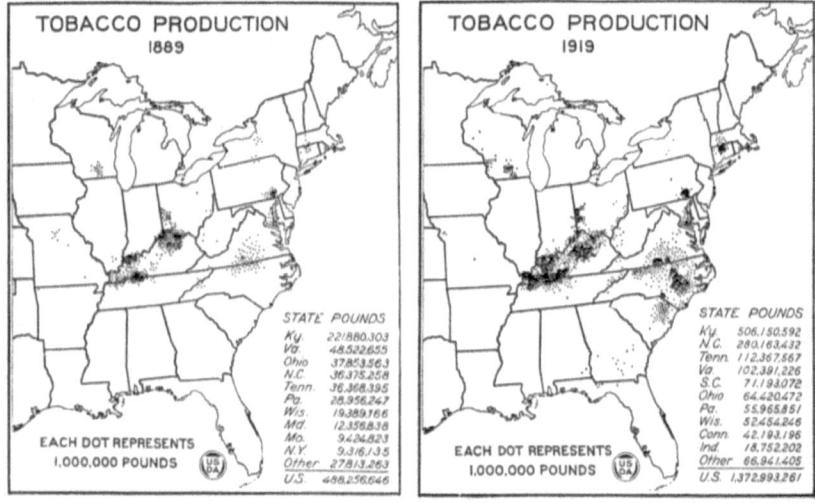

Figure 16. The expanding turn-of-the-century tobacco frontier not only produced more tobacco, but also drew vast new tracts, particularly in the South, into the global tobacco market. Although the Office of Tobacco Investigations discouraged this expansion, the office unintentionally facilitated it through biological innovation. W.W. Garner and E.G. Moss, "History and Status of Tobacco Culture," *United States Department of Agriculture Yearbook 1922* (Washington: GPO, 1923).

B.W. Kilgore, the group initially formed as the North Carolina Tobacco Growers Association before broadening its scope to include Virginia and South Carolina. In February 1922 they incorporated as the Tri-State Tobacco Growers Cooperative Association with the support of 64,000 growers.[141] Tri-State's founding goal was to overthrow the quality principle and the auction warehouse system that promoted it by pooling crops—a strategy growers had tested in various forms since the agrarian uprisings of the 1890s. By controlling the crop supply, Tri-State could, in the words of the lawyer and commodity-organizing expert Aaron Sapiro, control the "movement of crops into the markets of the world at such times and in such quantities that these markets can absorb the crops at fair prices."[142] Participating growers—mostly those in the traditional growing region of the Piedmont—would receive an advance payment, based on grade, for depositing tobacco in one of 139 Tri-State warehouses.[143] In order to coerce growers into participating, Tri-State relied on various state officials and their allies. The USDA played an essential role in Tri-State's founding, as Extension Service agents established 1,800 county-level clubs that formed Tri-State's organizational base.[144] Leading media figures including Poe, as well as the editors of the Raleigh *News & Observer*, Richmond *Times Dispatch*, and Greensboro *Daily News* enthusiastically supported the movement. Financial houses in New York and Richmond extended credit so Tri-State could make advance payments. It was by far the most ambitious organizing effort in the tobacco South's history.

Tri-State's emergence placed OTI in an awkward position. On one hand, the Warehouse Act had revealed OTI officials' recognition of the quality principle's shortcomings; on the other hand, the office remained wary of direct political action. With warehouses vehemently opposing Tri-State and a range of OTI allies supporting it—including USDA colleagues in the Extension Service and the state of North Carolina, the latter of which funded twenty percent of OTI activity—the office had little choice but to engage. Garner, expressing his doubts to other OTI officials, noted that crop pooling had failed in the past, most spectacularly in Kentucky, where a well-organized pool had been undone by free riders selling outside the cooperative.[145] Rather than taint their office by aligning with another "doomed" venture, he suggested to Moss, OTI should educate growers about supply and demand and propose an alternative to Tri-State, a regulation of "acreage to meet changing demand." This was the market preservation ideal that OTI had long promulgated. "[T]he great irregularity in recent market prices," Garner claimed, "should be attributed simply to over-production, and not to the system of marketing."[146]

Moss seemed to share Garner's concerns. Aware that the American tobacco hegemony remained vulnerable, he feared that "a lot of new territory will be developed not only in the Gulf States but possibly in the foreign countries" if Virginia and Carolina growers pooled their crops.[147] Yet unlike Garner, who maintained his critical distance from a safer perch in Washington, Moss was in North Carolina under the direct supervision of Tri-State leader and state agricultural commissioner B.W. Kilgore. Moss "did not feel that [he] could very well afford to refuse" when Kilgore asked him to become the cooperative's secretary.[148] It is possible that Moss feigned his hesitance, that he was concerned about saving face not before one of his bosses, Kilgore, but before the other, Garner. After all, he accepted Tri-State's argument that tobacco marketing had to change. Either way, as a fervent believer that tobacco's quality should determine its economic value, Moss recognized that the quality principle, as practiced by warehouses and manufacturers, did not actually promote improved cultivation or reward biological innovation.

Moss attempted to balance his commitment to the founding ideals of USDA tobacco science with his frustration over the political economy of the auction warehouse. In articles for Tri-State's monthly journal, he emphasized that growers' should continue to prioritize quality. "It must be remembered," he advised Tri-State members in 1923, "that a rank, coarse growth is often associated with poor quality and low returns per pound. Therefore a reduction in cost per pound through larger yields should not be encouraged to the extent of sacrificing quality."[149] Perhaps growers followed Moss's suggestion, but in the short term it didn't matter. Tri-State collapsed into receivership in 1926, a victim of external pressures and basic structural flaws. Most pressingly, Tri-State could not attract a majority of growers to join, as warehouses tempted non-members with higher prices, landlords barred tenants from joining, and members lost faith in the cooperative's mission.[150] In short, the concerns expressed by Garner in Moss in 1920 and 1921 came to fruition. In the same year Tri-State collapsed, however, Moss continued engaging with the association's members through *The Progressive Farmer*, offering advice that mirrored his suggestions from 1923. "The slogan that should be adopted in the future," he wrote, "should be 'quality rather than quantity.'"[151] In an ironic twist, biological innovation of the sort OTI orchestrated began producing far more dependable, and therefore larger, yields per acre precisely as Tri-State collapsed. By the end of the 1920s, OTI's scientific accomplishments had facilitated conditions that made it easier for growers to produce unprecedented yields per acre. This new biological reality, which became clear by the early 1930s, all but guaranteed a future of either massive overproduction or more authoritative crop controls. It also ensured a huge and steady supply of bright tobacco at the dawn of what Allan Brandt has called the "cigarette century."[152]

Although Moss continued to promote the disciplines of quality, the internal distinctions that had shaped USDA tobacco science for a quarter century eroded in the maelstrom of the 1920s. In 1925, nine years after Congress passed the Warehouse Act, the USDA released a plan identifying twenty-nine tobacco types organized into six principle tobacco classes, a schema that continues to exist today. As Barbara Hahn has suggested, the plan marked a zenith in the long process of tobacco's commodification—that is, its transformation from a wild plant into a standardized interchangeable good.[153] For OTI, this was a triumph. The legibility of soils, plant biology, and fertilizer compounds mattered a great deal more when they had the promise of reliably affecting price.

But OTI's recognition that supply and demand did not simply govern the tobacco market—that improving quality would not necessarily improve grower conditions—also represented a broader intellectual shift within the USDA. In the decade ahead, the Department would oversee the steady corrosion of the quality principle and the emergence of a new political economy, one shaped by the price supports, production allotments, and subsidies from the Agricultural Adjustment Administration. The path from the Tri-State era to the AAA's tobacco program was tortuous, as contingent on the political alliances of office holders or executives as on the broader context of Depression. Yet the origins of that path lay in the declining feasibility of the federal support for the quality principle.[154]

Conclusion

Revising Tobacco Politics in the Twentieth Century

The creation of federally backed tobacco grades marked a turning point in tobacco politics. From the 1930s forward, growers assumed greater influence over tobacco's political economy. In an era of acreage allotments and price supports, the tax-designated trade sectors that had shaped power dynamics since the Civil War era no longer marginalized growers. By contrast, growers assumed what Sarah Milov has described as a "corporatist" relationship with the federal state, meaning that while the federal state organized growers, growers in turn shaped tobacco marketing and regulation to suit their interests. Although many of these growers celebrated their familial connections to the smallholders and sharecroppers of the nineteenth century, most descendants of those families no longer grew tobacco. Between the 1940s and 1980s, as crop allotments limited the earning potential of small farms and federal administrators set production rules, most small growers, and nearly all Black growers, were dispossessed. Remaining farms were large, white-owned, and worked by immigrants. Their proprietors enjoyed a relationship to the state comparable to the associationalism set in motion by tobacconists during the Civil War era. And like its predecessor, grower corporatism shaped the power dynamics of tobacco's political economy, ensuring congressional and executive support for the most controversial American crop of the late twentieth century.[1]

Grade standardization helped set these changes in motion, but that was not the only turning point for tobacco politics during the 1920s. The age of prohibition also witnessed a cresting wave of anti-tobacco sentiment, which had been building alongside the tobacco industry's political development during the late nineteenth and early twentieth centuries. Reformers since the antebellum period had criticized Americans' attachments to tobacco, but those efforts were often subsumed under other priorities.[2] Anti-tobacco reform at the turn of the century, by contrast, was more formal, sophisticated, and independent from other crusades. At its center was the Anti-Cigarette League, founded by Lucy Page Gaston in 1899, which claimed 300,000 members by 1901. Among Gaston's supporters were the economist Irving Fisher, the scientist and president of Stanford University David Starr Jordan, the Food and Drug Administration's Harvey Wiley, and business leaders such as John Harvey Kellogg and Henry Ford.[3] Soon other groups emerged as well: the Non-Smokers' Protective League, the No-Tobacco League, and the Anti-Cigarette Smoking League. It was, as one writer has suggested, a "truly golden age" of anti-tobacco activism.[4]

Like their allies in the temperance movement, anti-tobacco reformers demanded legal prohibition and, although they never attained that ultimate goal, they achieved a remarkable legislative record: by the time the United States entered the First World War, eight states had banned cigarette sales and twenty-two others were considering similar legislation.[5] Where sales continued, other tobacco control measures circumscribed tobacco's distribution and consumption, such as age restrictions for the purchase of cigarettes, smoking bans in public spaces, obscenity laws that suppressed tobacco advertising, and prohibitively expensive license fees for tobacco retailers.[6] Nor were cigarettes, or even smoking, the only target. By 1910, hundreds of cities and thirteen states had outlawed public spitting in some form, thereby curtailing tobacco chewing—then the nation's most common form of tobacco consumption.[7]

It was not surprising, then, that in the wake of national alcohol prohibition in 1919 reformers and industry interests wondered if tobacco would, as one observer put it, "have its scalp added to the belt of the prohibitionist."[8] Many reformers certainly believed it would. The Woman's Christian Temperance Union, for example, circulated a pamphlet by economics professor Frederick W. Roman titled *Nicotine Next*, which emphasized both tobacco's immorality and its economic inefficiencies. "Man may raise useful things, such as wheat, potatoes, and cotton," argued Roman, "or he may disgrace himself and his neighbors by prostituting his fertile fields by growing tobacco."[9] The vehement anti-tobacco reformer and minister Calvin D. Crane argued that a tobacco ban should naturally follow alcohol prohibition because it was "the duty of the State to outlaw everything inimical to the welfare of its citizens."[10] But others discouraged the progression from prohibiting alcohol to banning tobacco. For many, smoking and chewing were so ubiquitous that they were simply woven into the fabric of daily life everywhere, including in prohibitionist circles. Further, as this book has shown, political and institutional development following the Civil War had entrenched tobacco within the nation's political economy. Attacking it would invite animosity from an even wider segment of the population than the anti-alcohol crusade. For these reasons, the Anti-Saloon League discouraged anti-tobacco activism as an inflammatory distraction, and Andrew Volstead, who authored the prohibition enforcement law that bore his name, openly chewed tobacco in the halls of

Congress while declaring his lack of support for tobacco suppression.[11] Indeed, in the wake of prohibition, tobacco consumption was likely more popular than it had ever been, with thousands of new smokers introduced to cigarettes during the war and the habit increasingly normalized by advertisements and film. The promise of outright prohibition dwindled throughout the 1920s, and by the end of the decade most state and local governments had repealed their anti-cigarette laws or let them fade into obscurity through poor enforcement.[12]

Ironically, one of the more enduring consequences of this "golden age" of anti-tobacco sentiment was the political mobilization it inspired within the tobacco industry. The tobacco trade had always monitored anti-tobacco developments, but throughout the late nineteenth and early twentieth centuries its concern rarely rose above mocking fascination. Trade journals during the 1880s and 1890s might have expressed annoyance at a prohibitory proposal, but they rarely showed real concern that reformers could actually affect their business. That tone changed during the prohibition era, and with the change came new trade associations whose explicit intention was to oppose anti-tobacco legislation. From its founding in 1919, for example, the Cincinnati-based Allied Tobacco League of America (ATL) pursued a "strenuous campaign...to cover the entire country and oppose the attack of the anti-tobacconists." "What the reformers are booked to encounter," argued one of ATL's founding members, "is the voice of a people weary of fanaticism, heckled to the end of all patience, and determined at last to clean house."[13]

The Tobacco Merchants Association (TMA) offered a similar approach, although its longevity and influence outpaced the Allied Tobacco League. Founded in 1915 by the industry's leading manufacturers, including American Tobacco, Lorillard, American Sumatra, and Richmond's Larus and Brother, TMA pursued an aggressive political agenda throughout the 1920s. Like its predecessors in the Civil War era, TMA hosted large annual conventions through which "leading factors" could "rub elbows and interchange interesting views," promoting a "spirit of fraternalism" among "competitors" and "buyer and seller."[14] At its conventions, TMA coordinated its messaging, devised committees to carry out various initiatives, and outlined the common interests of the general trade. In some cases, those interests were promotional, such as TMA's decision to vigorously champion the concept of Father's Day as a sales opportunity.[15] At other times, they were associational, as evidenced by TMA's overtures to W.W. Garner and the Office of Tobacco Investigations to improve leaf quality.[16] Most often, however, TMA used its resources to emphasize what it perceived as the industrywide threat of anti-tobacco reform.

Although the convenient bête noire of tobacco prohibition faded throughout the 1920s, a new "menace"—state taxation—proved an equally potent fuel for TMA's political mobilization.[17] State tobacco sales taxes, today a staple of tobacco control efforts, first appeared in the 1920s, nearly sixty years after the federal tobacco excises that transformed nineteenth-century tobacco politics.[18] They were a response to declining revenues, which made them attractive to nearly every state legislature, but they were also an outgrowth of anti-tobacco reformers' reconceptualization of tobacco's hazards. Like Frederick W. Roman, the economist behind the WCTU's *Nicotine Next*, social scientists increasingly framed tobacco as an economic, rather than moral, problem. In 1918, Irving Fisher, likely the most well-known American economist of the era, formed a "Committee to Study the Tobacco Problem" with the goal of establishing a "scientific" case for limiting tobacco consumption.[19] Fisher, "who rarely met a social problem he did not price," argued that tobacco was a problematic good because its social costs were not reflected in the prices consumers paid for tobacco products.[20] For Fisher, like Roman, those costs were internal, in that they posed health threats to consumers, but also external, in that they harmed society by removing fertile land from food production and diverting labor power from socially productive activities. This conclusion echoed the emerging welfare economics of British economist Arthur Cecile Pigou, a contemporary of Fisher's, whose influential treatises suggested that markets did not naturally optimize welfare but could be made socially beneficial through government intervention.[21] Nor did that intervention have to carry such an imposing burden as tobacco prohibition. Instead, smaller measures, like taxation, could correct market imperfections by aligning tobacco's economic costs with its social costs.

The underlying principles of state tobacco taxation therefore differed profoundly from the federal tax system of the late nineteenth century. After Iowa's legislature passed the first state tax in 1921, the Des Moines *Evening Tribune* noted that the "object of the law" was not, "primarily," to generate revenue but "to prevent the sale of cigarets to minors, and to enable the control of the sale of cigarets."[22] Yet it did generate revenue—more than one million dollars annually even in the early years of the Great Depression—and for cash-strapped states with both reform-minded constituents to court and growing populations of tobacco consumers, tobacco taxation was an obvious choice.[23]

TMA responded aggressively to the proliferation of state taxes. Under the direction of Charles Dushkind, an American Tobacco Company advertiser-turned-lawyer and TMA's managing director, the association firmly entrenched itself in the legislative politics of every state.[24] It published regular newsletters that contained lengthy analyses of tobacco taxation, and in 1921 it organized a poll of 13,000 newspaper editors to gauge public opinion of anti-tobacco reform. TMA also regularly circulated memos to thousands of dealers in any state considering a new tax. These memos emphasized the threats of empowered state revenue officials ("MERCHANTS DECLARE THEY ARE TREATED LIKE THIEVES," warned one such memo) and encouraged small businesses to organize themselves and their customers against taxation.[25] As one memo to Oregon dealers declared, "it will depend on your efforts, Mr. Dealer, and those of the other dealers in your State, as to whether or not this destructive and discriminatory tax measure shall become law."[26]

TMA's anti-tax efforts formed an ironic bookend for the tobacco politics of the previous sixty years, counterpoised as they were with the endeavors of the National Tobacco Association and its predecessors to construct the federal tobacco tax system during Reconstruction. In both cases, manufacturer-led associations initiated the rhetoric, strategies, and organization that profoundly influenced the broader American political economy. And in both cases, manufacturers professed a commitment to industrywide solidarity while generally alienating growers from decision making. There is little evidence that growers supported TMA, although some organizations, including the New England Tobacco Growers Association and the Burley Tobacco Growers' Co-operative, did voice concerns about prohibition and taxation. Nonetheless, TMA's rhetoric provided a foundation for industrywide mobilization unlike anything that had occurred in the postbellum period. "It is time for every one, in all divisions of the tobacco industry," argued TMA's President Chester Eisenlohr in 1920, "to constitute himself a guardian of the personal liberty involved in this issue, working for the common good and through the common center."[27]

Through the rest of the twentieth century, the two turning points of the 1920s—grower corporatism and industry defensiveness—embodied the new politics of tobacco. As they entrenched themselves in public power, growers joined manufacturers in their belligerent reactions to anti-tobacco reform that increasingly emphasized tobacco's human costs. The result was paradoxical, a political condition that permitted growers and manufacturers to wallow in grievance while reaping entitlements.[28]

Following TMA's example, tobacco interests deployed "a language of victimization" that promoted a "collective feeling of being transpired against" by public health reformers and, for an increasingly white population of growers, the Civil Rights Movement.[29] Why, tobacco interests demanded, couldn't more people just take care of themselves? If a consumer wanted to be healthy, then it was up to her to not smoke.

This was an ethic of "live and let live (or die)," as the anthropologist Peter Benson has put it.[30] It not only ignored a century of state management of the tobacco market, but also bore an uncanny resemblance to the logic of tobacco culture in the Gilded Age and Progressive Era, when tobacco capitalists benefited from state support while exploiting growers and then chastising them for failing to support themselves. The roles had shifted more than a century later, but this fusion of policy privilege and individualistic disdain continued to fortify tobacco's supremacy in American public life.

Acknowledgments

This book was made possible with generous financial support from the George and Jane Dennison Fellowship and the Moser-McKinney Fellowship at the University of Montana. These fellowships and their donors sustain the study of history at a public university. I am honored by their support. I am also grateful for generous fellowships and grants from the American Antiquarian Society, Virginia Historical Society, Agricultural History Society, the Society of Historians of the Gilded Age and Progressive Era, and the University of Montana's H. Duane Hampton Fund.

At Fordham University Press, I grateful for Andy Slap, who saw this book's potential and maintained interest long after we first discussed the project in Mississippi. Thanks as well to Frederic Nachbaur, Courtney Lee Adams Jr., Tom Lee, and Jeannie Whayne, each of whom nurtured the project through its final stages.

This book would not exist without the help of staff at numerous archives and libraries. Special thanks to everyone at the University of Montana's Maureen and Mike Mansfield Library. When I moved to Michigan, the University of Michigan's history department offered me access to their library system without hesitation; later, when I moved to Vermont, the history folks at the University of Massachusetts did the same. Each of these departments kept my work alive at critical junctures.

The Political Reconstruction of American Tobacco took shape in Missoula, Montana, far from any tobacco field, where friends and mentors gave me the confidence to get going and the encouragement to keep going. Thank you to Jeff Wiltse, Rob Saldin, and Anya Jabour for essential feedback on every aspect of this project. Thanks as well to Claire Arcenas, Richard Drake, Gillian Glaes, Dan Flores, Chris Pastore, and Jody Pavilack, each of whom taught me how to communicate my ideas about the past. My graduate colleagues at the University of Montana read many drafts of my work and were a source of encouragement during its inception. Thanks to Chelsea Chamberlain, Randall Williams, Sydney Gwynn-Williams, Sorn Jessen, Clinton Lawson, Tim Ballard, Jeff Meyer, Kayla Blackman, and Dylan Huisken. With his brilliance and humor, Robert H. Greene was an especially bright star for me as I became a historian. This book is dedicated to his memory.

Away from Montana, I benefited from the advice and kindness of numerous scholars, including Bart Elmore, Barbara Hahn, and Sloan Speck. I asked Ariel Ron to join my dissertation committee because his scholarship profoundly altered my thinking about agricultural science, government, and capitalism. After he graciously agreed, he read everything I sent him and offered incisive feedback.

As I tried to keep this project afloat after leaving Missoula, many friends and colleagues brought comfort and encouragement. I am especially thankful to Robert Ramaswamy, Anna Wood, Gary Clark, and Kate Knopp.

I missed my family very much during the years I was researching and writing. This book is for my aunts and uncles and cousins, my brother James O'Connor and sister-in-law Sarah O'Connor, my mother-in-law Ray Mulford and father-in-law Ward Mulford, and my parents, Jim O'Connor and Sue O'Connor.

Although Kyle Volk will scoff, it is absolutely the case that I completed this book because of his support. He had my back without condition or compromise. He is a once-in-a-lifetime teacher and friend.

Katie O'Connor has been by my side for each step in this process. The love we've known, as someone said, is the love of two people staring, not at each other but in the same direction. She is my everything.

Notes

Introduction

1. *Yearbook of the United States Department of Agriculture, 1916* (Washington: Government Printing Office, 1917): 544.
2. *Report of the Commissioner of Internal Revenue for the Fiscal Year Ended June 30, 1894* (Washington: GPO, 1894), 354-55.
3. Charles D. Bohannan and D.P. Campbell, *A Preliminary Study of the Marketing of Burley Tobacco in Central Kentucky* (Lexington, KY: State University Press, 1916), 226. On antebellum tobacco, see Christopher Clark, *The Roots of Rural Capitalism: Western Massachusetts, 1780-1860* (Ithaca: Cornell University Press, 1990), 294-303; Barbara Hahn, *Making Tobacco Bright: Creating an American Commodity, 1617-1937* (Baltimore: Johns Hopkins University Press, 2011), 45-64; Drew A. Swanson, *A Golden Weed: Tobacco and Environment in the Piedmont South* (New Haven: Yale University Press, 2014), 16-45.
4. "The Work Before Us," *Tobacco Leaf*, Oct. 14, 1874.
5. Total tobacco returns for this period can be found in *Report of the Commissioner of Internal Revenue for the Fiscal Year Ended June 30, 1882* (Washington: GPO, 1883), 122-125. Tobacco's percent of internal revenue can be found in *Report of the Commissioner of Internal Revenue for the Fiscal Year Ended June 30, 1879* (Washington: GPO, 1880), 175-177. For its percentage of total revenue, I have compared these numbers with receipts data found in various annual reports of the Secretary of the Treasury. For example, for the year in which tobacco accounted for fifteen percent of total revenue, see *Annual Report of the Secretary of the Treasury for the Year 1879* (Washington: GPO, 1880), iii.
6. W. Elliot Brownlee, *Federal Taxation in America: A History*, 3rd ed. (New York: Cambridge University Press, 2016), 72; see also Ajay Mehrotra, *Making the Modern American Fiscal State: Law, Politics, and the Rise of Progressive Taxation, 1877-1929* (New York: Cambridge University Press, 2013), 41-45. For the relationship between federal taxation, debt, and national solvency, see Richard Franklin Bensel, *Yankee Leviathan: The Origins of Central State Authority in America, 1859-1877* (New York: Cambridge University Press, 1990), 297-298.
7. Hahn, *Making Tobacco Bright*, 51.
8. On makeshift economies, see Steven Stoll, *Ramp Hollow: The Ordeal of Appalachia* (New York: Hill and Wang, 2017), 74-76.
9. Stoll, *Ramp Hollow*, 122.
10. "Very Doubtful," *United States Tobacco Journal*, Jul. 29, 1882. On the shift from web to chain, see Hahn, *Making Tobacco Bright*, 71-98.
11. Adrienne Monteith Petty, *Standing Their Ground: Small Farmers in North Carolina since the Civil War* (New York: Oxford University Press, 2013). On freeholders in Virginia, see Steven Hahn, *A Nation Under Our Feet: Black Political Struggles in the*

Rural South from Slavery to the Great Migration (Cambridge: Belknap Press of Harvard University Press, 2003), 365.

12. Jane Dailey, *Before Jim Crow: The Politics of Race in Postemancipation Virginia* (Chapel Hill: University of North Carolina Press, 2000). See also Hahn, *A Nation Under Our Feet*, 364-384.

13. On the Grange's white supremacy, see Charles Postel, *Equality: An American Dilemma, 1866-1896* (New York: Farrar, Strauss, and Giroux, 2019), 70-110.

14. Judgments of tobacco quality represented what William Cronon has called the "second nature" of commodification. It was a way of comprehending the social meaning and economic value of a product of rural nature, which rested "atop the original landscape that nature—'first nature'—had created as such an inconvenient jumble." William Cronon, *Nature's Metropolis: Chicago and the Great West* (New York: W.W. Norton & Company, 1991), 56.

15. My notion of "quality" builds upon Timothy Mitchell's criticism of "efficiency"—a justification for authoritarian technologies, such as oil pipelines, that circumvent the demands and basic needs of labor. Timothy Mitchell, *Carbon Democracy: Political Power in the Age of Oil* (New York: Verso, 2013). Tobacco "types" were not based on natural distinctions. That fact made the perpetuation of the quality principle even more significant for boosters hoping to expand their global markets. On the creation of tobacco "types," see Hahn, *Making Tobacco Bright*. In many respects, tobacco's unique quality standards are most like those of coffee. See Mario Samper K., "The Historical Construction of Quality and Competitiveness: A Preliminary Discussion of Coffee Commodity Chains," in William G. Clarence-Smith and Steven Topik, eds., *The Global Coffee Economy in Africa, Asia, and Latin America, 1500-1989* (New York: Cambridge University Press, 2003), 120-153. Analysis of cotton quality in the antebellum period is also an instructive parallel. See Walter Johnson, *River of Dark Dreams: Slavery and Empire in the Cotton Kingdom* (Cambridge: The Belknap Press of Harvard University Press, 2013), 250-251.

16. Archibald D. Shamel, "The Improvement of Tobacco by Breeding and Selection," *Yearbook of the United States Department of Agriculture*. 1904. (Washington: GPO, 1905), 436.

17. On techniques of government, see Michel Foucault, "Governmentality," in Graham Burchell, Colin Gordon, and Peter Miller, *The Foucault Effect: Studies in Governmentality* (Chicago: University of Chicago Press, 1991), 87-104.

18. Jeffrey Kerr-Ritchie, *Freedpeople in the Tobacco South: Virginia, 1860-1900* (Chapel Hill, NC: University of North Carolina Press, 1999), 154.

19. *Annual Reports of the Department of Agriculture for the Year Ended June 30, 1910* (Washington: GPO, 1911), 316.

20. Allan Brandt, *The Cigarette Century: The Rise, Fall, and Deadly Persistence of the Product that Defined America* (New York: Basic Books, 2009).

21. Alfred D. Chandler, *The Visible Hand: The Managerial Revolution in American Business* (Cambridge: The Belknap Press of Harvard University Press, 1977), 381-391; Howard Cox, *The Global Cigarette: Origins and Evolution of British American Tobacco 1880-1945* (New York: Oxford University Press, 2000). Nan Enstad's recent work retains the focus on firms and trusts, but challenges business historians' assumptions about

their rise and contextualizes their development within the racial hierarchies of the Jim Crow South and U.S. imperialism. Nan Enstad, *Cigarettes, Inc.: An Intimate History of Corporate Imperialism* (Chicago: University of Chicago Press, 2018). As Enstad has written elsewhere, the Chandlerian approach promoted the "myth" that Duke "was first to see the potential of the cigarette and the first to market it abroad." It was not genius or innovation, Enstad argues, that explains Duke's triumph, but subterfuge and manipulation, including of the Fourteenth Amendment's equal protection clause. Nan Enstad, "Debunking the Capitalist Cowboy," *Boston Review*, Mar. 21, 2019.

22. Brandt, *The Cigarette Century*; Richard Kluger, *Ashes to Ashes: America's Hundred-Year Cigarette War, the Public Health, and the Unabashed Triumph of Philip Morris* (New York: Vintage Books, 1997).

23. On commodity chains, see Mario Samper K., "The Historical Construction of Quality and Competitiveness: A Preliminary Discussion of Coffee Commodity Chains"; Steven C. Topik and Allen Wells, *Global Markets Transformed 1870-1945* (Cambridge: Harvard University Press, 2012); Gary Gereffi, Miguel Korzeniewicz, and Roberto P. Korzeniewicz, "Introduction: Global Commodity Chains," in Gary Gereffi and Miguel Korzeniewicz, eds. *Commodity Chains and Global Capitalism* (Westport, CT: Greenwood Press, 1994). A number of recent works have used commodities to explore broader questions of political development. For example, see Sven Beckert, *Empire of Cotton: A Global History* (New York: Vintage Books, 2014); Enstad, *Cigarettes, Inc.*; Scott Reynolds Nelson, *Oceans of Grain: How American Wheat Remade the World* (New York: Basic Books, 2022); Joshua Specht, *Red Meat Republic: A Hoof-to-Table History of How Beef Changed America* (Princeton: Princeton University Press, 2019).

24. Some examples of scholarship that emphasizes new sites and practitioners of politics include: Rebecca Edwards, *Angels in the Machinery: Gender in American Politics from the Civil War to the Progressive Era* (New York: Oxford University Press, 1997); Steven Hahn, *A Nation Under Our Feet*; Richard R. John, "Farewell to the 'Party Period': Political Economy in Nineteenth-Century America," *Journal of Policy History* 16, no. 2 (Apr. 2004), 117-125; Kate Masur, *An Example for All the Land: Emancipation and the Struggle over Equality in Washington, D.C.* (Chapel Hill: University of North Carolina Press, 2010); Johann Neem, *Creating a Nation of Joiners: Democracy and Civil Society in Early National Massachusetts* (Cambridge: Harvard University Press, 2008); Ariel Ron, *Grassroots Leviathan: Agricultural Reform and the Rural North in the Slaveholding Republic* (Baltimore: Johns Hopkins University Press, 2020); Kyle G. Volk, *Moral Minorities and the Making of American Democracy* (New York: Oxford University Press, 2014).

25. Richard L. McCormick, *The Party Period and Public Policy: American Politics from the Age of Jackson to the Progressive Era* (New York: Oxford University Press, 1986); Joel Silbey, *The American Political Nation, 1838-1893* (Stanford: Stanford University Press, 1991).

26. Elisabeth S. Clemens, *The People's Lobby: Organizational Innovation and the Rise of Interest Group Politics in the United States, 1890-1925* (Chicago: University of Chicago Press, 1997); Reeve Huston, *Land and Freedom: Rural Society, Popular Protest, and Party Politics in Antebellum New York* (New York: Oxford University Press, 2000); David Montgomery, *Citizen Worker: The Experience of Workers in the United States with Democracy and the Free Market during the Nineteenth Century* (New York: Cambridge

University Press, 1993); Charles Postel, *The Populist Vision* (New York: Oxford University Press, 2007); for corruption, see Richard White, *Railroaded: The Transcontinentals and the Making of Modern America* (New York: W.W. Norton & Co., 2011).

27. These relationships help situate the associational character of the American state solidly in the Civil War Era—decades earlier than the Progressive Era, New Deal, and postwar contexts that historians have traditionally affiliated with the associational state. For more on the braided nature of public and private authority, see Brian Balogh, *The Associational State: American Governance in the Twentieth Century* (Philadelphia: University of Pennsylvania Press, 2015); Ellis Hawley, "Herbert Hoover, the Commerce Secretariat, and the Vision of an 'Associative State,' 1921-1928," *The Journal of American History* 61, 1 (Jun. 1974): 116-140.

28. Gregory P. Downs and Kate Masur, eds., *The World the Civil War Made* (Chapel Hill: University of North Carolina Press, 2016), 7. Historians of lobbies have long recognized that important public function of these seemingly "private" interest groups. See, for example, Clemens, *The People's Lobby*; Gaines Foster, *Moral Reconstruction: Christian Lobbyists and the Federal Legislation of Morality, 1865-1920* (Chapel Hill: University of North Carolina Press, 2002); Daniel Peart, *Lobbying and the Making of U.S. Tariff Policy, 1816-1861* (Baltimore: Johns Hopkins University Press, 2018); Margaret Susan Thompson, *The 'Spider Web': Congress and Lobbying in the Age of Grant* (Ithaca: Cornell University Press, 1985).

29. Stefan Link and Noam Maggor, "The United States as a Developing Nation: Revisiting the Peculiarities of American History," *Past and Present* 246 (Feb. 2020), 70; see also Ron, *Grassroots Leviathan*. For an overview of developmental state scholarship, see Stephan Haggard, *Developmental States* (Cambridge: Cambridge University Press, 2018).

30. Nicolas Barreyre, *Gold and Freedom: The Political Economy of Reconstruction*, trans. Arthur Goldhammer (Charlottesville: University of Virginia Press, 2015), 83; W. Elliot Brownlee, *Federal Taxation in America*, 70; Bensel, *Yankee Leviathan*, 329-332; Romain D. Huret, *American Tax Resisters* (Cambridge: Harvard University Press, 2014), 13-77; Sidney Ratner, *American Taxation: Its History as a Social Force in Democracy* (New York: W.W. Norton & Company, 1942), 111-144; Heather Cox Richardson, *The Greatest Nation of the Earth: Republican Economic Policies during the Civil War* (Cambridge: Harvard University Press, 1997), 137.

31. Charles Maier, *Leviathan 2.0: Inventing Modern Statehood* (Cambridge: The Belknap Press of Harvard University Press, 2012); Jürgen Osterhammel, *The Transformation of the World: A Global History of the Nineteenth Century*, trans. Patrick Camiller (Princeton: Princeton University Press, 2014).

32. My use of "tobacco frontier" builds on the concept of commodity frontiers common to histories of capitalism. As Raj Patel and Jason Moore have argued, frontiers are "the encounter zones between capital and all kinds of nature," sites that "extended the zone of appropriation" and drew the surpluses of nature and labor into the global economy. Raj Patel and Jason W. Moore, *A History of the World in Seven Cheap Things: A Guide to Capitalism, Nature, and the Future of the Planet* (Berkeley: University of California Press, 2017), 18-19; Jason W. Moore, "The Capitolocene II: accumulation by appropriation and the centrality of unpaid work/energy," *The Journal of Peasant Studies* 42, 2 (2017): 13; Sven Beckert et al., "Commodity frontiers and the transformation of the global countryside: a research agenda," *Journal of Global History* 16, no. 3 (2021): 435-450.

33. Alan L. Olmstead and Paul W. Rhode, "Table Da755-765–Cotton, cottonseed, shorn wool, and tobacco," in Susan B. Carter et al., eds. *Historical Statistics of the United States Millennial Edition Online*. (New York, NY: Cambridge University Press, 2006).

34. This corroborates a growing consensus among historians of the Gilded Age and Progressive Era, which holds that traditional emphases on urbanization and industrialization have neglected the rural character of American capitalism into the twentieth century. Christopher Clark, "The Agrarian Context of American Capitalist Development," in Michael Zakim and Gary Kornblith, eds., *Capitalism Takes Command: The Social Transformation of Nineteenth-Century America* (Chicago: University of Chicago Press, 2012), 14. See also Deborah Fitzgerald, *Every Farm a Factory: The Industrial Ideal in American Agriculture* (New Haven: Yale University Press, 2003); Kristin L. Hoganson, *The Heartland: An American History* (New York: Penguin Press, 2019); Catherine McNicol Stock and Robert D. Johnston, eds., *The Countryside in the Age of the Modern State: Political Histories of Rural America* (Ithaca: Cornell University Press, 2001); Jamie Pietruska, *Looking Forward: Prediction and Uncertainty in Modern America* (Chicago: University of Chicago Press, 2017); Ariel Ron, "Farmers, Capitalism, and Government in the Late Nineteenth Century," *The Journal of the Gilded Age and Progressive Era* 15 (2016): 294-309; Specht, *Red Meat Republic*.

35. Brandt, *The Cigarette Century*, 487.

36. For more on this dynamic, see Sarah Milov, *The Cigarette: A Political History* (Cambridge: Harvard University Press, 2019).

1. "An Acknowledged Power in the Land": Tobacconists, Taxation, and the Politics of Market Creation, 1862-1872

1. "Our Washington Letter," *Tobacco Leaf* [hereafter, *TL*], Sep. 30, 1878. On the German monopoly controversy, see Fritz Stern, *Gold and Iron: Bismarck, Bleichröder, and the Building of the German Empire* (New York: Vintage Books, 1979), 419-420.

2. Total tobacco returns for this period can be found in *Report of the Commissioner of Internal Revenue for the Fiscal Year Ended June 30, 1882* (Washington: GPO, 1883), 122-125.

3. "Our Washington Letter," *TL*, Sep. 30, 1878; "Letter from Mr. Kimball," *TL*, Oct. 12, 1878; "Departure of the German Tobacco Commission," *TL*, Nov. 4, 1878; "As Others See Us," *TL*, Feb. 15, 1879.

4. "As Others See Us," *TL*, Feb. 15, 1879.

5. I have chosen the term "tobacconist" for several reasons. First, it is less cumbersome than "tobacco manufacturers" and more specific than "manufacturers." Second, it is capacious enough to capture the diversity of a group that included, among others, chewing and smoking tobacco manufacturers, cigar makers, and snuff makers. Third, while today the term indicates *dealers* of tobacco, during the Civil War era manufacturers regularly used it to describe themselves. Finally, although manufacturing would become highly specialized by the turn of the century—largely due to the tax policies I analyze in this chapter—manufacturers in the 1860s were not entirely distinct from other trade sectors, particularly dealers. For more on the trade's mid-century "commodity web," see Barbara Hahn, *Making Tobacco Bright: Creating an American Commodity, 1617-1937* (Baltimore: Johns Hopkins University Press, 2011), 49-70.

6. "A Happy New Year!," *TL*, Jan. 1, 1868.

7. Tobacconists' associations provided a valuable organizational example for the so-called "employers' associations" that emerged in most national industries after the 1880s. Like the tobacconists before them, employers' associations regularly convened, elected leaders, and published trade journals (such as *Oil and Paint Manufacturer*, the *National Bottlers' Gazette*, and *Manufacturer and Builder*). Unlike tobacconists' associations, which were consumed by questions of taxation, later employers' associations formed in response to labor organizing. See Sven Beckert, *The Monied Metropolis: New York City and the Consolidation of the American Bourgeoisie, 1850-1896* (New York: Cambridge University Press, 2001), 288-292; see also Clarence E. Bonnett, *Employers' Associations in the United States: A Study of Typical Associations* (New York: MacMillan, 1922).

8. The internal revenue system created between 1862 and 1872 achieved several key components of what Gabriel Kolko called "political capitalism." That is, it produced *stability* ("elimination of internecine competition and erratic fluctuations in the economy"), *predictability* ("the ability, on the basis of politically ... secured means, to plan for future economic action"), and *rationalization* ("the organization of the economy and the larger political and social spheres in a manner that will allow corporations to function in a predictable and secure environment"). As the next chapter indicates, the revenue system did not achieve *security* ("protection from the political attacks latent in any formally democratic political structure"). See Gabriel Kolko, *The Triumph of Conservatism: A Reinterpretation of American History, 1900-1916* (New York: The Free Press, 1963), 3.

9. As Barbara Hahn has written, "Federal taxation of the Civil War era did not alone create the trend to Big Business that gathered steam at the turn of the last century, but its impact on these Southern industries demonstrates that government policy, as well as the invisible hand of markets and the visible hand of managerial control, contributed to the great merger movement and the conglomerate tendencies of the age." Hahn, *Making Tobacco Bright*, 84.

10. Nancy Cohen writes, "The producerist vernacular of free labor ideology, widely popular among Northern workers, artisans, and farmers, held that economic independence, gained through the ownership of real property or the possession of a skill that could provide ... independence, was a precondition of true freedom." Tobacconists came to believe that the revenue system as it functioned prior to 1868 created a disadvantage for taxpaying businesses by allowing tax-avoidant competition to flourish. As such, the tax robbed tobacconists of the fruits of their skills and, subsequently, their independence. See Nancy Cohen, *The Reconstruction of American Liberalism, 1865-1914* (Chapel Hill: University of North Carolina Press, 2002), 29. See also Rosanne Currarino, *The Labor Question in America: Economic Democracy in the Gilded Age* (Urbana: University of Illinois Press, 2011).

11. On Republicans' sectional divisions, see Nicolas Barreyre, *Gold and Freedom: The Political Economy of Reconstruction*, trans. Arthur Goldhammer (Charlottesville: University of Virginia Press, 2015).

12. Brian Balogh, *The Associational State: American Governance in the Twentieth Century* (Philadelphia: University of Pennsylvania Press, 2015), 139.

13. Heather Cox Richardson, *The Greatest Nation of the Earth: Republican Economic Policies during the Civil War* (Cambridge: Harvard University Press, 1997), 115-116.

14. Richard Franklin Bensel, *Yankee Leviathan The Origins of Central State Authority in America, 1859-1877* (New York: Cambridge University Press, 1990), 169.

15. Frank L. Olmsted, "The Tobacco Tax," *The Quarterly Journal of Economics* 5, 2 (Jan. 1891): 193-195. Congress repealed the first federal tobacco duties, imposed under Hamilton's fiscal system, in 1802. Congress imposed a second tobacco tax—this time on smoking tobacco, cigars, and snuff—during the War of 1812, and repealed it soon after the war's conclusion. Although these duties provided precedence for federal tobacco taxation, they did not provide a clear blueprint for the successful operation of such a tax. See Max Edling, *A Hercules in the Cradle: War, Money, and the American State, 1783-1867* (University of Chicago Press, 2014), 115, 136.

16. The latter point was true as long as the tax did not apply to raw leaf tobacco. In a minor controversy that signaled more significant political disruptions to come, the legislatures of Kentucky and Ohio petitioned Congress in March and April to eliminate a proposed tax of three cents per pound on leaf tobacco. Such a tax, wrote Kentucky's legislators, would fall "with great severity upon portions of our State which are suffering from the present war, and [discriminate] most prejudicially against the agricultural interests of the State." U.S. Congress, Senate, *Resolutions of the Legislature of Kentucky in Relation to the Proposed Tax on Tobacco*, March 24, 1862, 37th Cong., 2d Sess., 1862, Mis. Doc. No. 68; U.S. Congress, Senate, *Resolution of the Legislature of Ohio, in Favor of a Modification of the Proposed Tax on Leaf Tobacco*, April 14, 1862, 37th Cong., 2d Sess., 1862, Mis. Doc. No. 89.

17. *Report of the Commissioner of Internal Revenue on the Operations of the Internal Revenue System for the Year Ending June 30, 1863* (Washington: GPO, 1864), 7.

18. For England and France, see U.S. Congress, House, *Report of the Special Commissioner of the Revenue*, Jan. 7, 1868, 40th Cong., 2d Sess., Ex. Doc. 8, 65-74. See also "The Tobacco Trade and the Public Revenue," *New York Times*, Sep. 18, 1867. Although American critics typically cited the British and French examples, most European states relied on tobacco for some portion of their public revenues. For a survey of European revenue systems during the nineteenth century, see José Luís Cardoso and Pedro Lains, *Paying for the Liberal State: The Rise of Public Finance in Nineteenth-Century Europe* (New York: Cambridge University Press, 2010). Two valuable book length studies are Martin Daunton, *Trusting Leviathan: The Politics of Taxation in Britain, 1799-1914* (New York: Cambridge University Press, 2001) and Yanni Kotsonis, *States of Obligation: Taxes and Citizenship in the Russian Empire and Early Soviet Republic* (University of Toronto Press, 2014).

19. *Report of the Commissioner of Internal Revenue 1863*, 7.

20. *Report of the Commissioner of Internal Revenue 1863*, 7; *Report of the Commissioner of the Internal Revenue* (Washington: GPO, 1864), 9-10. The latter source is the Commissioner's annual report for the fiscal year ending June 30, 1864, although the report's title, unlike the previous year's report, does not indicate that fact.

21. *Congressional Globe*, 38th Cong., 1st Sess., 1864, 2763. This quote comes from Senator Reverdy Johnson of Maryland. His opposition to the leaf tax was emblematic of the position held by representatives from Border States, which were home to established tobacco-growing elites who had long cultivated relationships with foreign markets.

22. Receivers and Exporters of Leaf Tobacco, *Petition of the Receivers and Exporters of American Leaf Tobacco to the Members of the Senate and House of Representatives in Congress Assembled* (New York: s.n., 1863).

23. U.S. Congress, Senate, Committee on Finance, *Letter of the Commissioner of Agriculture to the Chairman of the Committee on Agriculture, upon the subject of the taxation*, 38th Cong., 1st Sess., 1864, 1-4.

24. Ariel Ron, "Summoning the State: Northern Farmers and the Transformation of American Politics in the Mid-Nineteenth Century," *Journal of American History* 102, 2 (Sep. 2016): 347-374. Barbara Hahn has suggested that the leaf tax proposal failed because the "romantic view of farming that prevails in American political culture likely made even wartime, Republican, pro-business administration reluctant to lay a direct tax on farmers." This chapter argues that policymakers were not influenced so much by romance as by the policy demands of influential, organized stakeholders who viewed the leaf tax as a threat to their economic well-being. Hahn, *Making Tobacco Bright*, 85.

25. "Tobacco," *The Country Gentleman*, Feb. 18, 1864. The Kentucky State Agricultural Society had been organizing its state's tobacco growers since at least 1859, when it held a "tobacco convention" for the purpose of bringing "producers and purchasers together" in order to "learn what grades are best suited to the market, and will meet the most ready sale." "Southern Tobacco Convention," *De Bow's Review*, May 5, 1859, 581.

26. "Tobacco, the Cotton of the North," *Moore's Rural New Yorker* (Rochester, NY), Feb. 27, 1864.

27. "Taxing Tobacco—Interesting Facts," *Moore's Rural New Yorker*, Mar. 5, 1864; "No Tax on Leaf Tobacco," *The Prairie Farmer* (Chicago, IL), Mar. 19, 1864.

28. For antebellum agricultural politics, see Ron, "Summoning the State."

29. The fiscal crisis was characterized by rising expenditures—which, in 1864, surpassed one billion dollars for the first time in US history, and a ballooning national debt of over three billion dollars. U.S. Congress, House, *Letter from the Secretary of the Treasury, transmitting his annual report of the finances for the year 1864*, December 6, 1864, 38th Cong., 2d Sess., Ex. Doc. 3, 32. See also Edling, *A Hercules in the Cradle*, 179.

30. *Report of the Commissioner of Internal Revenue 1863*, 106; *Report of the Commissioner of Internal Revenue on the Operations of the Internal Revenue System for the Fiscal Year Ending June 30, 1865* (Washington: GPO, 1865), 36.

31. Hahn, *Making Tobacco Bright*, 86.

32. *Congressional Globe*, 38th Cong., 1st Sess., 1864, 2706.

33. My analysis of tobacco's epistemological problems draws from Marion Fourcade's study of the nineteenth-century French wine industry. Marion Fourcade, "The Vile and the Noble: On the Relation between Natural and Social Classifications in the French Wine World," *The Sociological Quarterly* 53, 4 (2012): 524-545.

34. As one legislator complained, tobacco men had "been thronging these lobbies ever since we have had this question under discussion." *Congressional Globe*, 38th Cong., 1st Sess., 1864, 2763.

35. *Congressional Globe*, 38th Cong., 1st Sess., 1864, 2706.

36. U.S. Congress, House, *Report of the Commissioner of Internal Revenue*, Jan. 5, 1871, 41st Cong., 3d Sess., Ex. Doc. 4, 308-309.

37. For pounds of tobacco taxed, see *Annual Report of the Commissioner of Internal Revenue for the Fiscal Year Ended June 30, 1900* (Washington: GPO, 1900), 431-432.

38. Cooper Union delegates were likely inspired by the United States Brewers Association, which had held its first annual meeting in Philadelphia in February 1863. Amy Mittelman, "The Politics of Alcohol Production: The Liquor Industry and the Federal Government, 1862-1900" (PhD Diss, Columbia Univ., 1986), 152-155.

39. "The Convention of the Cigar and Tobacco Manufacturers," *New York Herald*, Dec. 8, 1864.

40. J. Leander Bishop, *A History of American Manufactures from 1608 to 1860, Vol. III* (Philadelphia: Edward Young & Co., 1868), 511-532. For notable attendees, see "The Convention of the Cigar and Tobacco Manufacturers," *New York Herald*, Dec. 8, 1864.

41. Edward Burke, *Tobacco Manufacture in the United States: A Report Adopted in Convention of the Trade* (New York: American News Company, 1864), 23.

42. Olmsted, "The Tobacco Tax," 194-195.

43. *Congressional Globe*, 38th Cong, 1st Sess., 220-221.

44. Burke, *Tobacco Manufacture in the United States*, 13.

45. Burke, 31.

46. "The Tobacco Trade," *Chicago Tribune*, Dec. 13, 1864.

47. *A Word about the Tax on Tobacco* (Baltimore: Murphy and Co., 1864).

48. Burke, 26-29. Critics of the leaf tax often overlooked the Cooper Union delegates' insistence that tobacconists continue paying the tax, insisting instead that the "game of the manufacturers is simply a selfish effort to avoid taxation, and impose their own proper burdens upon the shoulders of the already impoverished planters." "Virginia on the Tax Question," *TL*, Feb. 3, 1866.

49. "The Tobacco Tax," *TL*, Sep. 30, 1865.

50. For these petitions, see Folders 1 and 2, Taxation of Cigars and Tobacco; HR38A-G24.15; 38th Cong.; Records of the Committee on Ways and Means; Records of the House of Representatives, RG 223; National Archives Building, Washington, D.C.

51. "Petition of cigar makers of St. Louis praying for a duty on leaf tobacco," Jan. 25, 1865 and "Petition of the Cigar Manufacturers of Windsor, Connecticut praying for a duty on leaf tobacco," Jan. 26, 1865; Folder 2, Taxation of Cigars and Tobacco; HR38A-G24.15; 38th Cong.; Records of the Committee on Ways and Means; Records of the House of Representatives, RG 223; National Archives Building, Washington, D.C.

52. For Ohio and West Virginia, see "Petition of citizens of the state of Ohio praying that leaf tobacco may not be taxed," Jan. 17, 1865 and "Petition of the citizens of Kanawha Valley, in the State of West Virginia," undated; Folder 2, Taxation of Cigars and Tobacco; HR38A-G24.15; 38th Cong.; Records of the Committee on Ways and Means; Records of the House of Representatives, RG 223; National Archives Building, Washington, D.C.; for Connecticut Valley, see "Tobacco Convention," *The Country Gentleman*, Jan. 19, 1865.

53. "Petition of the citizens of Kanawha Valley, in the State of West Virginia," undated; Folder 2, Taxation of Cigars and Tobacco; HR38A-G24.15; 38th Cong.; Records of the Committee on Ways and Means; Records of the House of Representatives, RG 223; National Archives Building, Washington, D.C. On the influence of Virginia's planter elite in antebellum state government, see Sean Patrick Adams, *Old Dominion, Industrial*

Commonwealth: Coal, Politics, and Economy in Antebellum America (Baltimore: Johns Hopkins University Press, 2004). The buyer monopsony feared by West Virginian growers became the defining crisis of the early twentieth century tobacco industry. See Tracy Campbell, *The Politics of Despair: Power & Resistance in the Tobacco Wars* (Lexington: University of Kentucky Press, 1993); see also Hahn, *Making Tobacco Bright*, 147-155.

54. "Delaney, Harris, and Co., Manufacturers of Plug Tobacco to Representative C.M. Harris," Dec. 30, 1864; Folder 2, Taxation of Cigars and Tobacco; HR38A-G24.15; 38th Cong.; Records of the Committee on Ways and Means; Records of the House of Representatives, RG 223; National Archives Building, Washington, D.C.

55. "Petition of Citizens of Chicago, in regard to taxation of tobacco," Jan. 27, 1865; Folder 2, Taxation of Cigars and Tobacco; HR38A-G24.15; 38th Cong.; Records of the Committee on Ways and Means; Records of the House of Representatives, RG 223; National Archives Building, Washington, D.C.

56. "Tax on Tobacco," *TL*, Jan. 13, 1866. This use of "capitalist" comports with Leon Fink's analysis of the term during the 1870s and 1880s. "In part," Fink writes, "what 'being considered a capitalist' implied was disregard for workers' self-respect, the open defense of the laws of classical political economy, the working assumption of labor as a commodity." In addition to those implications, the critics of Cooper Union tobacconists associated "capitalists" with monopolism, corruption, and the desire to consolidate the national market and business organizations. Leon Fink, *Workingmen's Democracy: The Knights of Labor and American Politics* (Urbana: University of Illinois Press, 1983), 10.

57. "The Tobacco Convention on Saturday," *The Daily Empire* (Dayton, OH), Dec. 12, 1865.

58. Herbert Ronald Ferleger, "David A. Wells and the American Revenue System, 1865-1870" (PhD diss., Columbia University, 1942), 31. For a brief and thorough account of Wells' career and economic theories, see Cohen, *The Reconstruction of American Liberalism*, 86-95.

59. Edward Burke, ed., *Proceedings of the Convention of Tobacconists Held at Cooper Institute in the City of New York, November 22, 1865* (New York: E.O. Jenkins, 1865), 3.

60. "Meeting of Cigar Manufacturers," *TL*, Sep. 23, 1865; "National Convention at Louisville," *TL*, Sep. 23, 1865.

61. "Tax on Tobacco," *TL*, Jan. 20, 1866.

62. It is unclear why manufacturers and dealers remained silent on Reconstruction and emancipation. They may have simply taken Southern labor politics for granted and imagined that their proposed revenue bureaucracy would manage the reconstruction of tobacco culture. They may also have viewed the leaf tax as means of cornering the market in leaf tobacco prior to Virginian manufacturers' reentry into the market. On the industrialization of tobacco production in antebellum Virginia, see Hahn, *Making Tobacco Bright*, 46-47.

63. "Louisville Tobacco Convention," *TL*, Feb. 10, 1866.

64. See Jeffrey Kerr-Ritchie, *Freedpeople in the Tobacco South: Virginia, 1860-1900* (Chapel Hill: University of North Carolina Press, 1999): 31-69. See also Thavolia Glymph, "Freedpeople and Ex-Masters: Shaping a New Order in the Postbellum South, 1865-1868," in Thavolia Glymph and John J. Kushma, eds., *Essays on the Postbellum Southern Economy* (College Station: Texas A&M University Press, 1985): 48-72.

65. U.S. Congress, House, *Revenue System of the United States*, Jan. 29, 1866, 39th Cong., 1st Sess., Ex. Doc. 34, 26.

66. "Tobacconists' National Association," *TL*, Feb. 10, 1866.

67. "The Tobacco Board of Trade of the City of New York," *TL*, Nov. 23, 1866.

68. With increased consolidation during the 1870s and 1880s, tobacco manufacturers turned from commission merchants to in-house peddlers and jobbers. That shift, as Nannie Mae Tilley noted, made "the interests of selling and manufacturing identical." By the end of the century, tobacco commission merchants had disappeared. See Nannie Mae Tilley, *The Bright Tobacco Industry, 1860-1929* (Chapel Hill: University of North Carolina Press, 1948): 528-536. For quote, see 532-533. See also Alfred D. Chandler, Jr., *The Visible Hand: The Managerial Revolution in American Business* (Cambridge: Harvard University Press, 1977): 382-383.

69. Cincinnati had developed into an important tobacco trade center during the antebellum years. Via the Ohio River and tributaries such as the Kanawha, Muskingum, Licking, and Kentucky rivers, Cincinnati's manufacturers and dealers spent years cultivating relationships with growers of various tobacco "types": the Virginia tobacco popular among plug manufacturers; the "heavily fired" tobacco of east-central Ohio; and the strong, dark tobacco of the "Black Patch" in Kentucky and Tennessee. Most important were the city's connections to growers of fine "cutting tobacco" in northern Kentucky and the seed-leaf growers of the Miami Valley, who knew no market but Cincinnati until the 1860s. Dozens of manufacturers and dealers in the city likewise enjoyed access to the growing markets along the Great Lakes and Mississippi River. By the end of the war the city's tobacco industry was well prepared to dominate the Western trade and resist encroachments from New York. "Tax on Smoking Tobacco," *TL*, Mar. 21, 1866; Manufacturers, Leaf Dealers, & Warehouseman of Cincinnati, Ohio, *An Argument in Favor of the Reduction of the Tax on Manufactured Tobacco, and Against the Transfer of the Tax to Leaf* (Cincinnati: s.n., 1867), 3.

70. "An Act to authorize the incorporation of boards of trade and chambers of commerce," *General and Local Laws and Joint Resolutions Passed by the Fifty-Seventh General Assembly of the State of Ohio* (Columbus, OH: 1866): 89-91. The syllabus of an 1883 case before the Supreme Court of Ohio indicates that the ATTC formed under this law. "Supreme Court of Ohio," *Weekly Cincinnati Law Bulletin* IX (Jan. 8, 1883): 9. The case concerned the ATTC's election of a tobacco inspector who was not a citizen of Ohio. *State v. Casey*, 38 Ohio St. 555 (1883). "Constitution of the Association of the Tobacco Trade of Cincinnati, *TL*, Feb. 6, 1867.

71. "Tax on Smoking Tobacco," *TL*, Mar. 21, 1866.

72. I am drawing on James C. Scott's conception of "legibility," or "a state's attempt to make a society legible, to arrange the population in ways that simplified the classic state functions of taxation, conscription, and prevention of rebellion." James C. Scott, *Thinking Like a State: How Certain Schemes to Improve the Human Condition Have Failed* (New Haven: Yale University Press, 1998), 2. See also Noam Maggor, "To Coddle and Caress These Great Capitalists: Eastern Money, Frontier Populism, and the Politics of Market-Making in the American West," *American Historical Review* 122, no. 1 (Feb. 2017): 77.

73. Congress disbanded the original Revenue Commission and appointed Wells "Special Commissioner of Revenue" in 1866. "Washington News," *New York Times*, July` 18, 1866.

74. Burke, ed., *Proceedings of the Convention of Tobacconists*, 7.

75. Edward Balleisen has described the deployment of "fraud" and associated aspersions as business owners' "rhetorical club." Balleisen argues that throughout the nineteenth century, "[e]mbattled business owners invoked the language of duplicity as a means of launching broadsides at nettlesome competitors." Balleisen, *Fraud: An American History from Barnum to Madoff* (Princeton: Princeton University Press, 2017): 11.

76. Balleisen, *Fraud*, 67.

77. Stephen Mihm has noted that antebellum "shovers" of counterfeit currency often exploited "petty entrepreneurs" who had adequate cash on hand to make change but were not so well versed in currency as to easily detect counterfeits. Tobacconists, like butchers, druggists, and other ubiquitous business owners, were thus common targets. Stephen Mihm, *A Nation of Counterfeiters: Capitalists, Con Men, and the Making of the United States* (Cambridge: Harvard University Press, 2007), 223.

78. Balleisen, *Fraud*, 77-78. See also Mark Wahlgren Summers, *The Era of Good Stealings* (New York: Oxford University Press, 1993), 62-85.

79. "Frauds on the Government," *Internal Revenue Record & Customs Journal*, Apr. 7, 1866; "The Congressional Committee's Report on Internal Revenue Frauds," *New York Times*, Feb. 26, 1867.

80. Members of the TNA and ATTC regularly described themselves as the nation's "legitimate" manufacturers. For example, see "Memorial of the Tobacco Cutters of Cincinnati," Feb. 28, 1866; Committee on Ways and Means March 2, 1866 to May 14 1866; HR 39A – H25.5 Tray 1; Records of the Committee on Ways and Means; Records of the House of Representatives, RG 223; National Archives Building, Washington, D.C.

81. "The Tobacco Tax," *TL*, Sep. 30, 1865.

82. "Petition of cigar manufacturers, journeyman cigar-makers, dealers in cigars, and growers of and dealers in seed-leaf tobacco of Dayton, Ohio," undated; Committee on Ways and Means Jan. 18, 1867 to Feb. 22 1867; HR 39 A – H25.5 Tray 1; Records of the Committee on Ways and Means; Records of the House of Representatives, RG 223; National Archives Building, Washington, D.C.

83. U.S. Congress, House, Committee of Ways and Means, *Report of the Special Commissioner of the Revenue*, 40th Cong., 2d Sess., 1868, 37-38.

84. U.S. Congress, House, *Frauds on the Revenue*, 39th Cong., 2d Sess., Feb. 25, 1867.

85. "The Tobacco Tax," *TL*, Sep. 30, 1865.

86. I am drawing upon David Gamage's conception of tax gaming, which he describes as "the subcategory of distortionary tax reduction behaviors that tend to be more idiosyncratic and contingent on exploiting the details of how tax systems are implemented." David Gamage, "How Should Governments Promote Distributive Justice?: A Framework for Analyzing the Optimal Choice of Tax Instruments," *Tax Law Review* 68, 1 (2014-2015): 5, n.18.

87. U.S. Congress, House, Committee of Ways and Means, *Report of the Special Commissioner of the Revenue*, 40th Cong., 2d Sess., 1868, 36. This was perhaps the most common, or at least most commonly criticized, brand of evasion. Cigar makers made essentially the same argument when they complained that competitors deceitfully priced their products to avoid higher tax brackets. See "Memorial of 7300 Cigar Manufacturers of Cincinnati for uniformity in taxing cigars," Jan. 25, 1867; Committee on Ways and

Means Jan 18, 1867 to Feb 22 1867 undated; HR 39 A – H25.5; 39th Congress; Records of the Committee on Ways and Means; Records of the House of Representatives, RG 223; National Archives Building, Washington, D.C.

88. U.S. Congress, House, Committee of Ways and Means, *Report of the Special Commissioner of the Revenue*, 40th Cong., 2d Sess., 1868, 36. As Nancy Cohen has suggested, Wells was deeply troubled by the postbellum economy's potential "eclipse of the moral order of proprietary capitalism." That fear underlay Wells' broader intellectual shift during the 1870s, in which he outlined a consumerist political economy that, Cohen argues, influenced liberal economics well into the twentieth century. It is likely that Wells' tenure as Special Commissioner of Revenue, and particularly his analysis of tobacco frauds and their effect on tobacconist proprietorships, influenced his later analyses. See Cohen, *The Reconstruction of American Liberalism*, 90.

89. Manufacturers, Leaf Dealers, & Warehouseman of Cincinnati, Ohio, *An Argument in Favor of the Reduction of the Tax*, 5. For more on "speculation," see Olmsted, "The Tobacco Tax," 198.

90. "Pressing Tobacco for Domestic Use," *The Country Gentleman*, Jul. 14, 1864; "The Tobacco Question," *The Country Gentleman*, Feb. 6, 1862.

91. Burke, ed., *Proceedings of the Convention of Tobacconists*, 11.

92. "Tax on Tobacco," *TL*, Jan. 27, 1866.

93. "Louisville Tobacco Convention," *TL*, Feb. 10, 1866.

94. "Tobacconists' National Association," *Tobacco Leaf*, Mar. 7 – Mar. 14, 1866. For Bollman, see Jamie L. Pietruska, *Looking Forward: Prediction and Uncertainty in Modern America* (Chicago: University of Chicago Press, 2017), 87.

95. For antimonopolism, see Gretchen Ritter, *Goldbugs and Greenbacks: The Antimonopoly Tradition and the Politics of Finance in America* (New York: Cambridge University Press, 1997), 104-109; see also Richard White, *Railroaded: The Transcontinentals and the Making of Modern America* (New York: W.W. Norton & Co., 2011), 111-113.

96. Burke, *Proceedings of the Convention of Tobacconists*, 9; see also "Memorial of the Tobacco Cutters of Cincinnati."

97. "The Tobacco Tax," *TL*, Sep. 30, 1865.

98. "The Tobacco Tax," *TL*, Sep. 30, 1865. Manufacturers routinely described themselves as "honest." The term was useful for two reasons. First, it helped propagate manufacturers' self-perception as the rightful public face of the tax reform process. Second, it distinguished their calls for federal control from the antimonopolist critique of state-sanctioned but unearned market dominance. On the rhetorical use of "honesty" in nineteenth-century political economy, see Richard R. John, *Network Nation: Inventing American Telecommunications* (Cambridge: Belknap Press of Harvard University Press, 2010), 67-68.

99. "The Tobacco Tax," *TL*, Sep. 30, 1865.

100. Burke, *Proceedings of the Convention of Tobacconists*, 11.

101. "Tax on Smoking Tobacco," *TL*, Mar. 21, 1866.

102. Burke, ed., *Proceedings of the Convention of Tobacconists*, 11.

103. "Grand Convention at the Cooper Institute," *TL*, Dec. 2, 1865.

104. Bensel, *Yankee Leviathan*, 285-302.

105. See, for example, *Proceedings of the National Convention of Manufacturers, Held at Cleveland, Ohio* (Cleveland: Sanford & Hayward, 1867). Tobacco manufacturers were not exempt from this mood. Despairing of the "fifteen, almost sixteen, million dollars drawn from [tobacco] in 1866," the editors of *Tobacco Leaf* concluded, "the Government to-day is feeding ... upon a carcass." "The Case as It Stands," *TL*, Aug. 28, 1867.

106. "Tradesmen and Congressmen," *TL*, Mar. 6, 1867.

107. *Congressional Globe*, 39th Cong., 1st Sess., 1866, 2436

108. Tobacco manufacturers' policy vision, and its embrace by legislators inclined to oppose such special privileges, is reminiscent of the federal government's embrace of fiat currency and numerous state governments' acceptance of corporate chartering as a means to rapidly generate capital and meet wartime demands. For fiat currency, see Mihm, *A Nation of Counterfeiters*; for corporate chartering, see Sean Patrick Adams, "Soulless Monsters and Iron Horses: The Civil War, Institutional Change, and American Capitalism," in Gary J. Kornblith and Michael Zakim, eds., *Capitalism Takes Command: The Social Transformation of Nineteenth-Century America* (Chicago: University of Chicago Press, 2011): 249-276.

109. "To the Public," *TL*, Mar. 4, 1865.

110. *Directory of Tobacco Men in the United States* (New York: C. Pfirshing, 1867).

111. "Tradesmen and Congressmen," *TL*, Mar. 6, 1867.

112. "Tradesmen and Congressmen," *TL*, Mar. 6, 1867. Several years later, Pfirshing referred to legislators who supported the trade as "Tobaccocrats." "The New Virginia U.S. Senator," *Tobacco Leaf*, Feb. 1, 1871.

113. "Convention of Tobacconists in Washington," *Tobacco Leaf*, Feb. 13, 1867.

114. As the war dwindled to an end, Mayo had helped organize supplies for the Army of Northern Virginia. He also ran for the Virginia House of Delegates in 1865. "Meeting of the People of Henrico," *Richmond Dispatch*, Mar. 9, 1865; "To the Voters of Henrico County," *Richmond Dispatch*, Mar. 22, 1865.

115. "Convention of Tobacconists in Washington," *TL*, Feb. 13, 1867.

116. "Convention of Tobacconists in Washington," *TL*, Feb. 13, 1867.

117. "Presentation," *TL*, May 29, 1867.

118. "The Lorillard Manufactories," *TL*, Apr. 17, 1867.

119. "Programme of the Second Annual Fair," *TL*, Feb. 13, 1867.

120. "Cincinnati Tobacco Fair," *TL*, Jul. 24, 1867.

121. "No Title," *The Daily Appeal* (Memphis, TN), Sep. 8, 1867.

122. "Convention of Tobacco Manufacturers," *The Evening Telegraph* (Philadelphia), Sep. 5, 1867.

123. "The Tobacco Interest," *TL*, May 1, 1867.

124. *Memorial of the Convention of Tobacco Manufacturers, Held at Cleveland, O., on the 17th and 18th of Sept., 1867* (St. Louis: Times Steam Printing Company, 1867), 3.

125. Lorillard was not at the convention, but delegates nominated him to the Executive Committee anyway, believing influential New Yorkers would "be of great service to us in carrying out our purposes." "The Cleveland Convention," *TL*, Oct. 9, 1867.

126. "National Tobacco Convention," *Daily Evening Telegraph*, Sep. 18, 1867.

127. *Memorial of the Convention of Tobacco Manufacturers*, 8.

128. *Memorial of the Convention of Tobacco Manufacturers*, 6-7.
129. These proposals appear in *Memorial of the Convention of Tobacco Manufacturers*. *Tobacco Leaf* captured much of the convention's debate. See "The Cleveland Convention," *TL*, Oct. 9, 1867. For the final draft of the convention's proposed law, which included the recommendation for a ten-thousand-dollar bond, see U.S. Congress, House, Committee of Ways and Means, *Report of the Special Commissioner of the Revenue*, 40th Cong., 2d Sess., 1868, 62-63.
130. "The Prevention of Fraud in Tobacco," *TL*, Sep. 11, 1867.
131. Delegates were clearly aware of this potential outcome. To avoid criticism, they asked Congress to institute the stamp system while dramatically reducing rates. As ATTC leader T.R. Spence told his colleagues, "There are many small manufacturers who would be very much opposed to prepaying the forty-cent tax." Spence warned that if delegates did not propose a low tax, small manufacturers' "combined influence will be great against our whole scheme." "The Cleveland Convention," *TL*, Oct. 9, 1867; see also *Memorial of the Convention of Tobacco Manufacturers*, 5.
132. "National Tobacco Convention," *Daily Evening Telegraph*, Sep. 18, 1867.
133. "The Cleveland Convention," *TL*, Oct. 9, 1867.
134. "New-York Tobacco Board of Trade," *TL*, Oct. 30, 1867.
135. F.A. Prague, "Proposed Plan for the Inspection and Collection of the Revenue on Manufactured Tobacco & Snuff," undated; Folder 11, Cigars and Tobacco Undated; HR 40A – H 19.5, 40th Cong.; Records of the Committee on Ways and Means; Records of the House of Representatives, RG 223; National Archives Building, Washington, D.C.
136. In 1867, the TNA changed its name to the "New York Fine-Cut Tobacco Manufacturers' Association." For clarity, I refer to the association as "TNA" throughout the rest of this chapter. "Resolutions of the Tobacco Trade," undated; Folder 1, Internal Revenue Taxation; HR 40A – F27.27, 40th Cong.; Records of the Committee on Ways and Means; Records of the House of Representatives, RG 223; National Archives Building, Washington, D.C.
137. "A Happy New Year!" *TL*, Jan. 1, 1868.
138. F. & J. Rives, "Public Acts of the Fortieth Congress of the United States," *Appendix to the Congressional Globe*, 40th Cong., 2d Sess., 1868, 537-542.
139. F. & J. Rives, "Public Acts."
140. Hahn, *Making Tobacco Bright*, 86-87. Barbara Hahn suggests that different rates for smoking and chewing tobacco "did not forestall fraud; they made it easier to accomplish." Although manufacturers fretted over such an outcome, evidence suggests that was not the case. Following the passage of the 1868 Revenue Act, the amount of chewing tobacco taxed annually shot up from twelve million pounds in 1867-1868 to nineteen million pounds in 1869-1870, the first full year under the new law. *Annual Report of the Commissioner of Internal Revenue for the Year Ending June 30, 1900* (Washington: GPO, 1900), 431.
141. Tobacco manufacturers of Oxford, NC to Robert Cumming Schenck, Feb. 10, 1868; Folder 1, Internal Revenue Taxation; HR 40A – F27.27, 40th Cong.; Records of the Committee on Ways and Means; Records of the House of Representatives, RG 223; National Archives Building, Washington, D.C.

142. T.R. Spence to John Sherman, Jun. 30, 1868; Folder 11, Cigars and Tobacco Undated; HR 40A – H19.5, 40th Cong.; Records of the Committee on Ways and Means; Records of the House of Representatives, RG 223; National Archives Building, Washington, D.C.

143. Pierre Lorillard to Robert Cumming Schenck, Mar. 5, 1868; Folder 11, Cigars and Tobacco Undated; HR 40A – H19.5, 40th Cong.; Records of the Committee on Ways and Means; Records of the House of Representatives, RG 223; National Archives Building, Washington, D.C.

144. "Proposed Amendments to the Internal Revenue Tax Bill," undated; Folder 2, Internal Revenue Taxation; HR 40A – F27.27, 40th Cong.; Records of the Committee on Ways and Means; Records of the House of Representatives, RG 223; National Archives Building, Washington, D.C. William E. Lawrence kept some distance between himself (and the New Yorkers he represented) and this pamphlet's criticism of monopoly. Under his signature, he appended a brief note endorsing the pamphlet's "general features, but especially in asking reduction."

145. J.P. Spence to Robert Cumming Schenck, Mar. 12, 1868; Folder 1, Internal Revenue Taxation; HR 40A – F27.27, 40th Cong.; Records of the Committee on Ways and Means; Records of the House of Representatives, RG 223; National Archives Building, Washington, D.C.

146. These meetings were called by a group of Chicago manufacturers hoping to rally the trade in favor of "free stamps." "Editor Tobacco Leaf," *TL*, Jan. 20, 1869. The fight for "free stamps" lasted through the spring and ended in the opening weeks of the Forty-first Congress. Although the House had passed a free stamp bill in the closing weeks of the Fortieth Congress, the Senate failed to take up the measure. During the opening weeks of the Forty-first Congress, newly appointed Revenue Commissioner Columbus Delano advised the Senate Finance Committee that free stamps would promote fraud, effectively killing the issue. U.S. Congress, Senate, *Statement Prepared in the Office of Internal Revenue in Relation to the Tax on Manufactured Tobacco*, 41st Congress, 1st Sess., Apr. 1, 1869.

147. Convention of Tobacconists, *Memorial of the Convention of Tobacconists to the Honorable Committee of Ways and Means* (Washington, D.C., 1869), 6.

148. *The National Tobacco Association of the United States: Its Organization and Proceedings up to December 8, 1871* (New York: Henry Spear, 1872), 19-23.

149. "The National Tobacco Association," *TL*, Jul. 4, 1869.

150. "The Cincinnati Tobacco Fair," *TL*, Aug. 11, 1869. Gallagher parlayed his leadership within NTA into a prominent position in the Connecticut Democratic Party. See "Again to the Front," *TL*, Oct. 7, 1882.

151. For tobacco revenue totals from 1872 to 1900, see *Annual Report of the Commissioner of Internal Revenue 1900*, 388-393.

152. "Obituary," *Irish World and American Industrial Liberator* (New York, NY), May 14, 1898.

153. *An Act to reduce Duties on Imports, and to reduce Internal Taxes, and for other purposes*. Public Law 315, *Statutes at Large of the United States of America* 17 (1873): 250.

154. *Appendix to the Congressional Globe*, 42nd Cong., 3d Sess., 1872, 1-2.

155. "The Assumed Representation of the Tobacco and Segar Trade," *United States Tobacco Journal*, Sep. 5, 1876.

Chapter 2. "A Hard Law at Best": The Political Economy of Tobacco Taxation from Depression to Surplus, 1873-1890

1. Frank Olmsted, "The Tobacco Tax," *The Quarterly Journal of Economics* 5, vol. 2 (Jan. 1891), 203-204.
2. Olmsted, "The Tobacco Tax," 208.
3. Olmsted.
4. Olmsted, 219.
5. Ajay Mehrotra, *Making the Modern American Fiscal State: Law, Politics, and the Rise of Progressive Taxation, 1877-1929* (New York: Cambridge University Press, 2013), 68.
6. "That Nuisance, the Internal Revenue Department," *Tobacco Leaf* (hereafter, *TL*), Sep. 15, 1875.
7. Memorial of the Tobacco Board of Trade of Louisville, KY to the Congress of the United States, Jan. 1878; Folder 1, Tax on Tobacco Jan. 14—Feb. 26, 1878, Box 184; SEN 45A - H7.7; 45th Cong.; Records of the Senate, RG 46; National Archives Building, Washington, D.C.; Olmsted, "The Tobacco Tax," 206.
8. For publication history of the *United States Tobacco Journal* (hereafter, *USTJ*), I am drawing from Hammerstein's deposition in a lawsuit brought by one of his creditors. "Oscar Hammerstein, Editor of the United States Tobacco Journal," *TL*, Mar. 3, 1883.
9. Memorial of the Tobacco Board of Trade of Louisville, KY, Jan. 1878.
10. The Bureau reorganized these divisions several times. During the mid-1870s, for instance, tobacco affairs were housed under the "Division of Law." Raum created the Division of Tobacco following his appointment in 1876. See *Report of the Secretary of the Treasury on the State of the Finances for the Year 1875* (Washington: GPO, 1875), 179. See also *Report of the Commissioner of Internal Revenue for the Year 1879* (Washington: GPO, 1879), C.
11. The 1868 Internal Revenue Act barred courts from hindering the collection of assessed taxes. Olmsted, "The Tobacco Tax," 206.
12. For a thorough overview of the Bureau's administrative structure between its founding in 1862 and Raum's administration, see Wilbur Miller, *Revenuers & Moonshiners: Enforcing Federal Liquor Law in the Mountain South, 1865-1900* (Chapel Hill: University of North Carolina Press, 1991), 61-126. Although Raum's administration seemed to exemplify the virtues of civil service reform, he was actually an opponent of that policy. Rather, as a stalwart Republican, Raum saw the Bureau as an extension of his party. To that end, successful revenue generation served the party's policy goals. It also kept a potentially unpopular government agency generally free of corruption charges—a critical task amid Liberal and Democratic accusations of Republican malfeasance. For more on civil service reform during Reconstruction, see Nicholas Barreyre, *Gold and Freedom: The Political Economy of Reconstruction* (Charlottesville: University of Virginia Press, 2015), 195; Morton Keller, *Affairs of State: Public Life in Nineteenth Century America* (Cambridge: Harvard University Press, 1977), 272-275.
13. *Report of the Commissioner of Internal Revenue for the Fiscal Year Ending June 30, 1880* (Washington: GPO, 1880): V.
14. Barbara Hahn, *Making Tobacco Bright: Creating an American Commodity, 1617-1937* (Baltimore: Johns Hopkins University Press, 2011), 89.

15. "North Carolina Tobacco Frauds," *New York Times*, Oct. 10, 1877; see also *Annual Report of the Commissioner of Internal Revenue for the Fiscal Year Ending June 30, 1877* (Washington: GPO, 1877): XXX.

16. "Revenue Defrauders," *USTJ*, May 25, 1878.

17. "Seized," *USTJ*, May 25, 1878; "The Seizure of a Tobacco Factory and Arrest of a Tobacco Manufacturer," *TL*, May 27, 1878. Raum's decision to release the factory illustrated the Bureau's approach to wealthier businesses that ran afoul of revenue law. Barbara Hahn describes a similar case eight years earlier, in which accused Richmond tobacconist J.B. Pace "settled all his difficulties with the Govt" by paying twenty thousand dollars. Taxpayers who lacked similar financial resources often found themselves embroiled in years of legal wrangling following a seizure. Hahn, *Making Tobacco Bright*, 89.

18. "Blockading in North Carolina," *TL*, Nov. 4, 1874.

19. "Blockading at a Discount," *TL*, Dec. 9, 1874.

20. "He Regulates," *USTJ*, Apr. 26, 1879.

21. "Very Doubtful," *USTJ*, Jul. 29, 1882.

22. In addition to Chapter One, see Hahn, *Making Tobacco Bright*, 84-91. The BIR did not use the term "tobacconist." It described tobacconists as "manufacturers," a term I avoided in chapter 1 because of its lack of specificity. Where possible, I continue to use "tobacconist" here.

23. *Public Laws of the United States of America, Passed at the Second Session of the Forty-Second Congress, 1871-2* (Boston: Little, Brown, and Company, 1872), 249-255; see also "He Regulates," *USTJ*, Apr. 26, 1879. The apparent simplicity of tobacco's commodity chain belied the incredible complexity of everyday business. The title "leaf dealer" was a particularly reductive characterization. As Nannie Mae Tilley noted, "leaf dealer" applied to a range of overlapping speculative roles, such as "operators of prize houses, rehandlers, order buyers, commissioner merchants, brokers, contract buyers, and exporters," although the last of these was treated differently under the revenue law. Region, custom, and perhaps even individual preference made it difficult to clearly define any of these terms without appending "a long list of exceptions or combinations." Nannie Mae Tilley, *The Bright Tobacco Industry 1860-1929* (Chapel Hill: University of North Carolina Press, 1948), 251-252.

24. Based upon revenue collected under the retailer dealer tax, the prohibition seems to have been effective. In the wake of the Panic of 1873, the Bureau collected $8,000 from the tax; that number declined steadily throughout the decade. By the early 1880s, only one or two growers found themselves penalized by the tax each year. *Annual Report of the Commissioner of Internal Revenue on the Operations of the Internal Revenue System for the Year Ending 1874* (Washington: GPO, 1874): 14-25; *Report of the Commissioner of Internal Revenue for the Fiscal Year Ended June 30, 1884* (Washington: GPO, 1884): 40.

25. "He Regulates," *USTJ*, Apr. 26, 1879.

26. For low prices during the 1870s, see Tilley, *Bright Tobacco Industry*, 397-398.

27. As Jeffrey Kerr-Ritchie has observed, capital in Virginia's tobacco-growing regions during the postbellum period was "significantly reduced" from antebellum levels. Jeffrey Kerr-Ritchie, *Freedpeople in the Tobacco South: Virginia, 1860-1900* (Chapel Hill: University of North Carolina Press, 1999), 158-160.

28. On the crop-lien system throughout the South, see Harold D. Woodman, *New South-New Law: The Legal Foundations of Credit and Labor Relations in the Postbellum Agricultural South* (Baton Rouge: Louisiana State University Press, 1995); on Virginia's crop lien law, see Kerr-Ritchie, *Freedpeople in the Tobacco South*, 157-180.

29. On the emergence of clerks, see Michael Zakim, "Producing Capitalism: The Clerk at Work," in Gary J. Kornblith and Michael Zakim, eds., *Capitalism Takes Command: The Social Transformation of Nineteenth-Century America* (Chicago: University of Chicago Press, 2012), 223-247.

30. "He Regulates," *USTJ*, Apr. 26, 1879. As Michael Zakim has noted, double entry "was an old technology" by the nineteenth century. Nonetheless, by mid-century it had proliferated as never before by proving "powerfully adept at calculating the overwhelming detail and unprecedentedly large numbers generated by industrial capitalism." Zakim, "Producing Capitalism," 228.

31. Neal Brothers, "To the Planters of Virginia and N. Carolina," 20 Jun. 1872, VA6, Broadsides and Ephemera Collection, David M. Rubenstein Rare Book & Manuscript Library, Duke University; see also Tilley, *The Bright Tobacco Industry, 1860-1929*, 202.

32. "He Regulates," *USTJ*, Apr. 26, 1879.

33. "Revenue Regulations," *USTJ*, Jun. 22, 1878. Similar provisions governed the liquor trade. Richard Hamm has noted that the Bureau demanded records of sales, inventory, and "the amount of fuel consumed," as well as gauging the amount of taxable alcohol in the product throughout its production. As with tobacco, "No detail was overlooked." Richard F. Hamm, *Shaping the Eighteenth Amendment: Temperance Reform, Legal Culture, and the Polity, 1880-1920* (Chapel Hill: University of North Carolina Press, 1995), 94.

34. On tobacco's "managerial revolution," see Alfred Chandler, *The Visible Hand: The Managerial Revolution in American Business* (Cambridge: Harvard University Press, 1977), 382-391. Chandler suggests that the American Tobacco Company's integration of purchasing and sales after 1885 represented the industry's managerial breakthrough. This is undoubtedly accurate, but the record-keeping provisions mandated by the Bureau of Internal Revenue had begun transforming management, particularly within manufacturing businesses, in the decade prior to ATC's consolidation.

35. Hahn, *Making Tobacco Bright*, 90. In 1885, a Pennsylvania tobacconist named Lewis Sylvester detailed his own experiences with potential investors: "Approach a man of means anxious to invest capital in any legitimate business," he wrote. "He is looking for an opportunity; he is assured of your knowledge of the business; has confidence in your integrity. He discovers that the placing of a Cigar stamp too close to the edge of the box, or the inadvertent omission of a data, puts his property in jeopardy. What will he do? Just what you or I would do—look for a different enterprise." "Why Tax on Tobacco Should be Abolished," *Western Tobacco Journal (WTJ)*, Apr. 6, 1885.

36. "Attention Segarmanufacturers!," *USTJ*, Jan. 30, 1877. On risk and autonomy in nineteenth-century workplaces, see Jonathan Levy, *Freaks of Fortune: The Emerging World of Capitalism and Risk* (Cambridge: Harvard University Press, 2012); Amy Dru Stanley, *From Bondage to Contract: Wage Labor, Marriage, and the Market in the Age of Revolution* (New York: Cambridge University Press, 1998); Barbara Young Welke, *Recasting American Liberty: Gender, Race, Law, and the Railroad Revolution, 1865-1920*

(New York: Cambridge University Press, 2001); and John Fabian Witt, *The Accidental Republic: Crippled Workingmen, Destitute Widows, and the Remaking of American Law* (Cambridge: Harvard, 2004).

37. "The Tobacco Industry," *TL*, Dec. 24, 1881.

38. Wm. R. Vidal, Advertisement, *Internal Revenue Record & Customs Journal*, Jan. 3, 1874; C. Jourgensen, Advertisement, *TL*, Oct. 17, 1877.

39. Bump's Annotated Internal Revenue Law, Advertisement, *Internal Revenue Record & Customs Journal*, Jan. 3, 1874.

40. "The Tinfoil War," *USTJ*, Jan. 31, 1880. From the passage of the 1868 Revenue Law forward, tinfoil packaging was a source of significant conflict between manufacturers in the West and East. Westerners did not package tobacco in tin foil because the cost of shipping it from Crooke's New York factory was too great. It was also a poor preservative for tobacco shipped to distant markets. Firms in New York, Boston, and Philadelphia, however, preferred tinfoil because it enabled them to sell small, single-ounce packages. During the 1870s, Eastern firms encouraged Congress to adopt a rule mandating tinfoil packaging, which would force Western firms to adapt to the Eastern way of business. Such a rule would have also forced Western firms to do business with Crooke, who had patented the manufacturing process for tinfoil. U.S. Congress, House, Committee on Ways and Means. *Proposal to Amend Regulations Regarding the Packaging of Chewing Tobacco: Hearing before the Committee on Ways and Means, House of Representatives*, May 13, 1876. 44th Cong. 1st Sess. [Unpublished, 1876]. 9-11.

41. "The Tinfoil War," *USTJ*, Jan. 31, 1880.

42. U.S. Congress, House, *John J. Crooke*, 49th Cong., 1st sess., 1886, H. Rep. 3445, serial 2445, 1.

43. "The Work Before Us," *TL*, Oct. 14, 1874.

44. Although friendship was an important part of Bureau-tobacco relations, it could not compare to the relationship between the Bureau and the alcohol industries. Those relations were so intimate that numerous individuals, including Revenue Commissioners Raum and John W. Yerkes, became liquor lobbyists following their tenures. Hamm, *Shaping the 18th Amendment*, 95.

45. For more on homosocial friendship in Gilded Age political economy, see Richard White, *Railroaded: The Transcontinentals and the Making of Modern America* (New York: W.W. Norton & Co., 2011), 93-133.

46. For an example of such a relationship, see "Tobacco on the Track," *Richmond Dispatch*, May 2, 1883. Richmond's collector, Otis H. Russell, allowed tobacconists to use his office to stamp their packages in his office—technically a violation of the law, because the packages had been removed from their factories without a stamp—if they were pressed for time. Russell even helped them attach the stamps.

47. "The Impromptu Meeting of Segar Manufacturers," *USTJ*, May 22, 1877.

48. "Historical," *USTJ*, Jul. 1, 1882.

49. "Israel Kimball," *USTJ*, Mar. 12, 1881.

50. "Requiescat in Pace," *USTJ*, Mar. 18, 1882.

51. "Historical," *USTJ*, Jul. 1, 1882.

52. Edward Burke, ed., *Proceedings of the Convention of Tobacconists Held at Cooper Institute in the City of New York, November 22, 1865* (New York: E.O. Jenkins, 1865), 11.

53. On the association between tax resistance and political ideology, see Romain D. Huret, *American Tax Resisters* (Cambridge: Harvard University Press, 2014).

54. On the criticism of patronage and corruption, see Mark Wahlgren Summers, *The Era of Good Stealings* (New York: Oxford University Press, 1993), 89-106; Maragret Susan Thompson, *The "Spider Web": Congress and Lobbying in the Age of Grant* (Ithaca: Cornell University Press, 1985).

55. "Repudiation Well Organized, and 'In Cold Blood,'" *Southern Planter and Farmer* (*SPF*) 36, 12 (Dec. 1875), 663.

56. *Proposal to Amend Regulations Regarding the Packaging of Chewing Tobacco*, 15.

57. "The Journal and Revenue Officials," *USTJ*, Sep. 5, 1876.

58. For a well-known contemporary criticism of "jobbery," see William Graham Sumner, *What Social Classes Owe to Each Other* (Caldwell, ID: Caxton Press, 2003), 122.

59. "Washington Letter," *WTJ*, Jan. 22, 1883.

60. "Not Decided," *USTJ*, Jul. 22, 1882.

61. "Those Who Object to Reduction of the Tobacco Tax," *USTJ*, Jan. 26, 1878.

62. "From Washington," *USTJ*, May 11, 1878.

63. I use "monopsonistic" because the system contained many sellers (growers) but few buyers (manufacturers/tobacconists). Critics of the tobacco tax, like many critics of postbellum political economy, used term "monopoly" to describe this imbalance. See Barbara Hahn, *Making Tobacco Bright*, 91-98; Olmsted, "The Tobacco Tax," 213-214.

64. I have calculated these totals by dividing the total revenue collected from manufacturers' license taxes by ten (the cost of a manufacturers' license was ten dollars).

65. For pounds taxed per year, see *Annual Report of the Commissioner of Internal Revenue for the Fiscal Year Ending June 30, 1900* (Washington: GPO, 1900), 431-432. The monopsonistic trend in tobacco manufacturing was inconsistent with other trends in the industry. During the same period, the number of cigar makers increased threefold, from nearly 7,000 to 21,000, while the number of cigars taxed (the equivalent of pounds of tobacco taxed for manufacturers) increased from nearly 600 million to more than 6 billion.

66. Richard Franklin Bensel, *The Political Economy of American Industrialization, 1877-1900* (New York: Cambridge University Press, 2000), 29.

67. "Abolishment of Internal Revenue Taxes and Its Results on the Tobacco Industry," *USTJ*, Nov. 4, 1882.

68. Barbara Hahn has made a similar claim. She argues that the tobacco trust, which formed in 1890, "resulted from the taxation policies of the wartime federal government and the end of flexibility among tobacco products." Hahn, *Making Tobacco Bright*, 91. The data I have compiled provides greater detail about the nature of the industry's "end of flexibility," particularly the lack of change among numbers of tobacconists.

69. Memorial of the Tobacco Board of Trade of Louisville, KY, Jan. 1878.

70. "Tobacco—Its Future in the South," *The Southern Review* 26, 51 (Jul. 1879): 385. On Ragland, see Hahn, *Making Tobacco Bright*, 118.

71. "The Tobacco Tax," *USTJ*, Dec. 7, 1878.

72. Petition of Members of Silver Grange, No. 140, of Pendleton County, Kentucky, approving the action of the National Grange, Feb. 1879; Folder unnumbered, Tax on Tobacco—Tabled Feb. 12-28, 1879, Box 219; SEN 45A – J6; 45th Cong.; Records of U.S. Senate, RG 46; National Archives Building, Washington, D.C.

73. Mehrotra, *Making the Modern American Fiscal State*, 61-65.

74. By the end of the 1870s, the revenue generated by the tobacco tax roughly equaled the cost of veterans' pensions. In 1880, for example, the tax generated thirty-eight million dollars, and the government paid thirty-six million dollars in pensions. For tobacco revenue, see *Report of the Commissioner of Internal Revenue for the Fiscal Year Ended June 30, 1880* (Washington, GPO, 1880), 50; for pension costs, see *Annual Report of the Secretary of the Treasury on the State of the Finances for the Year 1880* (Washington: GPO, 1880), 287. In the years following the Panic of 1873, tariff revenue declined significantly as tobacco and alcohol revenue increased, a situation that led internal taxes to effectively subsidize the tariff's protection for Northern industry.

75. "Tobacco Manufacture," *New York Times*, Apr. 11, 1874.

76. Kerr-Ritchie, *Freedpeople in the Tobacco South*, 129.

77. "From Washington," *USTJ*, Feb. 9, 1878.

78. "Tobacco—Its Future in the South," *The Southern Review* 26, 51 (Jul. 1879): 389.

79. On the growth of North Carolina's tobacco industry at the expense of Virginia's, see Tilley, *The Bright Tobacco Industry*, 545-565.

80. Petition of Citizens of Hanover County, Virginia, praying for the repeal of the law imposing a tax on tobacco, Feb. 1, 1879, Folder 4 Tax on Tobacco Jan. 7—Feb. 7, 1879, Box 184; SEN 45A – H7.7; 45th Cong.; Records of the Senate Finance Committee; Records of the Senate, RG 46; National Archives Building, Washington, D.C.

81. "To the Farmers and Planters of Virginia," *Southern Planter and Farmer* 37, 10 (Oct. 1876), 669.

82. "Repudiation Well Organized, and 'In Cold Blood,' Already Upon Us," *Southern Planter and Farmer* 36, 12 (Dec. 1875), 663.

83. Memorial of the Citizens of Lynchburg, VA, Jun. 11, 1878, Folder 2 Mar. 19 – Jun. 18, 1878, Box 184; SEN 45A – H7.7; 45th Cong.; Records of the Senate, RG 46; National Archives Building, Washington, D.C.

84. "From Washington," *USTJ*, May 11, 1878.

85. Charles Postel, *Equality: An American Dilemma, 1866-1896* (New York: Farrar, Straus and Giroux, 2019), 73.

86. Patrick Mulford O'Connor, "'The Festering Sores of Our Body Politic': Federal Tobacco Taxation, Race, and the Politics of Fear in Postemancipation Virginia," *Soundings: An Interdisciplinary Journal* 101, no. 1 (Jan. 2018): 41-51. See also Kerr-Ritchie, *Freedpeople in the Tobacco South*, 93-180; Jane Dailey, *Before Jim Crow: The Politics of Race in Postemancipation Virginia* (Chapel Hill: University of North Carolina Press, 2000).

87. Steven Hahn, *A Nation Under Our Feet: Black Political Struggles in the Rural South from Slavery to the Great Migration* (Cambridge: The Belknap Press of Harvard University Press, 2003), 384.

88. Custom receipts plummeted following the Panic, reaching as low as $130 million in 1876-1877. For comparison, receipts in 1871-1872 were $216 million. See *Annual Report of the Secretary of the Treasury on the State of the Finances for the Year 1877* (Washington: GPO, 1877), 3; *Annual Report of the Secretary of the Treasury on the State of the Finances for the Year 1872* (Washington: GPO, 1872), 3.

89. *Proposal to Amend Regulations Regarding the Packaging of Chewing Tobacco*, 31.

90. John Randolph Tucker, "The Tobacco Tax—A Thorough Explanation of What It Means," *Southern Planter and Farmer* 37, 9 (Sep. 1876), 598.

91. Although these bills were doomed, their ubiquity suggested the breadth and energy of opposition to the tax. "Crazy Tax Bills on Tobacco," *USTJ*, Jan. 12, 1878.

92. Memorial of M.H. Clark and other citizens of Tennessee asking Congress to reduce the tax on Manufactured Tobacco, Jan. 14, 1878, Folder 1 Tax on Tobacco Jan. 14 – Feb. 26, 1878, Box 184; SEN 45A – H7.7; 45th Cong.; Records of the Senate Finance Committee; Records of the Senate, RG 46; National Archives Building, Washington, D.C.

93. Resolutions adopted at a public meeting of the Citizens of Powhatan County, Virginia, in favor of the repeal of the tax on tobacco, Jan. 15, 1879, Folder 4 Tax on Tobacco Jan. 7—Feb. 7, 1879, Box 184; SEN 45A – H7.7; 45th Cong.; Records of the Senate Finance Committee; Records of the Senate, RG 46; National Archives Building, Washington, D.C.

94. A Memorial from the National Grange asking for the repeal or a reduction in the tax on Tobacco, Dec. 16, 1878, Folder 3 Tax on Tobacco Dec. 16-20, 1878, Box 184; SEN 45A – H7.7; 45th Cong.; Records of the Senate Finance Committee; Records of the Senate, RG 46; National Archives Building, Washington, D.C.

95. Smaller manufacturers, and even some larger firms who had grown weary of the post-1875 rate increase, also added their voices to this movement. One such organization, the "National Tobacco Manufacturers' Association," included members from Kentucky, Maryland, North Carolina, and Ohio, as well several former leaders of the National Tobacco Association. The vast majority of anti-tax energy, however, came from growers and leaf dealers whose economic fortunes had dwindled during the 1870s. "From Washington," *USTJ*, Jan. 19, 1878.

96. "From Washington," *USTJ*, Jan. 19, 1878.

97. "The Tobacco Tax," *USTJ*, Mar. 9, 1878.

98. "From Washington," *USTJ*, Jan. 19, 1878.

99. *Proposal to Amend Regulations Regarding the Packaging of Chewing Tobacco*, 50.

100. Petition of P. Lorillard & Co., May 21, 1878, Folder 3 Tax on Tobacco Mar. 19 – Jun. 18, 1878; SEN 95A – H7.7; 45th Cong.; Records of the Senate Finance Committee; Records of the Senate, RG 46; National Archives Building, Washington, D.C.

101. "The Tobacco Tax," *USTJ*, Mar. 9, 1878.

102. "From Washington," *USTJ*, Jun. 8, 1878.

103. "The Tobacco Tax," *USTJ*, Mar. 9, 1878.

104. On the "growing social antagonism," see Mehrotra, *Making the Modern American Fiscal State*, 38-85.

105. "Recommending Abolition of the Tobacco Tax," *WTJ*, Dec. 8, 1884.

106. Bensel, *The Political Economy of American Industrialization*, 472-473; see also Keller, *Affairs of State*, 381.

107. "Abolition of Tobacco Taxes," *USTJ*, Nov. 18, 1882.

108. "How to Abolish Taxes," *USTJ*, Aug. 12, 1882.

109. "Tax Reduction," *USTJ*, Jan. 28, 1882.

110. "Requiescat in Pace," *USTJ*, Mar. 18, 1882.

111. "From Washington," *USTJ*, Mar. 11, 1882.

112. Tilley, *The Bright Tobacco Industry*, 545-565.

113. "From Washington," *USTJ*, Mar. 11, 1882.

114. "Washington Letter," *USTJ*, Jan. 15, 1883; "Tax Abolition," *USTJ*, May 17, 1884.

115. "Washington Letter," *USTJ*, Jan. 15, 1883.

116. "The Convention in Washington," *TL*, Mar. 18, 1882.

117. "The Tax Question," *USTJ*, Dec. 9, 1882; "Tobacco Factories Stopping," *New York Times*, Dec. 2, 1882; "Tax Reduction," *New York Times*, Dec. 10, 1882; "Tobacco Men Anxious," *New York Times*, Dec. 19, 1882; "The Tobacco Tax Question," *New York Times*, Dec. 27, 1882.

118. Petition of the manufacturers and dealers in tobacco, cigars, and cigarettes of Des Moines, Jan. 1883, Folder 3 Jan. 5, 1883—Jan. 13, 1883, Box 109; SEN 47A—J8 Committee on Finance, Taxes General; 47th Cong.; Records of the Senate Finance Committee; Records of the Senate, RG 46; National Archives Building, Washington, D.C.

119. Theda Skocpol, *Protecting Soldiers and Mothers: The Political Origins of Social Policy in the United States* (Cambridge: Harvard University Press, 1992), 102.

120. Skocpol, *Protecting Soldiers and Mothers*, 108-109

121. Keller, *Affairs of State*, 381.

122. "Whiskey, Beer, and Tobacco Tax," *The National Tribune* (Washington, D.C.), Jun. 10, 1886.

123. "Washington Notes," *USTJ*, Apr. 8, 1882.

124. "'Truth' Sees No Reason for Expecting a Repeal of the Tobacco Tax at Present," *WTJ*, Nov. 29, 1886.

125. Mehrotra, *Making the Modern American Fiscal State*, 37.

126. On tariff politics during the 1880s, see Bensel, *The Political Economy of American Industrialization*, 457-509; Keller, *Affairs of State*, 376-380.

127. "The Washington Outlook," *USTJ*, Dec. 8, 1883.

128. "Tobacco Tax Repeal," *USTJ*, May 7, 1887; "Kentucky Congressmen and Why They Are Opposed to Tobacco Tax Abolition," *WTJ*, Jan. 24, 1887.

129. "Congress and the Tobacco Tax," *WTJ*, Jul. 16, 1884.

130. "Petitions for the Repeal of the Tobacco Tax," *WTJ*, Jan. 29, 1887.

131. "The Tobacco Tax," *WTJ*, Feb. 7, 1887.

132. "'Truth' Sees No Reason for Expecting a Repeal of the Tobacco Tax at Present" *WTJ*, Nov. 29, 1886.

133. "Why the Durham Plant Favors the Revenue Tax on Tobacco," *WTJ*, Dec. 27, 1886.

134. "The Country's Voice," *USTJ*, Jan. 22, 1887.

135. "The Repeal of the Tobacco Tax," *USTJ*, Aug. 31, 1889; "The Tobacco Tax," *USTJ*, Dec. 21, 1889.

136. See Chandler, *The Visible Hand*, 382-391.

137. Bensel, *The Political Economy of American Industrialization*, 477-478.

138. "The Internal Revenue Changes," *Tobacco*, Oct. 10, 1890; "The Dawn of a New Era," *Tobacco*, Oct. 3, 1890.

Chapter 3. Tobacco's "Imperfect Knowledge": Governance, Classification, and Conflict in the World Tobacco Market, 1865-1890

1. "Foreign Markets," *Western Tobacco Journal* (hereafter, *WTJ*), May 17, 1880; "Foreign Markets," *WTJ*, Aug 23, 1880; "Eastern Markets," *Tobacco Leaf* (hereafter, *TL*), Aug 14, 1880.

2. "On the Board," *Chicago Daily Tribune*, Sep. 2, 1882.

3. For a comprehensive analysis of knowledge infrastructures, see Paul N. Edwards, *A Vast Machine: Computer Models, Climate Data, and the Politics of Global Warming* (Cambridge: MIT Press, 2010), 1-25. See also Leigh Star and Karen Ruhleder, "Steps Toward an Ecology of Infrastructure: Design and Access for Large Information Spaces," *Information Systems Research* 7, no. 1 (1996): 111-134. On the effects of grain elevators and the Chicago Board of Trade, see William Cronon, *Nature's Metropolis: Chicago and the Great West* (New York: W.W. Norton & Company), 97-147. For an account of similar processes in the cotton trade, see Harold D. Woodman, *King Cotton and His Retainers: Financing & Marketing the Cotton Crop of the South, 1800-1925* (Lexington: University of Kentucky Press, 1968), 290-292.

4. Jonathan Levy, *Freaks of Fortune: The Emerging World of Capitalism and Risk in America* (Cambridge: Harvard University Press, 2012), 232-263. On the broader transformation of the global grain commodity chain, see Steven C. Topik and Allen Wells, *Global Markets Transformed 1870-1945* (Cambridge: Harvard University Press, 2012), 113-146.

5. Although tobacco markets never developed standardization of the sort that characterized other commodities markets, chapter five notes that the USDA did devise relatively coherent and universal standards by the 1930s. The 1890s were a pivotal moment, however, for several reasons. For one, U.S. tobacco production continued its steady shift towards domestic markets and away from exports. Moreover, the formation of the American Tobacco Company meant that domestic buyers were concentrating their ability to shape quality demands. Finally, as chapter four indicates, a constellation of domestic fertilizer and allied firms continued to exert significant influence over domestic quality ideals. The institutions described in this chapter operated in a transnational context, with power spread more diffusely and the ability to enforce quality ideals always slightly out of reach.

6. During the 1880s, tobacco exports averaged roughly $21 million annually. This was a far smaller total than cotton and wheat, but fairly comparable to corn and sugar. *Statistical Abstract of the United States, 1890.* (Washington: GPO, 1891), 130-142.

7. Coffee is the other major global commodity with a diffuse quality history. See Mario Samper K., "The Historical Construction of Quality and Competitiveness: A Preliminary Discussion of Coffee Commodity Chains," in William G. Clarence-Smith and Steven Topik, eds., *The Global Coffee Economy in Africa, Asia, and Latin America, 1500-1989* (New York: Cambridge University Press, 2009), 120-153.

8. Both this chapter and the next suggest how junction regimes exerted power of both export and domestic leaf markets. This chapter focuses particularly on export markets, which developed different quality standards and marketed tobacco in hogsheads rather than the unpackaged piles of bright-leaf auction houses. I draw my emphasis on junctions, or "nodes," from commodity chains analysis, which describes "processes or segments within a commodity chain" as "boxes or nodes." Nodes involve "the acquisition and/or organization of inputs (e.g., raw materials and semifinished products), labor power (and its provisioning), transportation, distribution (via markets or transfers), and consumption." In the postbellum tobacco economy, these nodes developed in the urban junctions that mediated between farmers on the tobacco frontier and consumers around the world. See Gary Gereffi, Miguel Korzeniewicz, and Roberto P. Korzeniewicz, "In-

troduction: Global Commodity Chains," in Gary Gereffi and Miguel Korzeniewicz, eds. *Commodity Chains and Global Capitalism* (Westport, CT: Greenwood Press, 1994), 2. This chapter also draws on Emily Rosenberg's argument that "currents"—that is, transnational flows of social, political, and cultural knowledge—shaped the late-nineteenth century world. Ideas about tobacco's quality represented one such current. Emily Rosenberg, "Transnational Currents in a Shrinking World," in Rosenberg, ed., *A World Connecting: 1870-1945* (Cambridge: The Belknap Press of Harvard University Press, 2012), 815-996.

9. The significance of these factors has been a topic of debate among recent scholars. Barbara Hahn has argued that tobacco types are technological and political—not "natural." That is, "nature, seed, and genetics" insufficiently explain tobacco's variety. Drew Swanson has countered by centering soil, and farmers' deep knowledge of its relationship to tobacco, as essential to each variety's specificity. My definition of "fictions of standardization" draws from both, suggesting that while criteria of quality depended on natural foundations, they existed to serve the institutions that devised them. Their boundaries were thus porous, drawn and redrawn as institutions required. Barbara Hahn, *Making Tobacco Bright: Creating an American Commodity, 1617-1937* (Baltimore: Johns Hopkins University Press, 2011); Drew Swanson, *A Golden Weed: Tobacco and Environment in the Piedmont South* (New Haven: Yale University Press, 2014), esp. 223.

10. I encountered this idea in Gavin Wright's *Old South, New South: Revolutions in the Southern Economy Since the Civil War* (New York: Basic Books, 1986), 188-189. Wright draws on the theory of "increasing returns," which suggests how "relatively small initial advantage produces a result that becomes more compelling and less arbitrary over time."

11. This was a common assertion and could be tracked down in *Tobacco Leaf*'s weekly Louisville market reports. For example, see "Western and Southern Markets," *TL*, Jan. 5, 1884.

12. Cronon, *Nature's Metropolis*, 132.

13. Middlemen were essential to Gilded Age commodity markets, as control of knowledge was of paramount concern for long-distance trade. Personifying this imperative were the era's globe-spanning army of weighers, brokers, assessors, samplers, and various other evaluative experts. On the broader significance of middlemen as experts, see David Roth Singerman, "Science, Commodities, and Corruption in the Gilded Age," *The Journal of the Gilded Age and Progressive Era* 15 (2016), 278-293.

14. As Edwards notes, without a knowledge infrastructure, "you are left with claims you can't back up, facts you can't verify, comprehension you can't share, and data you can't trust. Without the infrastructure, knowledge can decay or even disappear." Edwards, *A Vast Machine*, 19.

15. Ed. C. de Jesus, *The Tobacco Monopoly in the Philippines: Bureaucratic Enterprise and Social Change, 1766-1880* (Quezon City: Ateneo de Manila University Press, 1980), 4-11.

16. "Remarks of Mr. Dodge," *Daily National Intelligencer* (Washington, D.C.), May 29, 1840.

17. "Tobacco in France," *United States Tobacco Journal* (hereafter, *USTJ*), Jan. 8, 1881; "Imperial Tobacco Monopoly," *USTJ*, Jan. 21, 1881.

18. Charles Maier, *Leviathan 2.0: Inventing Modern Statehood* (Cambridge: The Belknap Press of Harvard University Press, 2012), 13.

19. E.W. Saunders, "The Tobacco Trade in Its Relation to Taxation and Government Monopolies," in *Report of the Industrial Commission on Agriculture and on Taxation in Various States: Volume XI* (Washington: GPO, 1901), 51-71; "Foreign Tobacco News," *TL*, Dec. 23, 1878; "The Tobacco Tax in Portugal," *TL*, Jun. 28, 1879; "A Greek Monopoly," *TL*, Sept. 29, 1883; "Tobacco in Egypt," *USTJ*, Jul. 28, 1888.

20. For export totals, see Douglas A. Irwin, "Exports of selected commodities: 1790–1989," Table Ee569-589, in Susan B. Carter et al, eds., *Historical Statistics of the United States, Earliest Times to the Present: Millennial Edition* (New York: Cambridge University Press, 2006). As Jeffrey Kerr-Ritchie has noted, exports declined as a share of U.S. tobacco production between the Civil War era and 1900. By the turn of the century, exports accounted for 38 percent of total production, down from 56 percent in the early 1870s. "Tobacco's Rubicon," as Kerr-Ritchie puts it, "appears to have been crossed after 1886 when exports never again exceeded figures for [domestic] manufacturing consumption." Jeffrey Kerr-Ritchie, *Freedpeople in the Tobacco South: Virginia, 1860-1900* (Chapel Hill: University of North Carolina Press, 1999), 132.

21. Here I am drawing on Timothy Mitchell's argument that the representation of "internal distinctions" as "external boundaries," such as that between state and economy or state and society, is a technique of governance specific to modern statehood. Such "boundaries," Mitchell writes, are more accurately understand as "a line drawn internally, within the network of institutional mechanisms through which a social and political order is maintained." The structure of tobacco taxation was thus an illustration of the ways various states maintained order and projected authority. Timothy Mitchell, "Society, Economy, and the State Effect," in Aradhana Sharma and Akhil Gupta, eds., *The Anthropology of the State: A Reader* (Malden, MA: Blackwell Publishing, 2006), 170.

22. "Tobacco in France," *USTJ*, Jan. 8, 1881; U.S. Congress, House, Committee of Ways and Means, *Report of the Special Commissioner of the Revenue*, 40th Cong., 2d Sess., 1868, 81.

23. The United States operated a portion of its tobacco economy in this manner by contracting the sale of tobacco to military forces and the Bureau of Indian Affairs to private manufacturers. P. Lorillard, for example, won the 1877 bid to supply the eastern branch of the U.S. Army with plug tobacco at 56 cents per pound; in the same year, the New York firm Buchanan & Lyall secured the "Indian contract" of 69,000 pounds. "Tobacco for the Army," *TL*, May 30, 1877.

24. "Tobacco in Italy," *USTJ* Apr. 30, 1881;

25. Fritz Stern, *Gold and Iron: Bismarck, Bleichröder, and the Building of the German Empire* (New York: Vintage Books, 1979), 419-420. For another example, see Melinda Plastas and Maria Rentetzi's analysis of Austria-Hungary's M.L. Herzog & Co, "Tobacco Roads: Histories of Technologies and a Transnational Economy," *Advances in Historical Studies* 5, no. 2 (Apr. 2016), 45-48.

26. "England's Custom Duties on Tobacco," *USTJ*, Feb. 4, 1888.

27. "Italian, Turkish, and Russian Tobaccos," *TL*, Dec. 8, 1875; "The Tobacco Question in Belgium," *TL*, Aug. 8, 1879.

28. American tobacco trade journals covered the German monopoly debate closely throughout the 1870s and early 1880s. The issue was significant because debates af-

fected demand for U.S. imports, and also because it reflected many of the same tensions that continued to shape debates about American tobacco taxation in the years after Reconstruction. For an overview of the tobacco monopoly's place in Bismarck's revenue schemes, see Stern, *Gold and Iron*, 194.

29. de Jesus, *The Tobacco Monopoly in the Philippines*, 178-196; Mansoor Moaddel, "Shi'i Political Discourse and Class Mobilization in the Tobacco Movement of 1890-1892," *Sociological Forum* 7, no. 3 (Sept. 1992), 447-468.

30. For tobacco's sacred and social uses, see especially Marcy Norton, *Sacred Gifts, Profane Pleasures: A History of Tobacco and Chocolate in the Atlantic World* (Ithaca: Cornell University Press, 2008).

31. "Latakia," *TL*, Sep. 30, 1874.

32. On the civilization-barbarity dynamic, see James C. Scott, *The Art of Not Being Governed: An Anarchist History of Upland Southeast Asia* (New Haven: Yale University Press, 2009), 98-126.

33. "Tobacco in Spain," *TL*, Aug. 23, 1884. According to one American visitor, the factories of Italy and France likewise employed "girls and women chiefly." "The Paris Exposition," *TL*, Sep. 23, 1878.

34. "The Regie, or Tobacco Monopoly, of Moldavia and Wallachia," *TL*, Aug. 30, 1876; "Imperial Tobacco Monopoly," *USTJ*, Jan. 21, 1882.

35. Nannie Mae Tilley, *The Bright-Tobacco Industry, 1860-1929* (Chapel Hill: University of North Carolina Press, 1948), 515; Jeffrey Kerr-Ritchie, *Freedpeople in the Tobacco South: Virginia, 1860-1900* (Chapel Hill: University of North Carolina Press, 1999), 192-193.

36. I explore this dynamic more fully in chapter 4. See also Steven Stoll, "The Captured Garden: The Political Ecology of Subsistence under Capitalism," *International Labor and Working Class History* 85 (Spring 2014): 77.

37. "An Inconvenient Spanish Regulation," *TL*, Aug. 28, 1880; "A Recent Decree as to the Importation of Tobacco into Portugal," *WTJ*, May 3, 1886. On the Treasury Department's enforcement of customs law and the persistence of smuggling during the Gilded Age, see Andrew Wender Cohen, "Smuggling, Globalization, and America's Outward State, 1870-1909," *The Journal of American History* 97, 2 (Sep. 2010), 371-398

38. "Statistics of Smoking in France," *TL*, Sep. 30, 1874.

39. "Tobacco Culture in Germany—Map of Producing Districts," *TL*, Aug. 5, 1885.

40. "Statistics of European Tobacco," *WTJ*, Oct. 4, 1880.

41. Timothy Mitchell, "Society, Economy, and the State Effect," 180.

42. "The New French Contract," *TL*, May 6, 1882"; "New Contract," *WTJ*, Jan. 7, 1884.

43. "A Breeze," *USTJ*, Sep. 13, 1879.

44. According to coverage in the American tobacco press, some states were more effective revenue collectors than others. In contrast with its descriptions of eager Spanish revenue inspectors, *Tobacco Leaf* often referenced "a formidable system of smuggling" in the Ottoman Empire. Yet these conclusions tended to come from the reports of foreign visitors—traveling merchants or consuls—and so it is difficult to say to what extent they accurately grasped the conditions of a given tobacco economy. "Foreign Tobacco News," *TL*, Jul. 25, 1885.

45. By "middlemen," I mean agents who, as Gary Biglaiser defines them, "trade but do not originally own a good, do not physically alter the good, and receive no consumption value from possessing the good." Biglaiser, "Middlemen as Experts," *RAND Journal of Economics* 24, no. 2 (Summer 1993): 212-223.
46. "Has the Boom in Western Leaf Tobacco a Solid Foundation," *TL*, Aug. 6, 1887.
47. "The Parsee and the Tobacco Regies," *TL*, Sep. 13, 1879.
48. "A Breeze," *USTJ*, Sep. 13, 1879.
49. "About the Regies" and "The Parsee and the Tobacco Regies," *TL*, Sep. 13, 1879
50. "A Breeze," *USTJ*, Sep. 13, 1879.
51. "'Regie' Tobacco Monopoly," *WTJ*, Aug. 2, 1886.
52. "Foreign Tobacco Monopolies," *New York Times*, May 8, 1880; "Commissioner of Agriculture on the 'Regie' System of Buying American Tobacco," *WTJ*, Jun. 8, 1886.
53. "Commissioner of Agriculture on the 'Regie' System of Buying American Tobacco," *WTJ*, Jun. 8, 1886.
54. In some cases, members of junction regimes included the regie correspondents who orchestrated procurement of U.S. tobacco. Max Abenheim, for instance, was a well-known correspondent of several regies and a member of the New York Tobacco Board of Trade. See, for example, "Unjust Tobacco Samples," *WTJ*, Jan. 24, 1881.
55. "An Export Bonded Warehouse," *TL*, Jan. 20, 1875.
56. "False Tobacco-Packing," *TL*, Apr. 21, 1883.
57. "How Tobacco is Marketed and Manufactured at Louisville, KY," *TL*, Oct. 1, 1887.
58. Kerr-Ritchie, *Freedpeople in the Tobacco South*, 138-139.
59. "Gov. Kemper of Virginia on Tobacco Inspection," *TL*, Dec. 23, 1874. For an overview of the inspection controversy see Tilley, *The Bright-Tobacco Industry*, 402-405.
60. "The Virginia Tobacco Inspection Laws," *TL*, Jan. 6, 1875.
61. "Tobacco Inspection in Baltimore," *TL*, Dec. 15, 1875.
62. State-appointed inspection regimes likewise existed in Kentucky and Tennessee. Tom Lee, "Southern Appalachia's Bright Tobacco Boom: Industrialization, Urbanization, and the Culture of Tobacco," *Agricultural History* 88, 2 (Spring 2014), 182; "Unjust Tobacco Samples," WTJ, Jan. 24, 1881.
63. "The Tobacco Inspection Law of Missouri—Petition for Its Repeal by the Tobacco Association of St. Louis," *TL*, Mar. 14, 1877.
64. On Wise's prominence in postbellum Virginia, see Robert H. Gudmestad, "Baseball, the Lost Cause, and the New South in Richmond, Virginia, 1883-1890," *The Virginia Magazine of History and Biography* 106, 3 (Summer, 1998): 267-300.
65. As one Virginia warehouseman put it, "Cotton is not inspected, nor are cattle or peanuts. Tobacco alone is an orphan and needs the protection of the Government." "Virginia Tobacco Inspections," *TL*, Jan. 27, 1875.
66. For more detail see chapter 4.
67. I address this process more fully in chapter 4. See also Drew A. Swanson, *A Golden Weed: Tobacco and Environment in the Piedmont South* (New Haven: Yale University Press, 2014), 187-189.
68. Maryland did not abolish state inspection during the Gilded Age, a decision that many observers blamed for the state's declining tobacco industry. For those who

idealized a laissez-faire market, Maryland became the preeminent example of state inspection's flaws. Deriding Maryland inspection as "a stench in the nostrils of decent folks at home," one critic argued that state inspection "must of necessity be liable to abuse, fraud and the evils entailed by incompetency of employees, growing worse as it grows older; any free system would regulate itself in these respects, growing better with time." "The Tobacco Question," *TL*, Jan. 12, 1876. In 1880, a Bryantown grower named Henry Turner challenged the law by exporting a hogshead from Baltimore to Bremen "without having procured the same to be weighed, passed, and marked by any inspector of tobacco." Under indictment for the offense, Turner claimed the state had inadvertently abolished inspection in 1872. The U.S. Supreme Court upheld Turner's conviction, and thus Maryland's inspection law, in 1883. *Henry A. Turner v. The State of Maryland*, 107 U.S. 38 (1883); "The Tobacco Inspection Laws of Maryland Sustained," *WTJ*, Jan. 24, 1881; "Washington Letter," *WTJ*, Feb. 12, 1883.

69. Kerr-Ritchie, *Freedpeople in the Tobacco South*, 143.

70. "Richmond (Virginia) Tobacco Trade," *WTJ*, Oct. 10, 1881; "Scheme of Inspection for the Richmond Tobacco Market," *TL*, Oct. 15, 1881.

71. "Dissatisfied with Inspection Laws," *TL*, Sep. 23, 1882. See also Tilley, *The Bright-Tobacco Industry*, 402-403.

72. Kerr-Ritchie, *Freedpeople in the Tobacco South*, 142-146.

73. "In Full Operation," *TL*, Apr. 4, 1885.

74. "The Tobacco Board of Trade," *TL*, Jan. 10, 1880.

75. "The Proposed Tobacco Inspection Law of Virginia," *WTJ*, Jan. 30, 1882.

76. Dara Orenstein, "Warehouses on Wheels," *Environment and Planning D: Society and Space* 36, no. 4 (2018): 649.

77. "A Day in the New York Tobacco Market," *TL*, Nov. 10, 1883; "The National Tobacco Inspection, Brooklyn, NY," *TL*, Oct. 25, 1876.

78. "Regrets and Congratulations," *TL*, Dec. 2, 1878.

79. "New York Naval Stores and Tobacco Exchange," *TL*, Jan. 24, 1885.

80. "Regrets and Congratulations," *TL*, Dec. 2, 1878; "Richmond Tobacco Inspection," *WTJ*, Oct. 9, 1882.

81. "A Day in the New York Tobacco Market," *TL*, Nov. 10, 1883.

82. See chapter 4 on the overlapping developments of ideas about quality, warehouse power, and growers' "ignorance" of markets.

83. Topik and Wells, *Global Markets Transformed*, 114.

84. "Richmond Tobacco Inspection," *WTJ*, Oct. 9, 1882.

85. "False Tobacco-Packing," *TL*, Apr. 21, 1883; "Serious Charges," *WTJ*, Apr. 24, 1883; "An Export Bonded Warehouse," *TL*, Jan. 20, 1875.

86. "Letter from Scotland," *WTJ*, Jun. 20, 1881; "Tobacco Inspection in Baltimore," *TL*, Dec. 15, 1875.

87. "First Annual Report," *TL*, Jan. 5, 1876.

88. "Maryland Tobacco Inspection," *WTJ*, Jan. 24, 1881.

89. "Unjust Tobacco Samples," *WTJ*, Jan. 24, 1881.

90. Charles Stuart Kennedy, *The American Consul: A History of the United States Consular Service, 1776-1914* (Westport, CT: Greenwood Press, 1990). See also Kristen L. Hoganson, *The Heartland: An American History* (New York: Penguin Press, 2019), 151-156.

91. "Tobacco in Baden, Germany," *WTJ*, Jan. 10, 1881.
92. "The Tobacco Trade of Rotterdam," *USTJ*, May 30, 1885.
93. "False Tobacco-Packing," *TL*, Apr. 21, 1883; "Serious Charges," *WTJ*, Apr. 24, 1883.
94. U.S. Congress, Senate, "Letter from the Secretary of State, communicating, in obedience to law, a statement of such fees as have been collected, accounted for, and reported by the various diplomatic and consular agents of the United States during the year ended December 31, 1877," December 9, 1878, 45th Cong., 3d Sess., 1878, S. Doc. 2, 4.; "Consul Grinnell's Departure from Bradford," *Bulletin of the National Association of Wool Manufacturers* XIX, III/IV (1889): 301.
95. "The Bremen Tobacco Trade," *USTJ*, Feb. 11, 1882.
96. "Maryland Tobacco Inspection," *WTJ*, Jan. 24, 1881.
97. "Unjust Tobacco Samples," *WTJ*, Jan. 24, 1881.
98. "The Unkindest Cut of All," *USTJ*, Jan. 15, 1881; "Maryland Tobacco Inspection," *WTJ*, Jan. 24, 1881.
99. "Unjust Tobacco Samples," *WTJ*, Jan. 24, 1881.
100. "The Baltimore Inspections," *TL*, Mar. 12, 1881.
101. "The Proposed Tobacco Inspection Law of Virginia," *WTJ*, Jan. 30, 1882.
102. "A Proud Achievement by the U.S. Tobacco Journal," *USTJ*, Oct. 12, 1889.
103. "Tobacco at Guatemala," *USTJ*, Oct. 6, 1888.
104. "Tobacco in Madras," *USTJ*, Nov. 9, 1889.
105. "Tobacco in Asia," *USTJ*, Oct. 12, 1889.

Chapter 4. "The Road to Prosperity": Power and the Politics of Quality on the Bright Tobacco Frontier, 1865-1900

1. John Ott, *The Position Tobacco Has Ever Held as the Chief Source of Wealth to Virginia* (Richmond: Southern Fertilizing Company, 1876); John Ott, *Tobacco in Virginia and North Carolina: Some Observations in Connection with the Several Types of Tobacco Now Produced in These Two States* (Richmond: Southern Fertilizing Company, 1877).
2. Ott, *The Position Tobacco Has Ever Held*, 10.
3. "Alliance Convention at Durham," *The Progressive Farmer* (hereafter, *PF*), Feb. 26, 1889.
4. "On the Road with a Live Tobacco Buyer," *Tobacco Leaf* (hereafter, *TL*), Mar. 24, 1883.
5. Alan Olmstead and Paul Rhode, *Creating Abundance: Biological Innovation and American Agricultural Development* (New York: Cambridge University Press, 2008), 203.
6. Graham Burchell, Colin Gordon, and Peter Miller, *The Foucault Effect: Studies in Governmentality* (Chicago: University of Chicago Press, 1991), x. By "disciplines" I mean, as Michel Foucault and Timothy Mitchell suggested, "those small-scale polymorphous methods of order." In the tobacco frontier, this could be everything from the tending of a crop to its arrangement on a warehouse floor to the growers' projection of class identity to neighbors or potential buyers. Timothy Mitchell, "Society, Economy, and the State Effect," in Aradhana and Akhil Gupta, eds., *The Anthropology of the State: A Reader* (Malden, MA: Blackwell Publishing, 2006), 177.
7. Burchell, Gordon, and Miller, *The Foucault Effect*, x. Not that the federal state was somehow unaware of these changes. As chapter 5 makes clear, the quality principle,

and the general distribution of judgment and control away from household growers, exemplified key aspects of the USDA's agricultural ideals. In this sense, as Colin Gordon has put it, "largely privatized micro-power structures none the less participate, from the viewpoint of government, in a coherent general policy of order." Burchell, Gordon, and Miller, *The Foucault Effect*, 27.

8. Barbara Jeanne Fields, "The Advent of Capitalist Agriculture: The New South in a Bourgeois World," in Thavolia Glymph and John J. Kushma, *Essays on the Postbellum Southern Economy* (College Station: Texas A&M Press, 1985), 73-94. For an overview of the histories of each of these groups, see Adrienne Monteith Petty, *Standing Their Ground: Small Farmers in North Carolina since the Civil War* (New York: Oxford University Press, 2013), 29-54. On Lumbee Indians since Malinda Maynor Lowery, *The Lumbee Indians: An American Struggle* (Chapel Hill: The University of North Carolina Press, 2018), 102-103; on Sappony tobacco growers, see Nick Martin, "A Family from High Plains," *Splinter*, Aug. 2, 2018, https://www.splinter.com/a-family-from-high-plains-1827707537.

9. Tracy Campbell, *The Politics of Despair: Power and Resistance in the Tobacco Wars* (Lexington: University Press of Kentucky, 1993), 6-20.

10. Crandall A. Shifflett, *Patronage and Poverty in the Tobacco South: Louisa County, Virginia, 1860-1900* (Knoxville: University of Tennessee Press, 1982), 18; see also Evan Bennett, "Of the Quest for the Golden Leaf: Black Farmers and Bright Tobacco in the Piedmont South," in Debra A. Reid and Evan Bennett, eds., *Beyond Forty Acres and Mule: African American Landowning Families since Reconstruction* (Gainesville: University Press of Florida, 2012), 179-204.

11. W.E.B. Du Bois, "The Negroes of Farmville, Virginia: A Social Study," *Bulletin of the Department of Labor* 14 (Jan. 1898): 4, 30.

12. Evan Bennett, *When Tobacco Was King: Families, Farm Labor, and Federal Policy in the Piedmont* (Gainesville: University Press of Florida, 2014), 9-18. Steven Stoll describes households as "co-owners" of male wages and crop revenue. Stoll also defines households as "any group of related people who live together, pool their resources, and eat from the same pot. Life under the roof and around the table is a cooperative venture and a struggle for power that has as its singular goal the survival of its members. This logic of survival leads agrarian households to self-exploit, meaning that they invest any and all labor necessary to feed and reproduce themselves, regardless of whether or not the monetary value of their crops or animals justifies the expenditure. In other words, the 'product' of the peasant household is the peasant household." Steven Stoll, "The Captured Garden: The Political Ecology of Subsistence under Capitalism," *International Labor and Working Class History* 85 (Spring 2014): 77. On the often overlooked role of women in world systems and commodity chain analysis, see Wilma A. Dunaway, "The Double Register of History: Situating the Forgotten Woman and Her Household in Capitalist Commodity Chains," *Journal of World Systems Research* 7, no. 1 (Spring 2001): 2-29.

13. "Advice about Tobacco Raising," *PF*, Dec. 9, 1902.

14. My use of "tobacco frontier" builds on the concept of commodity frontiers common to histories of capitalism. As Raj Patel and Jason Moore have argued, frontiers are "the encounter zones between capital and all kinds of nature," sites that "extended the zone of appropriation" and drew the surpluses of nature and labor into the global

economy. Raj Patel and Jason W. Moore, *A History of the World in Seven Cheap Things: A Guide to Capitalism, Nature, and the Future of the Planet* (Berkeley: University of California Press, 2017), 18-19; Jason W. Moore, "The Capitolocene II: accumulation by appropriation and the centrality of unpaid work/energy," *The Journal of Peasant Studies* 42, no. 2 (2017): 13.

15. Drew Swanson, *A Golden Weed: Tobacco and Environment in the Piedmont South* (New Haven: Yale University Press, 2014), 222. See also Roger Biles, "Tobacco Towns: Urban Growth and Economic Development in Eastern North Carolina," *The North Carolina Historical Review* 84, no. 2 (Apr. 2007): 156-190.

16. Swanson, *A Golden Weed*, 221. On the postbellum emergence of South Carolina tobacco culture, see Eldred E. Prince, Jr., *Long Green: The Rise and Fall of Tobacco in South Carolina* (Athens: University of Georgia Press, 2000), 46-77.

17. L.O. Howard, "The Principal Insects Affecting the Tobacco Plant," *Yearbook of the United States Department of Agriculture*. 1898. (Washington: GPO, 1899), 121-150. See also Swanson, *A Golden Weed*, 206-207.

18. Nannie Mae Tilley, *The Bright-Tobacco Industry, 1860-1929* (Chapel Hill: University of North Carolina Press, 1948), 39-40.

19. "The Bugs in the First District," *Western Tobacco Journal*, Apr. 26, 1880.

20. Tilley, *The Bright-Tobacco Industry*, 365.

21. Swanson, *A Golden Weed*, 207-208.

22. Price data drawn from Tilley, *The Bright-Tobacco Industry*, 353-357. Tilley herself recognized several problems with price data. For one, warehouses did not uniformly catalog or report annual prices, so data for much of the postbellum period is simply incomplete. Further, because speculators could purchase and resell tobacco on warehouse floors, the final prices reported by warehouses did not necessarily represent the prices paid to growers. The available price data is still valuable because it provides a rough illustration of growers' economic realities.

23. *Report of the Commissioner of Agriculture for the Year 1878* (Washington: GPO, 1879), 565.

24. On the postbellum decline of cotton prices, see Sven Beckert, *Empire of Cotton: A Global History* (New York: Vintage, 2015), 274-311; Gavin Wright, *Old South New South: Revolutions in the Southern Economy Since the Civil War* (New York: Basic Books, 1986), 55-57. Wright convincingly shows that aggregate tobacco demand increased as much as five percent annually through much of this period, which seems like it should have improved growers' fortunes. The conditions of the tobacco frontier made this unlikely, as production/supply skyrocketed along with indebtedness.

25. *Report of the Commissioner of Agriculture for the Year 1878*, 567.

26. "For Tobacco Inspectors," *PF*, Nov. 23, 1897.

27. "Raising Tobacco," *PF*, Jun. 18, 1889.

28. "Tobacco Growers Must Unite," *PF*, Jan. 27, 1901.

29. "Our Farmers' Clubs," *PF*, Jan. 19, 1887.

30. Petty, *Standing Their Ground*, 75-97.

31. Jeffrey Kerr-Ritchie, *Freedpeople in the Tobacco South: Virginia, 1860-1900* (Chapel Hill: University of North Carolina Press, 1999), 154.

32. On "open" versus "closed" system agriculture, see Edward Melillo, "The First Green Revolution: Debt Peonage and the Making of the Nitrogen Fertilizer Trade, 1840-1930," *American Historical Review* 117, no. 4 (Oct. 2012): 1031.

33. "A Plain Talk about Little Things," *PF*, Dec. 22, 1903.

34. Quoted in Petty, *Standing Their Ground*, 25.

35. In this sense tobacco capitalists were similar to other advocates of subsistence gardens, from British aristocrats to Appalachian mining companies. As Stoll has argued, landlords and their industrial successors "realized they could ensure adequate nutrition for their workers and reduce the sums they paid in wages by shifting the burden of survival onto laboring households." Stoll, "The Captured Garden," 76.

36. Sharon Ann Holt, *Making Freedom Pay: North Carolina Freedpeople, Working for Themselves* (Athens: University of Georgia Press, 2000), 14.

37. The historiography of postbellum stock laws is extensive. I rely on Petty, *Standing Their Ground*, 55-74, and R. Ben Brown, "Free Men and Free Pigs: Closing the Southern Range and the American Property Tradition," *Radical History Review* 108 (Fall 2010): 117-137. On related laws governing trespassing and timber cutting, see Emma Teitelman, "The Properties of Capitalism: Industrial Enclosures in the South and the West after the American Civil War," *The Journal of American History* (Mar. 2020): 888.

38. For example, the elite grower, seed salesman, and fertilizer promoter Robert Ragland targeted warehouses for poor returns. "Go into these modern tobacco marts," he wrote in 1889, "and see the number of warehousemen, weighers, auctioneers, clerks, canvassers, laborers and retainers every one of whom are paid far more for handling planters' tobacco than those who raise it!" Tilley, *Bright-Tobacco Industry*, 405.

39. Peruvian guano, sodium nitrate, and other amendments provided farmers with highly concentrated and inexpensive sources of nitrogen. Yet tobacco—particularly the light, combustible variety known as "bright leaf" that became so common in the southeast after the Civil War—grew well in nitrogen-depleted soils. In tobacco country, therefore, manufacturers marketed guanos and other fertilizers as low in nitrogen and high in phosphorous, which lent to tobacco a desirable burning quality. On the political economy of nitrogen-fixing agricultural inputs in the nineteenth and early-twentieth centuries, see Melillo, "The First Green Revolution." On the high phosphorous content of Bahamian guano and the mining of South Carolina phosphorous, see Richard Wines, *Fertilizer in America: From Waste Recycling to Resource Exploitation* (Philadelphia: Temple University Press, 1985), 105-106 and 112-124. On German potash as a component of tobacco fertilizer, see John Ott, *How Shall the Quality of Virginia Shipping Tobacco Be Improved?* (Richmond: Southern Fertilizing Company, 1874). On the importance of phosphorous in tobacco culture, see Swanson, *A Golden Weed*, 202. For more on the imperial significance of the antebellum guano trade, see Christina Duffy Burnett, "The Edges of Empire and the Limits of Sovereignty: American Guano Islands," *American Quarterly* 57, no. 3 (2005): 779-803.

40. Summary Description. Branch & Company, Richmond, Va. Records, 1837-1976. Virginia Historical Society.

41. Peter J. Rachleff, *Black Labor in the South: Richmond, Virginia, 1865-1890* (Philadelphia: Temple University Press, 1984), 4.

42. Tilley, *The Bright Tobacco Industry*, 157-159.

43. This passage comes from a Southern Fertilizing Company pamphlet announcing Allison & Addison's acquisition of SFC and its famous "Anchor Brand." Six years after this acquisition, Allison & Addison would be absorbed by the fertilizer trust, the Virginia-Carolina Chemical Company. Southern Fertilizing Company and Allison & Addison, *The Southern Fertilizing Co's Anchor Brand Fertilizer for Tobacco* (Richmond: Allison & Addison, 1889).

44. Ott, *How Shall the Quality of Virginia Shipping Tobacco Be Improved?*, 2.

45. Hahn, *Making Tobacco Bright*, 142.

46. Ott's analyses of global markets appeared in various tobacco trade journals and agricultural periodicals. "Crop Speculations," *TL*, Jan. 13, 1875.

47. Kerr-Ritchie, *Freedpeople in the Tobacco South*, 153.

48. Kerr-Ritchie, 150-155.

49. Raleigh Oil Mill and Fertilizer Company, "R.S.G. The Great Cotton, Tobacco, and Grain Fertilizer." Advertisement. *PF*, May 28, 1889.

50. Allison & Addison, "Allison & Addison's 'Star Brand' Special Tobacco Manure." Advertisement. *PF*, March 26, 1889.

51. S.S. Baker to Thomas Branch & Co., 24 August 1875; Box 138, Folder "Cat Island Guano Co. Letters of Recommendation," Branch & Company Records, Virginia Historical Society.

52. Swanson, *A Golden Weed*, 219-220.

53. Ariel Ron, "Farmers, Capitalism, and Government in the Late Nineteenth Century," *The Journal of the Gilded Age and Progressive Era* 15 (2016), 295-296. As Kristin Hoganson has argued, its champions also associated scientific agriculture with racial hierarchies. John Ott's conviction that freedpeople produced poor tobacco reflected this association. Kristin Hoganson, *The Heartland: An American History* (New York: Penguin Press, 2019), 173-176.

54. Ott, *Tobacco in Virginia and North Carolina*, 11-18.

55. David Richardson, *Allison & Addison's Agricultural Annual for 1878* (Richmond: Allison & Addison, 1878).

56. Robert L. Ragland, *Tobacco, from the Seed to the Salesroom* (Richmond: Wm. Ellis Jones, Steam Book & Job Printer, 1880), 2.

57. "More about Tobacco," *PF*, Sep. 22, 1887. In addition to his promotion of fertilizer, Ragland was a noted plant breeder. He claimed to have developed 29 varieties of bright tobacco as well as stands of dark, burley, and cigar leaf. Swanson, *A Golden Weed*, 220.

58. John Ott, *To the trade: depot of staple fertilizing materials* (Richmond: Southern Fertilizing Company, 1874).

59. Robert L. Ragland, *Cultivation and curing of fine yellow and shipping tobacco* (Richmond: Commissioner of Agriculture of Virginia, 1878).

60. Albert R. Ledoux, *Annual Report of the North Carolina Agricultural Experiment Station for 1879* (Raleigh: The Observer, State Printer, and Binder, 1879), 22.

61. Ledoux, *Annual Report*, 10.

62. North Carolina's fertilizer approval regulation was slightly different from the Bureau of Internal Revenue's entry regulations for tobacco manufacturers. In the latter

case, businesses entered the market upon payment of taxes and production of records, but the quality and effectiveness of their products had no bearing upon their entry. Fertilizer manufacturers entering North Carolina's market faced similar expectations, but they also submitted their products for analysis and required the state's approval of quality to sell their goods. As such, this market was more similar to twentieth-century pharmaceutical sales under the U.S. Food and Drug Administration. For that case, and a detailed analysis of the market-creating power of approval regulation, see Daniel Carpenter, "Confidence Games: How Does Regulation Constitute Markets?" in Edward J. Balleisen and David A. Moss, *Government and Markets: Toward a New Theory of Regulation* (New York: Cambridge University Press, 2010), 164-190.

63. Richard Franklin Bensel, *The Political Economy of American Industrialization, 1877-1900* (New York: Cambridge University Press, 2000), 37.

64. Tilley, *The Bright-Tobacco Industry*, 160-162; "Plain Talks on Fertilizers," *The Southern Planter and Farmer*, Apr. 1908.

65. Tilley, *The Bright-Tobacco Industry*, 160n27, 637.

66. "Money in Tobacco," *PF and Cotton Plant*, Feb. 21, 1905.

67. "Plain Talks on Fertilizers," *The Southern Planter and Farmer*, Apr. 1908.

68. Charles Dudley Warner, "The Industrial South," *Harper's Weekly*, Jan. 29, 1887.

69. Hahn, *Making Tobacco Bright*, 110-113. See also Biles, "Tobacco Towns," 164.

70. Tobacco auctions originated earlier in the nineteenth century but did not extend beyond a small number of Virginia communities until the 1870s. Tilly, *Bright-Tobacco Industry*, 201-202.

71. Warehouses charged growers for a variety of services, including weighing tobacco, placing it on the warehouse floor, and brokering sales. For one grower's analysis of this process, see "Vance County Notes," *PF*, Nov. 20, 1888.

72. Tilley, *Bright-Tobacco Industry*, 227.

73. Tilley, *Bright-Tobacco Industry*, 146-147.

74. Tilley, *Bright-Tobacco Industry*, 372-373.

75. In a remarkably frank illustration of the iniquitous relationship between growers and warehouse-town capitalists, John Ott argued that farmers' cultivation of tobacco was "tributary" to the merchants who furnished "a market at home for the products of all kinds raised by the farmer." Jeffrey Kerr-Ritchie built on Ott's claim to argue, "tributary was particularly precise because of the increased power of tobacco merchants over tobacco planter planters." Kerr-Ritchie, *Freedpeople in the Tobacco South*, 188.

76. For a similar process in French viticulture, see Marion Fourcade, "The Vile and the Noble: On the Relation between Natural and Social Classifications in the French Wine World," *The Sociological Quarterly* 53 (2012): 524-545.

77. Tilley, *The Bright-Tobacco Industry*, 633-638.

78. Kerr-Ritchie, *Freedpeople in the Tobacco South*, 148.

79. Scott Reynolds Nelson, *Iron Confederacies: Southern Railways, Klan Violence, and Reconstruction* (Chapel Hill: University of North Carolina Press, 1999), 163-178.

80. Tilley, *The Bright-Tobacco Industry*, 145.

81. Melillo, "The First Green Revolution," 1044; Tilley, *The Bright-Tobacco Industry*, 167.

82. Swanson, *A Golden Weed*, 204.

83. Bennett, "Of the Quest of the Golden Leaf," 190.

84. This was the reality of agrarian debt throughout the postbellum South, a point Gavin Wright has made specifically regarding sharecropper-planter relations. Gavin Wright, "The Strange Career of the New Southern Economic History," *Reviews in American History* 10, 4 (Dec. 1982): 174.

85. David Richardson, *Allison & Addison's Hand Book of the Garden, Seed Catalogue, and Almanac for 1874* (Richmond: Allison & Addison, 1874).

86. On the legal origins of credit and debt relations in postbellum Southern agriculture, see Harold D. Woodman, *New South—New Law: The Legal Foundations of Credit and Labor Relations in the Postbellum Agricultural South* (Baton Rouge: Louisiana State University, 1995). On North Carolina's crop lien law, the Landlord Tenant Act of 1875, see Petty, *Standing Their Ground*, 42. On Virginia's crop lien system, see Kerr-Ritchie, *Freedpeople in the Tobacco South*, 158-180.

87. Hahn, *Making Tobacco Bright*, 17-70. While antebellum tobacco culture was relatively flexible compared with the late nineteenth century, it was still capitalist and industrial. As Hahn carefully details, planters sought to achieve specific qualities and targeted particular markets when they sold their tobacco. And as Adrienne Monteith Petty has argued, North Carolina's planters and landless white farmers depended on extensive trade for their most basic staples, such as meat and corn. Under the new political economy of tobacco, however, the conditions of grower dependency shifted and the relative flexibility of the earlier period eroded. Further, under the influence of fertilizer manufacturers and warehouses, the standards of "quality" became more precise and uniform. Petty, *Standing Their Ground*, 24.

88. Kerr-Ritchie, *Freedpeople in the Tobacco South*, 142.

89. Kerr-Ritchie, *Freedpeople in the Tobacco South*, 100. See 93-123 for an analysis of emancipation's effect on tobacco culture during Reconstruction.

90. Holt, *Making Freedom Pay*, 1-24.

91. Tilley, *The Bright-Tobacco Industry*, 406.

92. Charles Postel, *The Populist Vision* (New York: Oxford University Press, 2007), 50-54. Growers' allies often included local elites, such as doctors, lawyers, and even furnishing merchants, leaf dealers, and manufacturers, a reality that suggests distinctions between tobacco's economic sectors, and the self-interest of those sectors, were not always clear.

93. The membership and leadership of these groups often overlapped. Tilley, *The Bright-Tobacco Industry*, 424. On the PF under Clarence Poe, see Elizabeth Herbin-Triant, "Southern Segregation South Africa-Style: Maurice Evans, Clarence Poe, and the Ideology of Rural Segregation," *Journal of Agricultural History* 87, no. 2 (Spring 2013), 170-193.

94. "President Grimes to the Tobacco Growers," PF, Feb. 20, 1900.

95. "Proceedings of the Convention of Tobacco Farmers," PF, Dec. 25, 1888.

96. Holt, *Making Freedom Pay*, 6. As Nan Enstad puts it, tobacco manufacturers staffed their factories by "raiding the local playground." Nan Enstad, *Cigarettes, Inc: An Intimate History of Corporate Imperialism* (Chicago: University of Chicago Press, 2018), 63.

97. Tilley, *Bright-Tobacco Industry*, 411; "Proceedings of the Convention of Tobacco Farmers," PF, Dec. 25, 1888.

98. No Title, *Durham Tobacco Plant*, Sep. 19, 1890.
99. "Vance County Notes," *PF*, Nov. 20, 1888.
100. See Campbell, *The Politics of Despair*; Hahn, *Making Tobacco Bright*, 147-155.
101. "Reduction of Tobacco Acreage as a Remedy for Low Prices," *PF*, Sep. 8, 1903.
102. John Ott, *Tobacco in Virginia and North Carolina: Some Observations in Connection with the Several Types of Tobacco Now Produced in These Two States* (Richmond: Southern Fertilizing Company, 1877), 3.
103. "President Grimes to the Tobacco Growers," *PF*, Feb. 20, 1900.
104. I am building on the work of several scholars here. Drew Swanson has argued that "'good' or 'bad' tobacco served as an indicator of a person's moral fiber," while Barbara Hahn has detailed how growers promoted "myths of varietals" that enabled them to market their products and create political associations. Regarding tobacco growers in the twenty-first century, Peter Benson has written of "the masculinity that over time has become embedded in tobacco farm management, the idea that this livelihood is the foundation of families that are icons of normalcy and part of an imagined mainstream, the material signs of being middle-class and the way that tobacco money permits access to things like new trucks and brick houses, and the values of heritage and tradition having to do with the longevity of family tobacco businesses." Swanson, *A Golden Weed*, 14; Hahn, *Making Tobacco Bright*, 130-139; Peter Benson, *Tobacco Capitalism: Growers, Migrant Workers, and the Changing Face of a Global Industry* (Princeton: Princeton University Press, 2012), 4. Pierre Bourdieu captured this process more generally: "Taste classifies," he wrote, "and it classifies the classifier." Pierre Bourdieu, *Distinction: A Social Critique of the Judgment of Taste* (Cambridge: Harvard University Press, 1984), 6.
105. "The Policy," *PF*, May 17, 1892.
106. "Meeting of Tobacco Growers," *PF*, Dec. 12, 1889.
107. "Advice about Tobacco Raising," *PF*, Dec. 9, 1902.
108. "The Policy," *PF*, May 17, 1892.

Chapter 5. The Health of the State: The USDA, Agricultural Hegemony, and the Federal Improvement of Tobacco Quality, 1890-1933.

1. Box 1, Crop-Experiment Reports, 1907-1920; Records of the Division of Tobacco and Plant Nutrition Investigations; Records of the Bureau of Plant Industry, Soils, and Agricultural Engineering, RG 54; National Archives Building, College Park, MD.
2. Paul Kramer, "Embedding Capital: Political-Economic History, the United States, and the World," *The Journal of the Gilded Age and Progressive Era* 15 (2016): 331-362. Kramer defines the United States as a "commodifying empire" because "the intrusion of capital's domain into social life and the biosphere, and the extent to which the world's resources served American's geopolitical interests and economic well-being, served as fundamental metrics of American power, global order, and the advancement of historical time itself." As it did domestically, the commodifying empire "required making unfamiliar social spaces legible, re-engineering production processes and labor relations, redrawing lines between public and private, sacred and profane, and imposing new technological and informational formats that locked in patterns of material dependence and expert authority, issuing intellectual monopolies on 'best practices.'"

3. Genetically speaking, all tobacco is the same. Nonetheless, because of its diverse forms of manufacture and consumption, it is reasonable to speak of, say, wrapper leaf for cigars and bright filler leaf for cigarettes as related but not identical plants. On tobacco genetics, see Barbara Hahn, *Making Tobacco Bright: Creating an American Commodity, 1617-1937* (Baltimore: Johns Hopkins University Press, 2011), 183-190.

4. *Report of the Commissioner of Agriculture for the Year 1877* (Washington: GPO, 1877), 21.

5. *Report of the Commissioner of Agriculture for the Year 1877*, 21.

6. Alan I. Marcus, *Agricultural Science and the Quest for Legitimacy: Farmers, Agricultural Colleges, and Experiment Stations, 1870-1890* (Ames: Iowa State University Press, 1985), 7-26.

7. Daniel Carpenter, *The Forging of Bureaucratic Autonomy: Reputations, Networks, and Policy Innovation in Executive Agencies, 1862-1928* (Princeton: Princeton University Press, 2001), 182-183.

8. Ariel Ron, "Henry Carey's Rural Roots: 'Scientific Agriculture,' and Economic Development in the Antebellum North," *Journal of the History of Economic Thought* 37, 2 (Jun. 2015): 263-275. On the Republican Party's continental ambitions, see Steven Hahn, "Slave Emancipation, Indian Peoples, and the Projects of a New American State," *Journal of the Civil War Era* 3, no. 3 (Sep. 2013): 307-330.

9. *Report of the Commissioner of Agriculture for the Year 1877*, 5.

10. *Report of the Commissioner of Agriculture for the Years 1881 and 1882* (Washington: GPO, 1882), 678. The collection, study, and distribution of "economic plants" were not new activities for the federal government. Throughout the nineteenth century, various individuals and agencies, including diplomats and the US Patent Office, worked to introduce new crops to American agriculture. See Nelson Klose, *America's Crop Heritage: The History of Foreign Plant Introduction by the Federal Government* (Ames: Iowa State College Press, 1950), 32-50; on the unintended consequences of crop introduction, including the spread of invasive pests, see Anne Effland, "International Programs of the USDA: Cross-Purposes or a Delicate Balance," *Agricultural History* 87 (Summer 2013): 349-358.

11. *Report of the Commissioner of Agriculture for the Year 1879* (Washington: GPO, 1880), 26-27.

12. *Report of the Commissioner of Agriculture for the Year 1883* (Washington: GPO, 1883), 5.

13. *Annual Report of the Commissioner of Agriculture for the Year 1880*, 22. For a full accounting of early commissioners' crop introduction interests, see Klose, *America's Crop Heritage*, 54-94.

14. Marcus, *Agricultural Science and the Quest for Legitimacy*, 13-18.

15. Jamie L. Pietruska, *Looking Forward: Prediction and Uncertainty in Modern America* (Chicago: The University of Chicago Press, 2017), 34-35.

16. *Report of the Commissioner of Agriculture for the Year 1873* (Washington: GPO, 1874), 10-11

17. Pietruska, *Looking Forward*, 37.

18. *Report of the Commissioner of Agriculture for the Year 1874* (Washington: GPO, 1875), 42.

19. Pietruska, *Looking Forward*, 27-70; see also Jonathan Levy, *Freaks of Fortune: The Emerging World of Capitalism and Risk in America* (Cambridge: Harvard University Press, 2012), 231-263.

20. "First Annual Report," *Tobacco Leaf* [*TL*], Jan. 5, 1876.

21. *Report of the Commissioner of Agriculture for the Year 1867* (Washington: GPO, 1868), 179-182.

22. Marcus, *Agricultural Science and the Quest for Legitimacy*, 16.

23. Marcus, *Agricultural Science and the Quest for Legitimacy*, 27-58.

24. On the creation and operations of the BAI, see Alan L. Olmstead and Paul W. Rhode, *Arresting Contagion: Science, Policy, and Conflicts over Animal Disease Control* (Cambridge: Harvard University Press, 2015), 42-93.

25. On the decades-long struggle preceding the Hatch Act, see Marcus, *Agricultural Science and the Quest for Legitimacy*.

26. Carpenter, *The Forging of Bureaucratic Autonomy*, 185.

27. Carpenter, *The Forging of Bureaucratic Autonomy*, 208-209. See also Klose, *America's Crop Heritage*, 109-119.

28. Ariel Ron, "Farmers, Capitalism, and Government in the Late Nineteenth Century," *The Journal of the Gilded Age and Progressive Era* 15 (2016): 294-309.

29. *Report of the Commissioner of Agriculture for the Year 1873*, 5.

30. *Report of the Commissioner of Agriculture for the Year 1878* (Washington: GPO, 1879), 566.

31. *Report of the Commissioner of Agriculture for the Year 1878*, 567.

32. *Report of the Commissioner of Agriculture. 1888.* (Washington: GPO, 1889), 647.

33. "South Carolina as a Tobacco-Growing State—Report of an Expert," *TL*, Mar. 5, 1887.

34. *Report of the Commissioner of Agriculture. 1888*, 659-660.

35. Milton Whitney, *Tobacco Soils of the United States: A Preliminary Report Upon the Soils of the Principal Tobacco Districts* (Washington: GPO, 1898), 5.

36. Appleby Cigar Machine Co., "Genuine Havana Flavoring," Advertisement. *TL*, Aug. 26, 1874.

37. "The Vuelta Abajo New Tobacco Flavoring," *TL*, Jan. 25, 1879.

38. *Annual Reports of the Department of Agricultural for the Fiscal Year Ended June 30, 1897* (Washington: GPO, 1897), xxviii; *Annual Reports of the Department of Agriculture for the Fiscal Year Ended June 30, 1902* (Washington: GPO, 1902), XLII

39. "American Cotton and Tobacco Cultivators Wanted in the Island of Corsica," *TL*, Nov. 11, 1874; "Tobacco Industries of Italy," *TL*, May 7, 1881; "Tobacco Culture in France," *TL*, Jul. 14, 1883.

40. American tobacco journals closely followed experiments in India. For representative examples, see "Tobacco in India," *TL*, Oct. 21, 1874; "Tobacco in India," *TL*, Sep. 15, 1875; "Tobacco Cultivation in India," *TL*, Oct. 11, 1879; "Tobacco Raising in India," *Western Tobacco Journal* [*WTJ*], Jun. 7, 1880; "Tobacco Culture in India," *TL*, Jul. 26, 1884; "Tobacco in Madras," *United States Tobacco Journal*, Nov. 23, 1889.

41. "Tobacco Culture in British Burma," *TL*, Jun. 23, 1883.

42. "Tobacco Growing in Sumatra," *WTJ*, May 17, 1880.

43. Klose, *America's Crop Heritage*, 130; Jeffrey R. Kerr-Ritchie, *Freedpeople in the Tobacco South: Virginia, 1860-1900* (Chapel Hill: University of North Carolina Press, 1999), 130.

44. Archibald D. Shamel, "The Improvement of Tobacco by Breeding and Selection," *Yearbook of the United States Department of Agriculture. 1904.* (Washington: GPO, 1905), 435.

45. See Deborah Fitzgerald, *Every Farm a Factory: The Industrial Ideal in American Agriculture* (New Haven: Yale University Press, 2003).

46. *Report of the Secretary of Agriculture* (Washington: GPO, 1896), 37; *Yearbook of the United States Department of Agriculture. 1897.* (Washington: GPO, 1898), 215.

47. U.S. Department of Agriculture. *Report No. 63: The Work of the Agricultural Experiment Stations on Tobacco.* (Washington: GPO, 1900), 5, 42-47.

48. Whitney, *Tobacco Soils of the United States*, 8.

49. Nannie Mae Tilley, *The Bright-Tobacco Industry, 1860-1929* (Chapel Hill: University of North Carolina Press, 1948), 590.

50. Drew Swanson, *A Golden Weed: Tobacco and Environment in the Piedmont South* (New Haven: Yale University Press, 2014), 221.

51. *Yearbook of the United States Department of Agriculture. 1894.* (Washington: GPO, 1895), 143-144.

52. Donald Worster, *Rivers of Empire: Water, Aridity, and the Growth of the American West* (New York: Oxford University Press, 1992), 5; *Annual Reports of the Department of Agriculture for the Fiscal Year Ended June 30, 1901* (Washington: GPO, 1901), XXXIX.

53. James C. Scott, *The Art of Not Being Governed: An Anarchist History of Upland Southeast Asia* (New Haven: Yale University Press, 2009), 41. This had been a concern of state governments since at least the 1870s, and several had begun working with land-grant universities on soils research in that decade. On the administrative history of the Bureau of Soils, see Douglas Helms, Anne B.W. Effland, and Patricia J. Durana, eds., *Profiles in the History of the U.S. Soil Survey* (Ames: Iowa State Press, 2002), 1-18. For a historical and scientific analysis of soil in agriculture history, see Douglas Helms, "Soil and Southern History," *Agricultural History* 74, 4 (Autumn, 2000), 723-758.

54. Note that this work preceded the federal experiment station network established under the Hatch Act of 1887. Connecticut and North Carolina were pioneering experiment station states and both, coincidentally, studied tobacco culture. *Annual Report of the North Carolina Agricultural Experiment Station, for 1886* (Raleigh: P.M. Hale, 1887), 10-11; The North Carolina Agricultural Experiment Station, *Report of the Director for the Year Ending June 30, 1899* (Raleigh: N.P., 1899), xviii.

55. Clarence W. Dorsey and J.A. Bonsteel, "Soil Survey in the Connecticut Valley," in Milton Whitney, ed., *Field Operations of the Division of Soils, 1899.* (Washington: GPO, 1900), 125; on Whitney's early work in Virginia, see Drew Swanson, *A Golden Weed: Tobacco and Environment in the Piedmont South* (New Haven: Yale University Press, 2014), 236.

56. Swanson, *A Golden Weed*, 236; *Annual Reports of the Department of Agriculture. Fiscal Year Ended June 30, 1900* (Washington: GPO, 1900), XLVIII.

57. *Annual Reports of the Department of Agriculture. Fiscal Year Ended June 30, 1898* (Washington: GPO, 1898), XLIII

58. *Annual Reports of the Department of Agriculture for the Fiscal Year Ended June 30, 1901*, XXXIX.
59. Carpenter, *Forging of Bureaucratic Autonomy*, 208.
60. *Report of the Secretary of Agriculture*, 15.
61. Carpenter, *Forging of Bureaucratic Autonomy*, 208.
62. Carpenter, *Forging of Bureaucratic Autonomy*, 218.
63. *Annual Reports of the Department of Agriculture. Fiscal Year Ended June 30, 1898*, 140.
64. *Annual Reports of the Department of Agriculture. Fiscal Year Ended June 30, 1900*, XLIII.
65. Archibald D. Shamel, "The Improvement of Tobacco by Breeding and Selection," *Yearbook of the United States Department of Agriculture. 1904.* (Washington: GPO, 1905), 435. While plant breeding had existed in various forms for thousands of years, the USDA's plant breeding efforts were part of a late-nineteenth century global trend by which imperial states sought to establish "economic botany" through systematic hybridization. See Noel Kingsbury, *Hybrid: The History and Science of Plant Breeding* (Chicago: The University of Chicago Press, 2009), 97-138.
66. A.D. Shamel, "Report of Committee on Tobacco Breeding," undated; Folder 149E, Miscellaneous; Box 35, General Correspondence, 1901-26; Records of the Bureau of Plant Industry, Soils, and Agricultural Engineering, RG 54; National Archives Building, College Park, MD.
67. "Tobacco Soil Report," *Southern Tobacco Journal*, Feb. 7, 1898.
68. *Annual Reports of the Department of Agriculture. Fiscal Year Ended June 30, 1898*, 139.
69. George T. McNess and E.H. Mathewson, "Dark Fire-Cured Tobacco of Virginia and the Possibilities for Its Improvement," *Yearbook of the United States Department of Agriculture. 1905.* (Washington: GPO, 1905), 220.
70. Scott, *The Art of Not Being Governed*, 40-64.
71. *Annual Reports of the Department of Agriculture for the Fiscal Year Ended June 30, 1906* (Washington: GPO, 1907), 12. In this sense, the USDA's tobacco program represented what Eli Cook has referred to as the "investmentality" of American public life in the Gilded Age and Progressive Era, by which government officials and business leaders analyzed political communities with "output-maximizing equations of economic growth." Eli Cook, *The Pricing of Progress: Economic Indicators and the Capitalization of American Life* (Cambridge: Harvard University Press, 2017), 2.
72. *Annual Reports of the Department of Agriculture for the Fiscal Year Ended June 30, 1901*, XLII.
73. *Annual Reports of the Department of Agriculture. Fiscal Year Ended June 30, 1900*, 78.
74. Andrew Wender Cohen, "Smuggling, Globalization, and America's Outward State, 1870-1909," *The Journal of American History* 97, no. 2 (Sept. 2010): 386.
75. "Statement of Marcus L. Floyd, of Tariffville, Conn.," *Tariff Hearings Before the Committee on Ways and Means of the House of Representatives. Sixtieth Congress 1908-1909. Vol. IV, Schedule F—Tobacco, and Manufactures of.* (Washington: GPO, 1909): 3552, 3558.
76. James F. O'Gorman, *A Connecticut Valley Vernacular: The Vanishing Landscape and Architecture of the New England Tobacco Fields* (Philadelphia: University of Pennsylvania Press, 2002), 22-23.

77. On the origins of Sumatran tobacco, see Jan Breman, *Taming the Coolie Beast: Plantation Society and the Colonial Order in Southeast Asia* (Delhi: Oxford University Press, 1989), 13-74.

78. Breman, *Taming the Coolie Beast*, 57-65.

79. "Statement of Marcus L. Floyd, of Tariffville, Conn.," 3551.

80. *Annual Reports of the Department of Agriculture for the Fiscal Year Ended June 30, 1902*. (Washington: GPO, 1902), LXX.

81. *Annual Reports of the Department of Agriculture 1902*, LXX-LXXIII.

82. *Annual Reports of the Department of Agriculture for the Fiscal Year Ended June 30, 1903* (Washington: GPO, 1903), 220.

83. *Annual Reports of the Department of Agriculture 1902*, LXXIII.

84. O'Gorman, *A Connecticut Valley Vernacular*, 23.

85. "Lancaster Trade Lively," *Tobacco Leaf*, May 25, 1905, 38.

86. *Annual Reports of the Department of Agriculture 1902*, LXXVI.

87. *Annual Reports of the Department of Agriculture 1903*, 220; "Tobacco Experts to Visit North Carolina," *Progressive Farmer (PF)*, Mar. 17, 1903.

88. "More Reports on North Carolina Farming," *PF and Cotton Plant*, May 30, 1905.

89. Swanson, *A Golden Weed*, 237.

90. "The Great Need of Southern Lands," *PF*, Dec. 20, 1898.

91. Seaman A. Knapp, "Causes of Southern Rural Conditions and the Small Farm as an Important Remedy," *Yearbook of the United States Department of Agriculture. 1908.* (Washington: GPO, 1909), 313-315.

92. *Annual Reports of the Department of Agriculture for the Year Ended June 30, 1907* (Washington: GPO, 1908), 272.

93. *Annual Reports of the Department of Agriculture for the Year Ended June 30, 1904* (Washington: GPO, 1904), XXXVI.

94. F.L. Stevens, "The History of the Tobacco Wilt in Granville County, North Carolina," in A.C. True, et al, eds., *Proceedings of the Seventeenth Annual Convention of the Association of American Agricultural Colleges and Experiment Stations Held at Washington, D.C., November 17-19, 1903.* (Washington: GPO, 1904); "More about the Tobacco Wilt," *PF*, Aug. 18, 1903; Tilley, *The Bright-Tobacco Industry*, 187.

95. Carpenter, *The Forging of Bureaucratic Autonomy*, 227-238; Natalie Ring, *The Problem South: Region, Empire, and the New Liberal State, 1880-1930* (Athens: The University of Georgia Press, 2012), 109-134.

96. *Annual Reports of the Department of Agriculture for the Year Ended June 30, 1910* (Washington: GPO, 1911), 316.

97. Willet M. Hays to Eugene G. Moss, Apr. 1, 1910; Folder 259, Eugene G. Moss; Box 58, General Correspondence, 1901-26; Records of the Bureau of Plant Industry, Soils, and Agricultural Engineering, RG 54; National Archives Building, College Park, MD.

98. E.G. Moss to W.W. Garner, Dec. 11, 1911; Folder 259B, Eugene G. Moss; Box 57; General Correspondence, 1901-26; Records of the Bureau of Plant Industry, Soils, and Agricultural Engineering, RG 54; National Archives Building, College Park, MD.

99. W.W. Garner to E.G. Moss, Nov. 25, 1919; Folder 259H, E.G. Moss, 1917-1919; General Correspondence, 1901-26; Records of the Bureau of Plant Industry, Soils, and Agricultural Engineering, RG 54; National Archives Building, College Park, MD.

100. W.W. Garner to E.G. Moss, Nov. 25, 1919.

101. Eugene G. Moss to W.W. Garner, Oct. 10, 1910; Folder 259A, Eugene G. Moss; Box 57, General Correspondence, 1901-26; Records of the Bureau of Plant Industry, Soils, and Agricultural Engineering, RG 54; National Archives Building, College Park, MD.

102. E.H. Mathewson, "Methods of Seed Saving and Selection as Factors in the Improvement of Tobacco," *The Bulletin of the North Carolina Department of Agriculture* (Oct., 1907): 49.

103. Eugene G. Moss to W.W. Garner, Jun. 21, 1912; Folder 259C, Eugene G. Moss; Box 56, General Correspondence, 1901-26; Records of the Bureau of Plant Industry, Soils, and Agricultural Engineering, RG 54; National Archives Building, College Park, MD.

104. Associate Chief, Bureau of Plant Industry, to David Houston Franklin, Secretary of Agriculture, October 16, 1918; Folder 149a-b-c-d misc.; Box 35; General Correspondence, 1901-26; Records of the Bureau of Plant Industry, Soils, and Agricultural Engineering, RG 54; National Archives Building, College Park, MD.

105. E.G. Moss, "*Progressive Farmer*—1922," undated; Folder 13, E.G. Moss, 1920-1925; Series 3, Manuscripts and News Releases; Oxford Tobacco Research Station Records; North Carolina State University Special Collections Research Center. The reference to Moss's cooperative work comes from his correspondence with W.W. Garner, his supervisor at OTI. See Folder 259, E.G. Moss; Box 58, General Correspondence, 1901-26; Records of the Bureau of Plant Industry, Soils, and Agricultural Engineering, RG 54; National Archives Building, College Park, MD. On the cooperative era in the tobacco South, see Sarah Milov, *The Cigarette: A Political History* (Cambridge: Harvard University Press, 2019), 36-45.

106. E.G. Moss to W.W. Garner, Jun. 21, 1912 and W.W. Garner to E.G. Moss, Jul. 1, 1912; Folder 259C, Eugene G. Moss; Box 56, General Correspondence, 1901-26; Records of the Bureau of Plant Industry, Soils, and Agricultural Engineering, RG 54; National Archives Building, College Park, MD.

107. Edward L. Ayers, *The Promise of the New South: Life after Reconstruction*, 2nd ed. (New York: Oxford University Press, 2007), 301-304; for a broader treatment of Jim Crow in North Carolina, see Glenda Gilmore, *Gender and Jim Crow: Women and the Politics of White Supremacy in North Carolina, 1896-1920* (Chapel Hill: University of North Carolina Press, 1996).

108. Adrienne Monteith Petty, *Standing Their Ground: Small Farmers in North Carolina Since the Civil War* (New York: Oxford University Press, 2013), 61.

109. Petty, *Standing Their Ground*, 64.

110. Petty, *Standing Their Ground*, 62-63.

111. For example, see Box 1, Crop Experiment Reports, 1907-20; Records of the Bureau of Plant Industry, Soils, and Agricultural Engineering, RG 54; National Archives Building, College Park, MD.

112. Swanson, *A Golden Weed*, 220.

113. B.G. Anderson, Tobacco Experiment Report, S.L. Ferguson Field, 1914; Box 1, Crop Experiment Reports, 1907-20; Records of the Bureau of Plant Industry, Soils, and Agricultural Engineering, RG 54; National Archives Building, College Park, MD.

114. E.G. Moss to W.W. Garner, Jul. 19, 1921; Folder 259, Eugene G. Moss; Box 58; E.G. Moss to James Johnson, Jun. 20, 1917; Folder 259H, E.G. Moss, 1917-1919; Box 58;

E.G. Moss to W.W. Garner, Jun. 2, 1913; Folder 259E, E.G. Moss; Box 57; W.W. Garner to E.G. Moss, Dec. 7, 1915; Folder 259F, E.G. Moss; Box 57; W.W. Garner to E.G. Moss, Jun. 26, 1919; Folder 259H, E.G. Moss, 1917-1919; Box 58; General Correspondence, 1901-26; Records of the Bureau of Plant Industry, Soils, and Agricultural Engineering, RG 54; National Archives Building, College Park, MD.

115. W.W. Garner to E.G. Moss, Dec. 9 1920; Folder 259, Eugene G. Moss; Box 58; General Correspondence, 1901-26; Records of the Bureau of Plant Industry, Soils, and Agricultural Engineering, RG 54; National Archives Building, College Park, MD.

116. Tilley, *The Bright-Tobacco Industry*, 396-448.

117. W.W. Green and R.P. Cocke, Fertilizer Tests Report, Virginia Agricultural Experiment Station, Dec. 22, 1909; Folder 1907-1908; Box 1, Crop-Experiment Reports, 1907-1920; Records of the Division of Tobacco and Plant Nutrition Investigations; Records of the Bureau of Plant Industry, Soils, and Agricultural Engineering, RG 54; National Archives Building, College Park, MD.

118. Allan M. Brandt, *The Cigarette Century: The Rise, Fall, and Deadly Persistence of the Product That Defined America* (New York: Basic Books, 2007), 23.

119. E.G. Moss to J.S. Cobb, Dec. 11, 1919; Folder 259H, E.G. Moss, 1917-1919; Box 58; General Correspondence, 1901-26; Records of the Bureau of Plant Industry, Soils, and Agricultural Engineering, RG 54; National Archives Building, College Park, MD.

120. Correspondence of W.W. Garner and Charles Dushkind, Jun., 1916; Folder 8, Correspondence re Mss; Box 5; General Correspondence, 1901-26; Records of the Bureau of Plant Industry, Soils, and Agricultural Engineering, RG 54; National Archives Building, College Park, MD.

121. E.G. Moss to W.W. Garner, Jul. 21, 1920; Folder 259, Eugene G. Moss; Box 58; E.H. Mathewson to E.G. Moss, Apr. 8, 1911; Folder 259A, Eugene G. Moss; Box 57; E.G. Moss to W.W. Garner, Sep. 25, 1920; Folder 259, Eugene G. Moss; Box 58; General Correspondence, 1901-26; Records of the Bureau of Plant Industry, Soils, and Agricultural Engineering, RG 54; National Archives Building, College Park, MD.

122. E.G. Moss to W.W. Garner, Sep. 25, 1920; Folder 259, Eugene G. Moss; General Correspondence, 1901-26; Records of the Bureau of Plant Industry, Soils, and Agricultural Engineering, RG 54; National Archives Building, College Park, MD.

123. Correspondence of E.G. Moss and F.A. Wolf, May, 1918; Folder 259H, E.G. Moss, 1917-1919; General Correspondence, 1901-26; Records of the Bureau of Plant Industry, Soils, and Agricultural Engineering, RG 54; National Archives Building, College Park, MD.

124. Correspondence of T.M. Carrington and E.H. Mathewson, 1909-1910; Folder 152 Tobacco Association of the U.S.; Box 35; General Correspondence, 1901-26; Records of the Bureau of Plant Industry, Soils, and Agricultural Engineering, RG 54; National Archives Building, College Park, MD.

125. David E. Hamilton, "Building the Associative State: The Department of Agriculture and American State-Building," *Agricultural History* 64, 2 (Spring 1990), 207-218; for a case study of the USDA's associationalism, see Brian Balogh, *The Associational State: American Governance in the Twentieth Century* (Philadelphia: University of Pennsylvania Press, 2015), 41-65.

126. E.G. Moss to W.W. Garner, Nov. 25, 1912; Folder 259D, Eugene G. Moss; Box 57; General Correspondence, 1901-26; Records of the Bureau of Plant Industry, Soils, and Agricultural Engineering, RG 54; National Archives Building, College Park, MD.

127. Correspondence of Walter D. Griffin and W.W. Garner, April 1914; Folder 88 Treasury Department; Box 26; General Correspondence, 1901-26; Records of the Bureau of Plant Industry, Soils, and Agricultural Engineering, RG 54; National Archives Building, College Park, MD.

128. E.G. Moss to W.W. Garner, Nov. 25, 1912; Folder 259D, Eugene G. Moss; Box 57; General Correspondence, 1901-26; Records of the Bureau of Plant Industry, Soils, and Agricultural Engineering, RG 54; National Archives Building, College Park, MD.

129. Daniel Carpenter has argued that Smith-Lever was not a new direction so much as a "statutory framing" of extension activity that had begun more than a decade earlier. Carpenter, *The Forging of Bureaucratic Autonomy*, 249. See also Elizabeth Sanders, *Roots of Reform: Farmers, Workers, and the American State, 1877-1917* (Chicago: University of Chicago Press, 1999), 333-335. For a powerful analysis of the biopolitical significance of the Extension Service and its associated 4-H programs, see Gabriel N. Rosenberg, *The 4-H Harvest: Sexuality and the State in Rural America* (Philadelphia: University of Pennsylvania Press, 2015).

130. On "bureaucratic pockets," see Carpenter, *The Forging of Bureaucratic Autonomy*, 248; Timothy Mitchell has identified historically and relationally constituted "internal distinctions" between state and non-state institutions (or, more specifically, the appearance of such distinctions), as the "distinctive technique of the modern political order." In clarifying OTI's legitimate jurisdictions, Garner and Moss were forging these distinctions, thereby constructing tobacco's political order. See Timothy Mitchell, "Society, Economy, and the State Effect," in Aradhana Sharma and Akhil Gupta, eds., *The Anthropology of the State: A Reader* (Malden, MA: Blackwell Publishing, 2006), 169-185.

131. On the Warehouse Act, see Tilley, *The Bright-Tobacco Industry*, 294-298. On buyers' collusion, see Milov, *The Cigarette*, 31.

132. Bourdieu, *Outline of a Theory of Practice*, 165.

133. Fitting with their historically furtiveness, manufacturers refused to stake a clear public position on the Warehouse Act. Although the quality principle and their tendency to collude gave them total control over growers, the American Tobacco Company claimed it approved of grading in 1929. Tilley, *The Bright-Tobacco Industry*, 294-298; see also Anthony J. Badger, *Prosperity Road: The New Deal, Tobacco, and North Carolina* (Chapel Hill: University of North Carolina Press, 1980), 19; Hahn, *Making Tobacco Bright*, 160-161.

134. E.G. Moss, "The Way to Make Money Growing Tobacco," *Tri-State Tobacco Grower*, Nov., 1923.

135. E.G. Moss to W.W. Garner, Mar. 21, 1921; Folder 259, Eugene G. Moss; Box 58; General Correspondence, 1901-26; Records of the Bureau of Plant Industry, Soils, and Agricultural Engineering, RG 54; National Archives Building, College Park, MD.

136. Pete Daniel, *Breaking the Land: The Transformation of Cotton, Tobacco, and Rice Cultures Since 1880* (Urbana: University of Illinois Press, 1985), 35.

137. Hahn, *Making Tobacco Bright*, 160.

138. United States Department of Agriculture, *Yearbook 1920* (Washington: GPO, 1921), 645.

139. Milov, *The Cigarette*, 29; Tilley, *The Bright-Tobacco Industry*, 450-451.

140. Moss's correspondence with Garner suggests the foundational role of Poe and B.W. Kilgore, the North Carolina Commissioner of Agriculture. E.G. Moss to W.W. Garner, October 7, 1920; Folder 259, Eugene G. Moss; Box 58, General Correspondence, 1901-26; Records of the Bureau of Plant Industry, Soils, and Agricultural Engineering, RG 54; National Archives Building, College Park, MD.

141. Tilley, *The Bright-Tobacco Industry*, 454. See also Milov, *The Cigarette*, 39-44.

142. Sarah Milov, "Little Tobacco: The Business and Bureaucracy of Tobacco Farming in North Carolina, 1920-1965," Ph.D. Diss., Princeton Univ., 2013, 61.

143. Tilly, *The Bright-Tobacco Industry*, 464.

144. Milov, "Little Tobacco," 71.

145. See Tracy Campbell, *The Politics of Despair: Power and Resistance in the Tobacco Wars* (Lexington: University Press of Kentucky, 1993).

146. W.W. Garner to E.G. Moss, Feb. 24, 1921; Folder 259, Eugene G. Moss; Box 58, General Correspondence, 1901-26; Records of the Bureau of Plant Industry, Soils, and Agricultural Engineering, RG 54; National Archives Building, College Park, MD.

147. E.G. Moss to W.W. Garner, Feb. 1, 1921; Folder 259, Eugene G. Moss; Box 58, General Correspondence, 1901-26; Records of the Bureau of Plant Industry, Soils, and Agricultural Engineering, RG 54; National Archives Building, College Park, MD.

148. E.G. Moss to W.W. Garner, Oct. 16, 1920; Folder 259, Eugene G. Moss; Box 58, General Correspondence, 1901-26; Records of the Bureau of Plant Industry, Soils, and Agricultural Engineering, RG 54; National Archives Building, College Park, MD.

149. Moss, "The Way to Make Money Growing Tobacco."

150. Sarah Milov has analyzed the causes of Tri-State's failure and placed them in the broader context of the political economy of the 1920s. Despite its collapse, she argues, Tri-State represented Herbert Hoover's associationalist ideals and laid the foundation for the "corporatist" farmer-state relations initiated by the New Deal. She suggests that the crucial link in this process was the Extension Service. "For at least a decade" prior to the Agricultural Adjustment Act, "government officials had been trying to contour the relationship between landowners, tenants, and manufacturers in order to give producers more power in the market." Milov, "Little Tobacco," 77. OTI offers a different lens, suggesting not only the significance of their connections to future policy but also their breaks with the past.

151. E.G. Moss, "Article for *Progressive Farmer*," Jan. 23, 1926; Folder 7, E.G. Moss, 1926-1930s, Box 13; Series 3, Manuscripts and News Releases; Oxford Tobacco Research Station Records; North Carolina State University Special Collections Research Center.

152. Brandt, *The Cigarette Century*.

153. Attentive to the political contests that continued into and after the New Deal, Hahn argues that this "process of commodification remains incomplete," as tobacco continues to lack a futures market and "no one can bid a leaf's price without seeing it, touching it, examining it." Hahn, *Making Tobacco Bright*, 166.

154. On the politics of agricultural adjustment, see Daniel, *Breaking the Land*, esp. 110-133 and Badger, *Prosperity Road*.

Conclusion. Revising Tobacco Politics in the Twentieth Century

1. Sarah Milov, *The Cigarette: A Political History* (Cambridge: Harvard University Press, 2019). On the dispossession of black growers, see Evan P. Bennett, "Of the Quest of the Golden Leaf: Black Farmers and Bright Tobacco in the Piedmont South" in Debra A. Reid and Evan P. Bennett, *Beyond Forty Acres and a Mule: African American Landowning Families since Reconstruction* (Gainesville, FL: University Press of Florida, 2012), 179-204.

2. Shane A. Smith, "The Pernicious Weed: Anti-Tobacco Sentiments in Periodical Literature, 1800-1870," *The Historian* 77, no. 1 (Spring 2015), 26-54.

3. Cassandra Tate, *Cigarette Wars: The Triumph of "The Little White Slaver"* (New York: Oxford University Press, 1999), 39-64.

4. Gordon Dillow, "Thank You For Not Smoking," *American Heritage Magazine* 32, 2 (Feb.-Mar. 1981).

5. Tate, *Cigarette Wars*, 65.

6. For a thorough overview of this legislation, see Marc Linder, *"Inherently Bad, and Bad Only": A History of State-Level Regulation of Cigarettes and Smoking in the United States since the 1880s, Volume 1* (Iowa City: privately printed, 2012), 1504-1569.

7. Philip P. Jacobs, ed., *A Tuberculosis Directory* (New York: The National Association for the Study and Prevention of Tuberculosis, 1911).

8. "Tobacco's Foes Losing Ground," *McNairy County Independent* (TN), Jun. 10, 1921.

9. Frederick William Roman, *Nicotine Next*, (Evanston, IL: National Woman's Christian Temperance Union, 1918), 6.

10. Calvin D. Crane, *Tobacco: An Assassin of Liberty* (Dayton, Ohio: 1921), 20.

11. Tate, *Cigarette Wars*, 123.

12. Tate, *Cigarette Wars*, 132.

13. "Allied Tobacco League to Fight Forces of Fanaticism; Officers Elected and Strenuous Campaign Planned," *Tobacco Record* (Brooklyn, NY), Oct. 15, 1919; "Tobacco Men Unite to Fight W.C.T.U.," *New York Times*, Oct. 10, 1919.

14. "Call for Fourth Tobacco Men's National Convention," *Southern Tobacco Journal* (*STJ*), Feb. 3, 1925.

15. Tobacco Merchants Association of the United States [TMA], "Father's Day," memorandum, 1927, file News Sheets and Memoranda, General Collection folio, Virginia Museum of History & Culture, Richmond, VA.

16. "U.S. Department of Agriculture to Investigate Cigar Leaf Crops," *STJ*, Jan. 13, 1926.

17. TMA, "The State Tax Menace: Forty-Four Legislatures to Meet in the Coming Season," memorandum, 1926, file News Sheets and Memoranda, General Collection folio, Virginia Museum of History & Culture, Richmond, VA.

18. Linder, *"Inherently Bad and Bad Only,"* 1939-1940.

19. Tate, *Cigarette Wars*, 125

20. Eli Cook, *The Pricing of Progress: Economic Indicators and the Capitalization of American Life* (Cambridge: Harvard University Press, 2017), 3.

21. Ian Kumekawa, *The First Serious Optimist: A.C. Pigou and the Birth of Welfare Economics* (Princeton: Princeton University Press, 2017).

22. Linder, *"Inherently Bad and Bad Only,"* 1929.
23. Linder, *"Inherently Bad and Bad Only,"* 1931.
24. "Charles Dushkind, Tobacco Executive," *New York Times*, May 30, 1945.
25. TMA, "Shall your Tobacco Tax Law Be Perpetuated?," memorandum, 1926, file News Sheets and Memoranda, General Collection folio, Virginia Museum of History & Culture, Richmond, VA.
26. TMA, "Save Your Business from Menacing Taxation," memorandum, 1926, file News Sheets and Memoranda, General Collection folio, Virginia Museum of History & Culture, Richmond, VA.
27. "Tobacco Merchants Association Protests Against Additional Tobacco Taxes and Opposes Re-Use of Cigar Boxes," *United States Tobacco Journal*, May 22, 1920.
28. For more on this condition, see Milov, *The Cigarette*.
29. Peter Benson, *Tobacco Capitalism: Growers, Migrant Workers, and the Changing Face of a Global Industry* (Princeton: Princeton University Press, 2012), 4, 15.
30. Benson, *Tobacco Capitalism*, 23.

Bibliography

Manuscript Collections
College Park, Maryland
National Archives II
Record Group 54, Records of the Bureau of Plant Industry, Soils, and Agricultural Engineering
Durham, North Carolina
David M. Rubenstein Rare Book, Manuscript, and Special Collections Library, Duke University, Broadsides and Ephemera Collection
Raleigh, North Carolina
Special Collections Research Center, North Carolina State University
Oxford Tobacco Research Station Records
Richmond, Virginia
Virginia Museum of History and Culture
Virginia Historical Society, Branch & Company, Richmond, Va. Records
General Collection folio
Hannah Family Papers
Washington, DC
National Archives I
Record Group 223, Records of the House of Representatives
Record Group 46, Records of the Senate

Newspapers and Periodicals
Bulletin of the National Association of Wool Manufacturers [Boston, MA]
Chicago Daily Tribune [Chicago, IL]
Country Gentleman [Albany, NY]
The Daily Appeal [Memphis, TN]
Daily National Intelligencer [Washington, DC]
The Daily Empire [Dayton, OH]
Daily Evening Telegraph [Philadelphia, PA]
De Bow's Review [New Orleans, LA]
Durham Tobacco Plant [Durham, NC]
Evening Tribune [Des Moines, IA]
Harper's Weekly [New York, NY]
Internal Revenue Record & Customs Journal [New York, NY]
Irish World and American Industrial Liberator [New York, NY]
McNairy County Independent [McNairy County, TN]

Moore's Rural New Yorker [Rochester, NY]
The National Tribune [Washington, DC]
New York Herald [New York, NY]
New York Times [New York, NY]
The Prairie Farmer [Chicago, IL]
The Progressive Farmer [Raleigh, NC]
The Progressive Farmer and Cotton Plant [Raleigh, NC]
Richmond Dispatch [Richmond, VA]
Southern Planter and Farmer [Richmond, VA]
The Southern Review [Baltimore, MD]
Southern Tobacco Journal [Winston, NC]
Tobacco: An Illustrated Weekly Journal [New York, NY]
Tobacco Leaf [New York, NY]
Tobacco Record [Brooklyn, NY]
Tri-State Tobacco Grower [Raleigh, NC]
United States Tobacco Journal [New York, NY]
Western Tobacco Journal [Cincinnati, OH]
Weekly Cincinnati Law Bulletin [Cincinnati, OH]

Published Primary Sources

Bishop, J. Leander. *A History of American Manufactures from 1608 to 1860, Vol. III.* Philadelphia, PA: Edward Young & Co., 1868.

Bohannan, Charles D., and D.P. Campbell. *A Preliminary Study of the Marketing of Burley Tobacco in Central Kentucky.* Lexington, KY: State University Press, 1916.

Bureau of Statistics. *Statistical Abstract of the United States, 1890.* Washington: GPO, 1891.

Burke, Edward, ed., *Proceedings of the Convention of Tobacconists Held at Cooper Institute in the City of New York, November 22, 1865.* New York: E.O. Jenkins, 1865).

———. *Tobacco Manufacture in the United States: A Report Adopted in Convention of the Trade.* New York, NY: American News Company, 1864.

Convention of Tobacconists. *Memorial of the Convention of Tobacconists to the Honorable Committee of Ways and Means.* Washington, DC: s.n., 1869.

Crane, Calvin D. *Tobacco: An Assassin of Liberty.* Dayton, Ohio: 1921.

Dailey, Jane. *Before Jim Crow: The Politics of Race in Postemancipation Virginia.* Chapel Hill: University of North Carolina Press, 2000.

Directory of Tobacco Men in the United States. New York, NY: C. Pfirshing, 1867.

Du Bois, W.E.B. "The Negroes of Farmville, Virginia: A Social Study," *Bulletin of the Department of Labor* no. 14 (January 1898).

Jacobs, Philip P., editor. *A Tuberculosis Directory.* New York: The National Association for the Study and Prevention of Tuberculosis, 1911.

Knapp, Seaman A. "Causes of Southern Rural Conditions and the Small Farm as an Important Remedy." In *Yearbook of the United States Department of Agriculture. 1908.* Washington, DC: GPO, 1909.

Ledoux, Albert R. *Annual Report of the North Carolina Agricultural Experiment Station for 1879.* Raleigh, NC: The Observer, State Printer, and Binder, 1879.

Garner, W.W. and E.G. Moss. "History and Status of Tobacco Culture," *United States Department of Agriculture Yearbook 1922* (Washington: GPO, 1923).
Manufacturers, Leaf Dealers, & Warehouseman of Cincinnati, Ohio. *An Argument in Favor of the Reduction of the Tax on Manufactured Tobacco, and Against the Transfer of the Tax to Leaf.* Cincinnati, OH: s.n., 1867.
Mathewson, E.H. "Methods of Seed Saving and Selection as Factors in the Improvement of Tobacco." In *The Bulletin of the North Carolina Department of Agriculture* 28, no. 10 (October 1907).
———. *Virginia Agricultural Experiment Stations Bulletin 205: Summary of Ten Years' Experiments with Tobacco.* Blacksburg, VA: June 1914.
McNess, George T. and E.H. Mathewson. "Dark Fire-Cured Tobacco of Virginia and the Possibilities for Its Improvement." *Yearbook of the United States Department of Agriculture. 1905.* Washington, DC: GPO, 1905.
Memorial of the Convention of Tobacco Manufacturers, Held at Cleveland, O., on the 17th and 18th of Sept., 1867. St. Louis, MO: Times Steam Printing Company, 1867.
Memorial of the Tobacco Board of Trade of Louisville, KY, Jan. 1878.
National Tobacco Association. *National Tobacco Association of the United States: Its Organization and Proceedings up to December 8, 1871.* New York, NY: Henry Spear, 1872.
North Carolina Agricultural Experiment Station. *Report of the Director for the Year Ending June 30, 1899.* Raleigh, NC: North Carolina Department of Agriculture, 1899.
———. *Annual Report of the North Carolina Agricultural Experiment Station, for 1886.* Raleigh, NC: P.M. Hale, 1887.
Ott, John. *How Shall the Quality of Virginia Shipping Tobacco Be Improved?* Richmond: Southern Fertilizing Company, 1874.
———. *The Position Tobacco Has Ever Held as the Chief Source of Wealth to Virginia.* Richmond: Southern Fertilizing Company, 1876.
———. *Tobacco in Virginia and North Carolina: Some Observations in Connection with the Several Types of Tobacco Now Produced in These Two States.* Richmond: Southern Fertilizing Company, 1877.
———. *To the trade: depot of staple fertilizing materials.* Richmond: Southern Fertilizing Company, 1874.
Proceedings of the National Convention of Manufacturers, Held at Cleveland, Ohio. Cleveland, OH: Sanford & Hayward, 1867.
Public Laws of the United States of America, Passed at the Second Session of the Forty-Second Congress, 1871-2. Boston, MA: Little, Brown, and Company, 1872.
Ragland, Robert L. *Tobacco, from the Seed to the Salesroom.* Richmond, VA: Wm. Ellis Jones, Steam Book & Job Printer, 1880.
———. *Cultivation and curing of fine yellow and shipping tobacco.* Richmond, VA: Commissioner of Agriculture of Virginia, 1878.
Receivers and Exporters of Leaf Tobacco. *Petition of the Receivers and Exporters of American Leaf Tobacco to the Members of the Senate and House of Representatives in Congress Assembled.* New York, NY: s.n., 1863.
Richardson, David. *Allison & Addison's Hand Book of the Garden, Seed Catalogue, and Almanac for 1874.* Richmond, VA: Allison & Addison, 1874.

———. *Allison & Addison's Agricultural Annual for 1878*. Richmond, VA: Allison & Addison, 1878.

Rives, F. & J., editors. "Public Acts of the Fortieth Congress of the United States." *Appendix to the Congressional Globe*. Washington, DC: F. & J. Rives, 1868.

Roman, Frederick William. *Nicotine Next*. Evanston, IL: National Woman's Christian Temperance Union, 1918.

Saunders, E.W. "The Tobacco Trade in Its Relation to Taxation and Government Monopolies." In *Report of the Industrial Commission on Agriculture and on Taxation in Various States: Volume XI*. Washington: GPO, 1901.

Stevens, F.L. "The History of the Tobacco Wilt in Granville County, North Carolina." In *Proceedings of the Seventeenth Annual Convention of the Association of American Agricultural Colleges and Experiment Stations Held at Washington, D.C., November 17-19, 1903*, edited by A.C. True, et al. Washington, DC: GPO, 1904.

Southern Fertilizing Company and Allison & Addison. *The Southern Fertilizing Co's Anchor Brand Fertilizer for Tobacco*. Richmond, VA: Allison & Addison, 1889.

U.S. Congress. *Congressional Globe*. 10 vols. Washington, DC, 1862-1872.

———. House. Committee of Ways and Means. *Report of the Special Commissioner of the Revenue*. 40th Cong., 2d Sess., January 7, 1868.

———. House. *Frauds on the Revenue*. 39th Cong., 2d Sess., Feb. 25, 1867.

———. House. *John J. Crooke*. 49th Cong., 1st sess., July 27, 1886.

———. House. *Letter from the Secretary of the Treasury, transmitting his annual report of the finances for the year 1864*. 38th Cong., 2d Sess., December 6, 1864.

———. House. *Revenue System of the United States*. 39th Cong., 1st Sess., January 29, 1866.

———. House. *Report of the Commissioner of Internal Revenue*. 41st Cong., 3d Sess., January 5, 1871.

———. House. *Report of the Commissioner of Internal Revenue for the Year 1879*. Washington: GPO, 1879.

———. House. "Statement of Marcus L. Floyd, of Tariffville, Conn." In *Tariff Hearings Before the Committee on Ways and Means of the House of Representatives. Sixtieth Congress 1908-1909. Vol. IV, Schedule F—Tobacco, and Manufactures of*. Washington, DC: GPO, 1909.

———. Senate. *Resolutions of the Legislature of Kentucky in Relation to the Proposed Tax on Tobacco*. 37th Cong., 2d Sess., March 24, 1862.

———. Senate. *Resolution of the Legislature of Ohio, in Favor of a Modification of the Proposed Tax on Leaf Tobacco*. 37th Cong., 2d Sess., April 14, 1862.

———. Senate. Committee on Finance. *Letter of the Commissioner of Agriculture to the Chairman of the Committee on Agriculture, upon the subject of the taxation*. 38th Cong., 1st Sess., January 21, 1864.

———. Senate. "Letter from the Secretary of State, communicating, in obedience to law, a statement of such fees as have been collected, accounted for, and reported by the various diplomatic and consular agents of the United States during the year ended December 31, 1877," December 9, 1878, 45th Cong., 3d Sess., 1878.

———. Senate. *Statement Prepared in the Office of Internal Revenue in Relation to the Tax on Manufactured Tobacco*. 41st Cong., 1st Sess., April 1, 1869.

BIBLIOGRAPHY

United States Department of Agriculture. *Annual Report of the Commissioner of Agriculture for the Year 1880.* Washington, DC: GPO, 1881.
———. *Annual Reports of the Department of Agricultural for the Fiscal Year Ended June 30, 1897.* Washington, DC: GPO, 1897.
———. *Annual Reports of the Department of Agriculture. Fiscal Year Ended June 30, 1898* (Washington: GPO, 1898
———. *Annual Reports of the Department of Agriculture. Fiscal Year Ended June 30, 1900.* Washington, DC: GPO, 1900.
———. *Annual Reports of the Department of Agriculture for the Fiscal Year Ended June 30, 1901.* Washington, DC: GPO, 1901.
———. *Annual Reports of the Department of Agriculture for the Fiscal Year Ended June 30, 1902.* Washington, DC: GPO, 1902.
———. *Annual Reports of the Department of Agriculture for the Fiscal Year Ended June 30, 1903.* Washington, DC: GPO, 1903.
———. *Annual Reports of the Department of Agriculture for the Year Ended June 30, 1904.* Washington, DC: GPO, 1904.
———. *Annual Reports of the Department of Agriculture for the Fiscal Year Ended June 30, 1906.* Washington, DC: GPO, 1907.
———. *Annual Reports of the Department of Agriculture for the Year Ended June 30, 1907.* Washington, DC: GPO, 1908.
———. *Annual Reports of the Department of Agriculture for the Year Ended June 30, 1910.* Washington, DC: GPO, 1911.
———. *Report No. 63: The Work of the Agricultural Experiment Stations on Tobacco.* Washington, DC: GPO, 1900.
———. *Report of the Commissioner of Agriculture for the Year 1867.* Washington, DC: GPO, 1868.
———. *Report of the Commissioner of Agriculture for the Year 1873.* Washington, DC: GPO, 1874.
———. *Report of the Commissioner of Agriculture for the Year 1874.* Washington, DC: GPO, 1875.
———. *Report of the Commissioner of Agriculture for the Year 1877.* Washington, DC: GPO, 1877.
———. *Report of the Commissioner of Agriculture for the Year 1878.* Washington, DC: GPO, 1879.
———. *Report of the Commissioner of Agriculture for the Year 1879.* Washington, DC: GPO, 1880.
———. *Report of the Commissioner of Agriculture for the Years 1881 and 1882.* Washington, DC: GPO, 1882.
———. *Report of the Commissioner of Agriculture for the Year 1883.* Washington, DC: GPO, 1883.
———. *Report of the Commissioner of Agriculture. 1888.* Washington, DC: GPO, 1889.
———. *Report of the Secretary of Agriculture.* Washington, DC: GPO, 1896.
———. *Yearbook of the United States Department of Agriculture. 1894.* Washington, DC: GPO, 1895.

———. *Yearbook of the United States Department of Agriculture*. 1897. Washington, DC: GPO, 1898.
———. *Yearbook of the United States Department of Agriculture*. 1898. Washington, DC: GPO, 1899.
———. *Yearbook of the United States Department of Agriculture*. 1904. Washington, DC: GPO, 1905.
———. *Yearbook of the United States Department of Agriculture, 1916*. Washington, DC: Government Printing Office, 1917.
———. *Yearbook 1920*. Washington, DC: GPO, 1921.
———. *Yearbook 1922*. Washington, DC: GPO, 1923.
United States Department of the Treasury. *Annual Report of the Commissioner of Internal Revenue on the Operations of the Internal Revenue System for the Year Ending 1874*. Washington, DC: GPO, 1874.
———. *Annual Report of the Commissioner of Internal Revenue for the Fiscal Year Ending June 30, 1877*. Washington, DC: GPO, 1877.
———. *Annual Report of the Commissioner of Internal Revenue for the Fiscal Year Ended June 30, 1900*. Washington, DC: GPO, 1900.
———. *Annual Report of the Secretary of the Treasury on the State of the Finances for the Year 1872*. Washington, DC: GPO, 1872.
———. *Annual Report of the Secretary of the Treasury on the State of the Finances for the Year 1877*. Washington, DC: GPO, 1877.
———. *Annual Report of the Secretary of the Treasury for the Year 1879*. Washington, DC: GPO, 1880.
———. *Annual Report of the Secretary of the Treasury on the State of the Finances for the Year 1880*. Washington: GPO, 1880.
———. *Report of the Commissioner of Internal Revenue on the Operations of the Internal Revenue System for the Year Ending June 30, 1863*. Washington, DC: GPO, 1864.
———. *Report of the Commissioner of the Internal Revenue*. Washington, DC: GPO, 1864.
———. *Report of the Commissioner of Internal Revenue for the Fiscal Year Ending June 30, 1865*. Washington, DC: GPO, 1865.
———. *Annual Report of the Commissioner of Internal Revenue for the Fiscal Year Ending June 30, 1877*. Washington: GPO, 1877.
———. *Report of the Commissioner of Internal Revenue for the Fiscal Year Ended June 30, 1879*. Washington, DC: GPO, 1880.
———. *Report of the Commissioner of Internal Revenue for the Fiscal Year Ending June 30, 1880*. Washington, DC: GPO, 1880.
———. *Report of the Commissioner of Internal Revenue for the Fiscal Year Ended June 30, 1882*. Washington, DC: GPO, 1883.
———. *Report of the Commissioner of Internal Revenue for the Fiscal Year Ended June 30, 1884*. Washington, DC: GPO, 1884.
———. *Report of the Commissioner of Internal Revenue for the Fiscal Year Ended June 30, 1894*. Washington, DC: GPO, 1894.

———. *Report of the Secretary of the Treasury on the State of the Finances for the Year 1875.* Washington, DC: GPO, 1875.
Virginia-Carolina Chemical Company. *Where Guano Is Made: Some of the Plants of Virginia-Carolina Chemical Company.* Richmond, VA: Virginia-Carolina Chemical Company, n.d.
Clarence W. Dorsey and J.A. Bonsteel. "Soil Survey in the Connecticut Valley." In *Tobacco Soils of the United States: A Preliminary Report Upon the Soils of the Principal Tobacco Districts,* edited by Milton Whitney. Washington, DC: GPO, 1898.
A Word about the Tax on Tobacco. Baltimore, MD: Murphy and Co., 1864.

Legal Cases, Public Laws, and Unpublished Testimony

An Act to reduce Duties on Imports, and to reduce Internal Taxes, and for other purposes. Public Law 315, Statutes at Large of the United States of America 17 (1873).
State v. Casey, 38 Ohio St. 555 (1883).
General and Local Laws and Joint Resolutions Passed by the Fifty-Seventh General Assembly of the State of Ohio. Columbus, OH: L.D. Myers & Bro., State Printers, 1866.
Henry A. Turner v. The State of Maryland, 107 U.S. 38 (1883).
U.S. Congress. House. Committee on Ways and Means. *Proposal to Amend Regulations Regarding the Packaging of Chewing Tobacco: Hearing before the Committee on Ways and Means, House of Representatives.* 44th Cong, 1st Sess., May 13, 1876.

Books and Journal Articles

Adams, Sean Patrick. *Old Dominion, Industrial Commonwealth: Coal, Politics, and Economy in Antebellum America.* Baltimore, MD: Johns Hopkins University Press, 2004.
Adams, Sean Patrick. "Soulless Monsters and Iron Horses: The Civil War, Institutional Change, and American Capitalism." In *Capitalism Takes Command: The Social Transformation of Nineteenth-Century America* edited by Gary J. Kornblith and Michael Zakim. University of Chicago Press, 2011.
Ayers, Edward L. *The Promise of the New South: Life after Reconstruction,* 2nd ed. New York, NY: Oxford University Press, 2007.
Badger, Anthony J. *Prosperity Road: The New Deal, Tobacco, and North Carolina.* Chapel Hill, NC: University of North Carolina Press, 1980.
Balleisen, Edward J. *Fraud: An American History from Barnum to Madoff.* Princeton, NJ: Princeton University Press, 2017.
———, and David A. Moss, editors. *Government and Markets: Toward a New Theory of Regulation.* New York, NY: Cambridge University Press, 2010.
Balogh, Brian. *The Associational State: American Governance in the Twentieth Century.* Philadelphia, PA: University of Pennsylvania Press, 2015.
Barreyre, Nicolas. *Gold and Freedom: The Political Economy of Reconstruction,* trans. Arthur Goldhammer. Charlottesville, VA: University of Virginia Press, 2015.
Beckert, Sven. *Empire of Cotton: A Global History.* New York, NY: Vintage, 2015.

———. *The Monied Metropolis: New York City and the Consolidation of the American Bourgeoisie, 1850-1896*. New York, NY: Cambridge University Press, 2001.

Bennett, Evan P. *When Tobacco Was King: Families, Farm Labor, and Federal Policy in the Piedmont*. Gainesville, FL: University Press of Florida, 2014.

Bensel, Richard Franklin. *The Political Economy of American Industrialization, 1877-1900*. New York, NY: Cambridge University Press, 2000.

———. *Yankee Leviathan: The Origins of Central State Authority in America, 1859-1877.* New York, NY: Cambridge University Press, 1990.

Benson, Peter. *Tobacco Capitalism: Growers, Migrant Workers, and the Changing Face of a Global Industry*. Princeton, NJ: Princeton University Press, 2012.

Biglaiser, Gary. "Middlemen as Experts." *RAND Journal of Economics* 24, no. 2 (Summer 1993): 212-223.

Bonnett, Clarence E. *Employers' Associations in the United States: A Study of Typical Associations*. New York, NY: MacMillan, 1922.

Bourdieu, Pierre. *Distinction: A Social Critique of the Judgment of Taste*. Cambridge, MA: Harvard University Press, 1984.

Brandt, Allan. *The Cigarette Century: The Rise, Fall, and Deadly Persistence of the Product that Defined America*. New York, NY: Basic Books, 2009.

Breman, Jan. *Taming the Coolie Beast: Plantation Society and the Colonial Order in Southeast Asia*. Delhi, India: Oxford University Press, 1989.

Brown, R. Ben. "Free Men and Free Pigs: Closing the Southern Range and the American Property Tradition." *Radical History Review* no. 108 (Fall 2010): 117-137.

Brownlee, W. Elliot. *Federal Taxation in America: A History*, 3rd ed. New York, NY: Cambridge University Press, 2016.

Burchell, Graham and Colin Gordon and Peter Miller, editors. *The Foucault Effect: Studies in Governmentality*. Chicago, IL: University of Chicago Press, 1991.

Burnett, Christina Duffy. "The Edges of Empire and the Limits of Sovereignty: American Guano Islands." *American Quarterly* 57, no. 3 (September 2005): 779-803.

Campbell, Tracy. *The Politics of Despair: Power & Resistance in the Tobacco Wars*. Lexington, KY: University Press of Kentucky, 1993.

Cardoso, José Luís, and Pedro Lains, *Paying for the Liberal State: The Rise of Public Finance in Nineteenth-Century Europe*. New York, NY: Cambridge University Press, 2010.

Carpenter, Daniel. "Confidence Games: How Does Regulation Constitute Markets?" In *Government and Markets: Toward a New Theory of Regulation*, edited by Edward J. Balleisen and David A. Moss. New York, NY: Cambridge University Press, 2010.

———. *The Forging of Bureaucratic Autonomy: Reputations, Networks, and Policy Innovation in Executive Agencies, 1862-1928*. Princeton, NJ: Princeton University Press, 2001.

Carter, Susan B. et al, editors. *Historical Statistics of the United States, Earliest Times to the Present: Millennial Edition*. New York, NY: Cambridge University Press, 2006.

Chandler, Alfred D. *The Visible Hand: The Managerial Revolution in American Business*. Cambridge, MA: The Belknap Press of Harvard University Press, 1977.

Clarence-Smith, William G. and Steven Topik, editors. *The Global Coffee Economy in Africa, Asia, and Latin America, 1500-1989*. New York, NY: Cambridge University Press, 2003.

Clark, Christopher. *The Roots of Rural Capitalism: Western Massachusetts, 1780-1860*. Ithaca, NY: Cornell University Press, 1990.

Clemens, Elisabeth S. *The People's Lobby: Organizational Innovation and the Rise of Interest Group Politics in the United States, 1890-1925*. Chicago, IL: University of Chicago Press, 1997.

Cohen, Andrew Wender. "Smuggling, Globalization, and America's Outward State, 1870-1909." *The Journal of American History* 97, no. 2 (September 2010): 371-398.

Cohen, Nancy. *The Reconstruction of American Liberalism, 1865-1914*. Chapel Hill, NC: University of North Carolina Press, 2002.

Cook, Eli. *The Pricing of Progress: Economic Indicators and the Capitalization of American Life*. Cambridge, MA: Harvard University Press, 2017.

Cox, Howard. *The Global Cigarette: Origins and Evolution of British American Tobacco 1880-1945*. New York, NY: Oxford University Press, 2000.

Cronon, William. *Nature's Metropolis: Chicago and the Great West*. New York, NY: W.W. Norton & Company, 1991.

Currarino, Rosanne. *The Labor Question in America: Economic Democracy in the Gilded Age* Urbana, IL: University of Illinois Press, 2011.

Daniel, Pete. *Breaking the Land: The Transformation of Cotton, Tobacco, and Rice Cultures since 1880*. Urbana, IL: University of Illinois Press, 1985.

Daunton, Martin. *Trusting Leviathan: The Politics of Taxation in Britain, 1799-1914*. New York, NY: Cambridge University Press, 2001.

de Jesus, Ed. C. *The Tobacco Monopoly in the Philippines: Bureaucratic Enterprise and Social Change, 1766-1880*. Quezon City, Philippines: Ateneo de Manila University Press, 1980.

Dillow, Gordon. "Thank You For Not Smoking." *American Heritage Magazine* 32, no. 2 (February—March. 1981): 94.

Downs, Gregory P., and Kate Masur, editors. *The World the Civil War Made*. Chapel Hill, NC: University of North Carolina Press, 2016.

Dunaway, Wilma A. "The Double Register of History: Situating the Forgotten Woman and Her Household in Capitalist Commodity Chains." *Journal of World Systems Research* VII, no. I (Spring 2001): 2-29.

Edling, Max. *A Hercules in the Cradle: War, Money, and the American State, 1783-1867*. Chicago, IL: University of Chicago Press, 2014.

Edwards, Paul N. *A Vast Machine: Computer Models, Climate Data, and the Politics of Global Warming*. Cambridge, MA: MIT Press, 2010.

Edwards, Rebecca. *Angels in the Machinery: Gender in American Politics from the Civil War to the Progressive Era*. New York: Oxford University Press, 1997.

Effland, Anne. "International Programs of the USDA: Cross-Purposes or a Delicate Balance?," *Agricultural History* 87 (Summer 2013): 349-358.

Enstad, Nan. *Cigarettes, Inc.: An Intimate History of Corporate Imperialism*. Chicago, IL: University of Chicago Press, 2018.

———. "Debunking the Capitalist Cowboy." *Boston Review*, Mar. 21, 2019.

Fields, Barbara Jeanne. "The Advent of Capitalist Agriculture: The New South in a Bourgeois World." In *Essays on the Postbellum Southern Economy* edited by Thavolia Glymph and John J. Kushma. College Station, TX: Texas A&M University Press, 1985.

Fink, Leon. *Workingmen's Democracy: The Knights of Labor and American Politics.* Urbana, IL: University of Illinois Press, 1983.
Fitzgerald, Deborah. *Every Farm a Factory: The Industrial Ideal in American Agriculture.* New Haven, CT: Yale University Press, 2003.
Foster, Gaines. *Moral Reconstruction: Christian Lobbyists and the Federal Legislation of Morality, 1865-1920.* Chapel Hill, NC: University of North Carolina Press, 2002.
Foucault, Michel. "Governmentality," in *The Foucault Effect: Studies in Governmentality,* edited by Graham Burchell, Colin Gordon, and Peter Miller. Chicago: University of Chicago Press, 1991)
Fourcade, Marion. "The Vile and the Noble: On the Relation between Natural and Social Classifications in the French Wine World." *The Sociological Quarterly* 53, no. 4 (Autumn 2012): 524-545.
Gamage, David. "How Should Governments Promote Distributive Justice?: A Framework for Analyzing the Optimal Choice of Tax Instruments." *Tax Law Review* 68, no. 1 (2014-2015): 1-87.
Gereffi, Gary, Miguel Korzeniewicz, and Roberto P. Korzeniewicz, "Introduction: Global Commodity Chains." In *Commodity Chains and Global Capitalism,* edited by Gereffi, Gary and Miguel Korzeniewicz. Westport, CT: Greenwood Press, 1994.
Gilmore, Glenda. *Gender and Jim Crow: Women and the Politics of White Supremacy in North Carolina, 1896-1920.* Chapel Hill, NC: University of North Carolina Press, 1996.
Glymph, Thavolia and John J. Kushma, editors. *Essays on the Postbellum Southern Economy.* College Station, TX: Texas A&M University Press, 1985.
Gudmestad, Robert H. "Baseball, the Lost Cause, and the New South in Richmond, Virginia, 1883-1890." *The Virginia Magazine of History and Biography* 106, no. 3 (Summer 1998): 267-300.
Haggard, Stephan. *Developmental States.* Cambridge: Cambridge University Press, 2018.
Hahn, Barbara. *Making Tobacco Bright: Creating an American Commodity, 1617-1937* Baltimore, MD: Johns Hopkins University Press 2011.
Hahn, Steven. *A Nation Under Our Feet: Black Political Struggles in the Rural South from Slavery to the Great Migration.* Cambridge, MA: Belknap Press of Harvard University Press, 2003.
———. "Slave Emancipation, Indian Peoples, and the Projects of a New American State." *Journal of the Civil War Era* 3, no. 3 (September 2013): 307-330.
Hamilton, David E. "Building the Associative State: The Department of Agriculture and American State-Building." *Agricultural History* 64, no. 2 (Spring 1990): 207-218.
Hamm, Richard F. *Shaping the Eighteenth Amendment: Temperance Reform, Legal Culture, and the Polity, 1880-1920.* Chapel Hill, NC: University of North Carolina Press, 1995.
Hawley, Ellis. "Herbert Hoover, the Commerce Secretariat, and the Vision of an 'Associative State,' 1921-1928." *The Journal of American History* 61, 1 (June 1974): 116-140.
Helms, Douglas. "Soil and Southern History," *Agricultural History* 74, 4 (Autumn 2000).
Helms, Douglas, Anne B.W. Effland and Patricia J. Durana, editors. *Profiles in the History of the U.S. Soil Survey.* Ames, IA: Iowa State Press, 2002.

Herbin-Triant, Elizabeth. "Southern Segregation South Africa-Style: Maurice Evans, Clarence Poe, and the Ideology of Rural Segregation." *Journal of Agricultural History* 87, no. 2 (Spring 2013): 170-193.

Hoganson, Kristin L. *The Heartland: An American History*. New York, NY: Penguin Press, 2019.

Holt, Sharon Ann. *Making Freedom Pay: North Carolina Freedpeople Working for Themselves, 1865-1900*. Athens, GA: The University of Georgia, 2000.

Huret, Romain D. *American Tax Resisters*. Cambridge, MA: Harvard University Press, 2014.

Huston, Reeve. *Land and Freedom: Rural Society, Popular Protest, and Party Politics in Antebellum New York*. New York, NY: Oxford University Press, 2000.

Irwin, Douglas A. "Exports of selected commodities: 1790–1989." Table Ee569-589, In *Historical Statistics of the United States, Earliest Times to the Present: Millennial Edition*, edited by Susan B. Carter et al. New York: Cambridge University Press, 2006.

John, Richard R. "Farewell to the 'Party Period': Political Economy in Nineteenth-Century America," *Journal of Policy History* 16, no. 2 (Apr. 2004): 117-125.

———. *Network Nation: Inventing American Telecommunications*. Cambridge, MA: Belknap Press of Harvard University Press, 2010.

Johnson, Walter. *River of Dark Dreams: Slavery and Empire in the Cotton Kingdom*. Cambridge, MA: The Belknap Press of Harvard University Press, 2013.

Keller, Morton. *Affairs of State: Public Life in Nineteenth Century America*. Cambridge, MA: Harvard University Press, 1977.

Kennedy, Charles Stuart. *The American Consul: A History of the United States Consular Service, 1776-1914*. Westport, CT: Greenwood Press, 1990.

Kerr-Ritchie, Jeffrey. *Freedpeople in the Tobacco South: Virginia, 1860-1900*. Chapel Hill, NC: University of North Carolina Press, 1999.

Kingsbury, Noel. *Hybrid: The History and Science of Plant Breeding*. Chicago, IL: The University of Chicago Press, 2009.

Klose, Nelson. *America's Crop Heritage: The History of Foreign Plant Introduction by the Federal Government*. Ames, IA: Iowa State College Press, 1950.

Kluger, Richard. *Ashes to Ashes: America's Hundred-Year Cigarette War, the Public Health, and the Unabashed Triumph of Philip Morris*. New York, NY: Vintage Books, 1997.

Kolko, Gabriel. *The Triumph of Conservatism: A Reinterpretation of American History, 1900-1916*. New York, NY: The Free Press, 1963.

Kornblith, Gary J., and Michael Zakim, editors. *Capitalism Takes Command: The Social Transformation of Nineteenth-Century America*. Chicago, IL: University of Chicago Press, 2011.

Kotsonis, Yanni. *States of Obligation: Taxes and Citizenship in the Russian Empire and Early Soviet Republic*. University of Toronto Press, 2014.

Kramer, Paul. "Embedding Capital: Political-Economic History, the United States, and the World." *The Journal of the Gilded Age and Progressive Era* 15 no. 3 (July 2016): 331-362.

Kumekawa, Ian. *The First Serious Optimist: A.C. Pigou and the Birth of Welfare Economics*. Princeton, NJ: Princeton University Press, 2017.

Lee, Tom. "Southern Appalachia's Bright Tobacco Boom: Industrialization, Urbanization, and the Culture of Tobacco." *Agricultural History* 88, no. 2 (Spring 2014): 175-206.

Levy, Jonathan. *Freaks of Fortune: The Emerging World of Capitalism and Risk.* Cambridge, MA: Harvard University Press, 2012.

Linder, Marc. *"Inherently Bad, and Bad Only": A History of State-Level Regulation of Cigarettes and Smoking in the United States since the 1880s, Volume 1.* Iowa City, IA: privately printed, 2012.

Link, Stefan and Noam Maggor. "The United States as a Developing Nation: Revisiting the Peculiarities of American History," *Past and Present* 246 (Feb. 2020): 269-306.

Lowery, Malinda Maynor. *The Lumbee Indians: An American Struggle.* Chapel Hill, NC: The University of North Carolina Press, 2018.

Maggor, Noam. "To Coddle and Caress These Great Capitalists: Eastern Money, Frontier Populism, and the Politics of Market-Making in the American West." *American Historical Review* 122, no. 1 (February 2017): 55-84.

Maier, Charles. *Leviathan 2.0: Inventing Modern Statehood.* Cambridge, MA: The Belknap Press of Harvard University Press, 2012.

Marcus, Alan I. *Agricultural Science and the Quest for Legitimacy: Farmers, Agricultural Colleges, and Experiment Stations, 1870-1890.* Ames, IA: Iowa State University Press, 1985.

Martin, Nick. "A Family from High Plains," *Splinter*, Aug. 2, 2018.

Masur, Kate. *An Example for All the Land: Emancipation and the Struggle over Equality in Washington, D.C.* Chapel Hill, NC: University of North Carolina Press, 2010.

McCormick, Richard L. *The Party Period and Public Policy: American Politics from the Age of Jackson to the Progressive Era.* New York, NY: Oxford University Press, 1986.

Mehrotra, Ajay. *Making the Modern American Fiscal State: Law, Politics, and the Rise of Progressive Taxation, 1877-1929.* New York, NY: Cambridge University Press, 2013.

Melillo, Edward. "The First Green Revolution: Debt Peonage and the Making of the Nitrogen Fertilizer Trade, 1840-1930." *American Historical Review* 117, no. 4 (October 2012): 1028-1060.

Mihm, Stephen. *A Nation of Counterfeiters: Capitalists, Con Men, and the Making of the United States.* Cambridge, MA: Harvard University Press, 2007.

Miller, Wilbur. *Revenuers & Moonshiners: Enforcing Federal Liquor Law in the Mountain South, 1865-1900.* Chapel Hill, NC: University of North Carolina Press, 1991.

Milov, Sarah. *The Cigarette: A Political History.* Cambridge, MA: Harvard University Press, 2019.

Milov, Sarah. "Smoking as Statecraft: Promoting American Tobacco Production and Global Cigarette Consumption, 1947-1970." *The Journal of Policy History* 28, no. 4 (October 2016): 707-747.

Mitchell, Timothy. *Carbon Democracy: Political Power in the Age of Oil.* New York, NY: Verso, 2013.

——. "Society, Economy, and the State Effect." In *The Anthropology of the State: A Reader*, edited by Aradhana Sharma and Akhil Gupta. Malden, MA: Blackwell Publishing, 2006.

Moaddel, Mansoor. "Shi'i Political Discourse and Class Mobilization in the Tobacco Movement of 1890-1892," *Sociological Forum* 7, no. 3 (September 1992): 447-468.

Montgomery, David. *Citizen Worker: The Experience of Workers in the United States with Democracy and the Free Market during the Nineteenth Century.* New York, NY: Cambridge University Press, 1993.

Moore, Jason W. "The Capitolocene Part II: accumulation by appropriation and the centrality of unpaid work/energy." *The Journal of Peasant Studies* 42, no. 2 (2017): 237-239.

Neem, Johann. *Creating a Nation of Joiners: Democracy and Civil Society in Early National Massachusetts.* Cambridge, MA: Harvard University Press, 2008.

Nelson, Scott Reynolds. *Iron Confederacies: Southern Railways, Klan Violence, and Reconstruction.* Chapel Hill, NC: University of North Carolina Press, 1999.

Nelson, Scott Reynolds. *Oceans of Grain: How American Wheat Remade the World.* New York: Basic Books, 2022.

Norton, Marcy. *Sacred Gifts, Profane Pleasures: A History of Tobacco and Chocolate in the Atlantic World.* Ithaca, NY: Cornell University Press, 2008.

O'Connor, Patrick Mulford. "'The Festering Sores of Our Body Politic': Federal Tobacco Taxation, Race, and the Politics of Fear in Postemancipation Virginia." *Soundings: An Interdisciplinary Journal* 101, 1 (Jan. 2018): 41-51.

O'Gorman, James F. *A Connecticut Valley Vernacular: The Vanishing Landscape and Architecture of the New England Tobacco Fields.* Philadelphia, PA: University of Pennsylvania Press, 2002.

Olmstead Alan L., and Paul W. Rhode. *Arresting Contagion: Science, Policy, and Conflicts over Animal Disease Control.* Cambridge, MA: Harvard University Press, 2015.

———. *Creating Abundance: Biological Innovation and American Agricultural Development.* New York, NY: Cambridge University Press, 2008.

Olmsted, Frank L. "The Tobacco Tax." *The Quarterly Journal of Economics* 5, no. 2 (January 1891): 193-219.

Orenstein, Dana. "Warehouses on Wheels." *Environment and Planning D: Society and Space* 36, no. 4 (2018): 648-665.

Osterhammel, Jürgen. *The Transformation of the World: A Global History of the Nineteenth Century.* Translated by Patrick Camiller. Princeton: Princeton University Press, 2014.

Patel, Raj and Jason W. Moore. *A History of the World in Seven Cheap Things: A Guide to Capitalism, Nature, and the Future of the Planet.* Berkeley, CA: University of California Press, 2017.

Peart, Daniel. *Lobbying and the Making of U.S. Tariff Policy, 1816-1861.* Baltimore, MD: Johns Hopkins University Press, 2018.

Petty, Adrienne Monteith. *Standing Their Ground: Small Farmers in North Carolina since the Civil War.* New York, NY: Oxford University Press, 2013.

Pietruska, Jamie. *Looking Forward: Prediction and Uncertainty in Modern America.* Chicago, IL: University of Chicago Press, 2017.

Plastas, Melinda and Maria Rentetzi. "Tobacco Roads: Histories of Technologies and a Transnational Economy." *Advances in Historical Studies* 5, no. 2 (Apr. 2016): 45-48.

Charles Postel, *Equality: An American Dilemma, 1866-1896* (New York: Farrar, Strauss, and Giroux, 2019)

Postel, Charles. *The Populist Vision*. New York, NY: Oxford University Press, 2007.

Prince, Jr., Eldred E. *Long Green: The Rise and Fall of Tobacco in South Carolina*. Athens, GA: University of Georgia Press, 2000.

Rachleff, Peter J. *Black Labor in the South: Richmond, Virginia, 1865-1890*. Philadelphia, PA: Temple University Press, 1984.

Ratner, Sidney. *American Taxation: Its History as a Social Force in Democracy*. New York, NY: W.W. Norton & Company, 1942.

Reid, Debra A., and Evan P. Bennett. *Beyond Forty Acres and a Mule: African American Landowning Families since Reconstruction*. Gainesville, FL: University Press of Florida, 2012.

Richardson, Heather Cox. *The Greatest Nation of the Earth: Republican Economic Policies during the Civil War*. Cambridge, MA: Harvard University Press, 1997.

Ring, Natalie. *The Problem South: Region, Empire, and the New Liberal State, 1880-1930*. Athens, GA: The University of Georgia Press, 2012.

Ritter, Gretchen. *Goldbugs and Greenbacks: The Antimonopoly Tradition and the Politics of Finance in America*. New York, NY: Cambridge University Press, 1997.

Ron, Ariel. "Farmers, Capitalism, and Government in the Late Nineteenth Century." *The Journal of the Gilded Age and Progressive Era* 15, no. 3 (July 2016): 294-309.

———. *Grassroots Leviathan: Agricultural Reform and the Rural North in the Slaveholding Republic*. Baltimore: Johns Hopkins University Press, 2020.

———. "Henry Carey's Rural Roots: 'Scientific Agriculture,' and Economic Development in the Antebellum North." *Journal of the History of Economic Thought* 37, no. 2 (June 2015), 263-275

———. "Summoning the State: Northern Farmers and the Transformation of American Politics in the Mid-Nineteenth Century," *Journal of American History* 103, no. 2 (September 2016): 347-374.

Rosenberg, Emily, "Transnational Currents in a Shrinking World." In *A World Connecting: 1870-1945*, edited by Emily Rosenberg. Cambridge, MA: The Belknap Press of Harvard University Press, 2012.

Rosenberg, Gabriel N. *The 4-H Harvest: Sexuality and the State in Rural America*. Philadelphia, PA: University of Pennsylvania Press, 2015.

Samper, Mario K. "The Historical Construction of Quality and Competitiveness: A Preliminary Discussion of Coffee Commodity Chains." In *The Global Coffee Economy in Africa, Asia, and Latin America, 1500-1989*, edited by Clarence-Smith, William G. and Steven Topik, New York, NY: Cambridge University Press, 20

Sanders, Elizabeth. *Roots of Reform: Farmers, Workers, and the American State, 1877-1917.* Chicago, IL: University of Chicago Press, 1999.

Scott, James C. *The Art of Not Being Governed: An Anarchist History of Upland Southeast Asia*. New Haven, CT: Yale University Press, 2009.

Scott, James C. *Thinking Like a State: How Certain Schemes to Improve the Human Condition Have Failed*. New Haven, CT: Yale University Press, 1998.

Sharma, Aradhana and Akhil Gupta, editors. *The Anthropology of the State: A Reader*. Malden, MA: Blackwell Publishing, 2006.

Shifflett, Crandall A. *Patronage and Poverty in the Tobacco South: Louisa County, Virginia, 1860-1900.* Knoxville, TN: University of Tennessee Press, 1982.
Silbey, Joel. *The American Political Nation, 1838-1893.* Stanford, CA: Stanford University Press, 1991.
Singerman, David Roth. "Science, Commodities, and Corruption in the Gilded Age," *The Journal of the Gilded Age and Progressive Era* 15, no. 3 (July 2016): 278-293.
Skocpol, Theda. *Protecting Soldiers and Mothers: The Political Origins of Social Policy in the United States.* Cambridge, MA: Harvard University Press, 1992.
Smith, Shane A. "The Pernicious Weed: Anti-Tobacco Sentiments in Periodical Literature, 1800-1870." *The Historian* 77, no. 1 (Spring 2015): 26-54.
Specht, Joshua. *Red Meat Republic: A Hoof-to-Table History of How Beef Changed America.* Princeton, NJ: Princeton University Press, 2019.
Stanley, Amy Dru. *From Bondage to Contract: Wage Labor, Marriage, and the Market in the Age of Revolution.* New York, NY: Cambridge University Press, 1998.
Star, Leigh and Karen Ruhleder. "Steps Toward an Ecology of Infrastructure: Design and Access for Large Information Spaces." *Information Systems Research* 7, no. 1 (1996): 111-134.
Stern, Fritz. *Gold and Iron: Bismarck, Bleichröder, and the Building of the German Empire.* New York, NY: Vintage Books, 1979.
Stock, Catherine McNicol and Robert D. Johnston, eds., *The Countryside in the Age of the Modern State: Political Histories of Rural America.* Ithaca, NY: Cornell University Press, 2001.
Stoll, Steven. "The Captured Garden: The Political Ecology of Subsistence under Capitalism." *International Labor and Working Class History* 85 (Spring 2014): 75-96.
———. *Ramp Hollow: The Ordeal of Appalachia.* New York, NY: Hill and Wang, 2017.
Summers, Mark Wahlgren. *The Era of Good Stealings.* New York, NY: Oxford University Press, 1993.
Sumner, William Graham. *What Social Classes Owe to Each Other.* Caldwell, ID: Caxton Press, 2003.
Swanson, Drew A. *A Golden Weed: Tobacco and Environment in the Piedmont South.* New Haven, CT: Yale University Press, 2014.
Tate, Cassandra. *Cigarette Wars: The Triumph of "The Little White Slaver."* New York, NY: Oxford University Press, 1999.
Teitelman, Emma. "The Properties of Capitalism: Industrial Enclosures in the South and West after the American Civil War," *The Journal of American History* (Mar. 2020): 879-900.
Thompson, Margaret Susan. *The "Spider Web": Congress and Lobbying in the Age of Grant.* Ithaca, NY: Cornell University Press, 1985.
Tilley, Nannie Mae. *The Bright-Tobacco Industry 1860-1929.* Chapel Hill, NC: University of North Carolina Press, 1948.
Topik, Steven C., and Allen Wells, *Global Markets Transformed 1870-1945.* Cambridge, MA: Harvard University Press, 2012.
Welke, Barbara Young. *Recasting American Liberty: Gender, Race, Law, and the Railroad Revolution, 1865-1920.* New York, NY: Cambridge University Press, 2001.`

White, Richard. *Railroaded: The Transcontinentals and the Making of Modern America.* New York, NY: W.W. Norton & Co., 2011.

Whitney, Milton. *Tobacco Soils of the United States: A Preliminary Report Upon the Soils of the Principal Tobacco Districts.* Washington, DC: GPO, 1898.

Wines, Richard. *Fertilizer in America: From Waste Recycling to Resource Exploitation.* Philadelphia, PA: Temple University Press, 1985.

Woodman, Harold D. *King Cotton and His Retainers: Financing & Marketing the Cotton Crop of the South, 1800-1925.* Lexington, KY: University of Kentucky Press, 1968.

———. *New South—New Law: The Legal Foundations of Credit and Labor Relations in the Postbellum Agricultural South.* Baton Rouge, LA: Louisiana State University Press, 1995.

Worster, Donald. *Rivers of Empire: Water, Aridity, and the Growth of the American West.* New York, NY: Oxford University Press, 1992.

Wright, Gavin. *Old South, New South: Revolutions in the Southern Economy Since the Civil War.* New York, NY: Basic Books, 1986.

———. "The Strange Career of the New Southern Economic History." *Reviews in American History.* 10, no. 4 (Dec. 1982): 164-180.

Volk, Kyle G. *Moral Minorities and the Making of American Democracy.* New York, NY: Oxford University Press, 2014.

Zakim, Michael. "Producing Capitalism: The Clerk at Work." In *Capitalism Takes Command: The Social Transformation of Nineteenth-Century America*, edited by Gary J. Kornblith and Michael Zakim. Chicago: University of Chicago Press, 2012

Databases

Carter, Susan B., and Richard Sutch, general editors. *Historical Statistics of the United States: Millennial Edition Online.*

Dissertations

Ferleger, Herbert Ronald. "David A. Wells and the American Revenue System, 1865-1970." Ph.D. Dissertation, Columbia University, 1942.

Mittelman, Amy. "The Politics of Alcohol Production: The Liquor Industry and the Federal Government, 1862-1900." Ph.D. Dissertation, Columbia University, 1986.

Index

A.H. Mickle & Sons, 18
Agricultural Adjustment Administration, 143, 199n150
alcohol: breweries and, 43; distilleries and, 42; industry and, 49; taxation and, 14, 40, 58. *See also* Prohibition
Allen and Ginter, 70
Allison & Addison, 97–100, 102, 106. *See also* fertilizer
Allied Tobacco League of America, 146
American Agriculturist, 117–118
American Sumatra Tobacco Company, 146
American Tobacco Company, 6, 64, 101, 105, 109–111, 127, 139, 147, 171n34, 177n5, 198n133. *See also* Tobacco Trust
antebellum tobacco industry, 2, 12, 18, 25, 28, 49, 53, 76–77, 107, 144, 163n69, 170n27, 189n87
antimonopolism, 27, 35, 51, 63, 109
Anti-Saloon League, 145. *See also* Prohibition
anti-tobacco movement, 144–148
Antwerp, Belgium, 65, 71, 83
Argentina, 68
Arrears Act of 1879, 61
Arthur, Chester A., 63
Association of the Tobacco Trade of Cincinnati, 11, 24–25, 29–32, 34–36, 80, 82, 163n70, 164n80
Astor House, 30
Atzeroth, Julia, 117
auctions: junction regimes and, 79–80, 177n8; Office of Tobacco Investigations and, 113, 128, 135; origins of, 188n70; tobacco growers and, 3, 91, 101, 138; tobacco quality and, 4, 107, 113, 139–140, 142; warehouses and, 1, 46, 103
Austria-Hungary, 68, 70

Bagley, John J., 22
Balleisen, Edward, 164n75
Baltimore, MD, 10, 18, 20, 30, 65–66, 76, 96, 102, 105; tobacco board of trade and, 30, 78, 85; tobacco inspection and, 85
banking, 5, 89–90, 102, 105, 109
Benson, Peter, 109n104
Bleichröder, Gerson, 69
border states, 15, 18, 21, 159n21
Boston, MA, 30
Bowie, W.W.W., 18
Bradford, L.J., 15, 22–23, 27
Brazil, 68, 117
bright tobacco, 90–93, 99, 129, 132, 134, 139, 142
Buchanan & Lyall, 43, 179n23
Bureau of Animal Industry, 119, 125
Bureau of Internal Revenue, 2, 10, 13, 28; occupational licensing and, 42–45, 64; regulating tobacco industry and, 38, 41–42, 45, 47, 57, 79, 115, 126, 187n62; relations with tobacconists and, 30, 49–50; Revenue Commission and, 22–24, 163n73; revenue inspectors and, 18, 26, 30; tax collectors and, 32, 37, 42, 49, 55, 64, 172n46; Tobacco Division and, 10, 61, 169n10
Bureau of Plant Industry, 123, 125–126, 130–131, 133–134
Bureau of Soils, 125–128, 134, 137
bureaucracy, 10–11, 23, 41
Burke, Edward, 10, 18, 20, 23, 26–28, 30, 33, 37, 48–49, 75
burley tobacco, 67; Burley Tobacco Growers' Co-operative and, 148

Carey, Henry, 116
Carpenter, Daniel, 198n129
Carr, Julian, 105
Carrington, Tazewell, 136. *See also* Tobacco Association of the United States
Cat Island Guano Company, 96, 98
cattle, 119, 131, 133–134
Census Bureau, 5, 71, 94, 116
Chandler, Alfred D, 6, 155n21, 171n34
chewing tobacco, 1, 13, 14, 16, 18, 26, 34, 52, 124, 145, 157n5, 167n140
Chicago, IL, 10, 15, 21, 31, 35–36, 61, 75; board of trade and, 65, 67
Chicago Tribune, 31
China, 122, 127
cigarettes, 1, 8, 71, 72, 129; age restrictions and, 145
Cigarmakers' Union, 36
cigars, 1, 13–14, 36, 61, 71–72, 122, 127, 159n15, 173n65
Cincinnati, OH, 1, 12, 28, 34–36, 55, 59, 61, 65, 76, 81, 146, 163n69. *See also* Association of the Tobacco Trade of Cincinnati; *Western Tobacco Journal*
citrus industry, 117
Clark, Christopher, 8
Clark, Daniel, 16
Clarksville, TN, 74, 76, 92, 124
Cleveland, Grover, 63, 103
Cleveland, OH, 31–32. *See also* conventions
coffee, 117, 154n15, 177n7
Cohen, Nancy, 158n10, 165n88
Colorado, 121
commission merchants, 13, 24, 29–30, 78, 163n68
commodity chain, 1–2, 4, 6–7, 20, 27–28, 37, 41, 43–45, 52, 59, 61, 68–69, 105, 110, 115, 177n8
Congress, U.S., 1–2, 12–18, 20, 22–23, 25–26, 30, 32–39, 41–42, 44, 46, 52–53, 55–57, 59, 63–64, 137, 142, 144, 146, 159n15, 168n146; Department of Agriculture, U.S. and, 116, 119–120, 125, 127–128. *See also* petitions

Congressional Globe, 11
Connecticut, 14, 18, 25, 36, 126–128, 135; experiment station and, 125, 193n54
Connecticut Leaf Tobacco Corporation, 128
Connecticut River Valley, 21, 127–128
Connecticut Tobacco and Trading Company, 128
Consular Service, U.S., 84–86
conventions, 2, 7, 11–12, 22–23, 58–59, 146; Cleveland, OH 1867 and, 31–34; Cooper Union 1864 and, 17–19, 21, 36; Washington, D.C. 1867 and, 29–30
cooperatives, 110, 132, 135. *See also* Tri-State Tobacco Growers' Cooperative Association
corn, 65, 90, 94–95, 131
corporatism, 8, 144, 148, 199n150
cotton, 66, 90, 93, 96, 104, 106, 111, 120, 125, 130–131, 154n15, 177n6, 181n65, 185n24
Country Gentleman, 27
Covington, KY, 24
Crane, Calvin D., 145. *See also* anti-tobacco movement
credit, 80, 89–90, 96, 106, 141, 189n86; scarcity in postbellum South and, 45
Crédit Mobilier scandal, 38
crop lien, 45
Cuba, and cigars, 121–122, 129
customs, 40, 55, 58, 71–72, 81

Daily Tobacco Plant, 105
Danville, VA, 3, 4, 55, 77, 93, 98, 101, 104–105, 108, 121; Danville Tobacco Association and, 45
debt, 90–91, 93–94, 96, 100, 105–108, 110, 185n24, 189n84. *See also* crop lien; tenancy
democracy, 7, 11–13, 32–34, 54
Democratic Party, 3, 37, 39, 51, 54–55, 62–63, 102, 133
Department of Agriculture, U.S., 5, 8, 27, 90, 111–112, 113; Bureau of Statistics and, 71; formation and growth, 116–119; tobacco and, 120–143. *See also* Bureau

of Plant Industry; Bureau of Soils; Congress, U.S.; growers; Office of Tobacco Investigations
Department of State, U.S., 84–86. *See also* Consular Service, U.S.
Detroit, MI, 1, 22, 35
Dodge, J.R., 118
double entry accounting, 46, 171n30
Du Bois, W.E.B., 91
Duke, Benjamin, 105, 109
Duke, James Buchanan, 6, 45, 64, 109, 154n21. *See also* American Tobacco Company; W. Duke Sons & Company
Durham, North Carolina, 1, 3, 43, 59–60, 63, 81, 89, 94, 98, 104, 105, 109
Dushkind, Charles, 147
Dutch East Indies, 86, 122, 127

Edwards, Paul N., 65, 177n3, 178n14
Egypt, 68; cotton and, 120
emancipation, 1–3, 23, 54, 66, 70, 88, 91, 96–97, 120, 133, 162n62, 189n89
Enstad, Nan, 154n21, 189n96
Export Leaf Tobacco Company, 135. *See also* Tobacco Trust
exports: tobacco and, 7, 14–15, 38, 44–46, 65–66, 68–69, 72–73, 76–80, 82–85, 107, 177n5, 179n20, 181n68
Extension Service, 131, 134, 137, 141, 198n129, 199n150

factories, 3, 10, 24, 31, 56–57, 71, 77, 100, 110, 124, 127; Bureau of Internal Revenue regulations and, 32, 43–44, 47, 53; fertilizer and, 100, 102; France and, 68–69; labor and, 54, 70, 109, 180n33, 189n96
Farmers' Alliance, 108–110
Farmers Union, 135
fertilizer, 5–6, 89–90, 94, 96–108, 110–111, 116, 123–124, 130–131, 134–136, 142, 187n62
fine-cut tobacco, 16, 30, 34

Fisher, Irving, 144, 147. *See also* anti-tobacco movement
Florida, 89, 117, 139
Food and Drug Administration, 145, 188n62
Ford, Henry, 145. *See also* anti-tobacco movement
Foucault, Michel, 183n6
France, 14, 68, 85, 117, 180n33; Paris Exposition of 1900 and, 125; tobacco monopoly and, 20, 69, 71–72
fraud: crop reporting and, 118; fertilizer and, 100; taxation and, 13, 25–28, 34–35, 46, 49, 61, 168n146; tobacco inspection and, 67, 78, 83–84, 181n68
Freedmen's Bureau, 23
freedpeople, 3, 23, 45, 54, 94, 97–98, 107–108, 187n53
freeholders, 3
free leaf proposal, 59, 61
free trade, 62, 74, 127

Gail & Ax, 20
Gamage, David, 164n86
Gaston, Lucy Page, 144. *See also* anti-tobacco movement
Germany: American exports and, 124; Bleichröder, Gerson and, 69; Bremen tobacco market and, 65–66, 71, 76, 83, 85, 181n68; Consular Service, U.S., and, 84–85; fertilizer and, 96; revenue system and, 10, 68, 69, 71
George, Henry, 62
Galloway, Beverly, 125
Gordon, Colin, 183n7
grades, tobacco and, 5, 65, 75, 82, 93–94, 97–99, 110–111, 121, 133, 138, 139–140, 144, 160n25, 198n133
Grand Army of the Republic, 62
Grange (Patrons of Husbandry), 3, 53, 54, 56, 80, 108, 154n13
Granville, NC, 92, 95
Graphic Company, 47
Great Britain, 14, 68
Greece, 68

greenbacks, 28, 64, 95, 101
Greensboro Daily News, 141
Greensboro, NC, 141
Grimes, J. Bryan, 109–111
Grinnell, William F., 85–86. *See also* Consular Service, U.S.
growers, 1–5, 7–8, 13–15, 25, 31, 75, 91, 104, 113, 149; criticism of and, 75, 95, 108; crop reports and, 105; debt and, 93, 106; Department of Agriculture, U.S., and, 113, 115, 118, 120–121, 123–124, 126, 128–129, 130, 132–139; fertilizer and, 97–101, 106; grading and, 74; insects and, 92; inspection and, 77–79; junction regimes and, 67, 76, 82, 90; labor and, 66, 96; occupational licensing and, 37–39, 45–46, 52, 103; organizing and 21–22, 42, 56, 58–59, 110, 140–143, 148; race and, 54–55, 89, 91, 109–110, 130, 133, 144; revenue systems and, 13–15, 17, 20–24, 27, 40–41, 44, 50–52, 53–59, 61, 63, 68–71; tobacco prices and, 93–94, 106, 108; tobacco quality and, 75, 86, 88, 90, 107, 111, 115; Tobacco Trust and, 64. *See also* cooperatives; Farmers' Alliance; Grange; *The Progressive Farmer*
guano, 96, 98, 111–112, 186n39. *See also* Cat Island Guano Company; fertilizer

Hahn, Barbara, 142, 154n15, 158n9, 160n24, 167n140, 170n17, 173n68, 178n9, 199n153
Hall, Joseph, 18–19
Hammerstein, Oscar, 41. *See also* *United States Tobacco Journal*
Hartford, CT, 128
Hatch Act of 1887, 119, 193n54
Henderson, NC, 104–105
hops, 120
House of Representatives, U.S., 37–38, 55, 168n146; Foreign Affairs Committee and, 75; Ways and Means Committee and, 21, 28, 33

Illinois, 21–22
India, 70, 86, 88, 122

inspection, 23, 25, 76–86, 107, 138, 182n68
Internal Revenue Act of 1862, 12–15, 18
Internal Revenue Act of 1864, 15, 17–18, 25–28
Internal Revenue Act of 1868, 13, 34–35, 40, 44, 52, 168n140, 169n11, 172n40
Internal Revenue Act of 1872, 12, 36–37, 40, 44, 47
The Internal Revenue Record and Customs Journal, 47
Interstate Commerce Commission, 119
Inter-State Tobacco Growers' Protective Association, 135
Iowa, 147
Iran, 69
Italy, 84, 124, 180n33; tobacco monopoly and, 68–69, 73–74

Jersey City, NJ, 3, 10
Jim Crow, 133
John J. Crooke and Company, 47–48, 172n40
Johnson, Andrew, 34
Johnson, Reverdy, 159n21
Jordan, David Starr, 145. *See also* anti-tobacco movement
junction regimes, 66–67, 76–86, 88–89, 177n8, 181n54
Judd, Orange, 117
jute, 117

Kanawha River Valley, 21, 163n69
Kentucky, 23, 27, 35, 37, 41, 44, 54, 56–57, 67, 73–74, 76, 81, 101, 110, 130, 141, 159n16, 181n62; State Agricultural Society and, 15, 22
Kellogg, John Harvey, 145. *See also* anti-tobacco movement
Kelley, William, 57
Kerr-Ritchie, Jeffrey, 170n27, 179n20, 188n75
Kilgore, B.W., 140–141
Killebrew, Joseph, 94. *See also* Census Bureau
Kimball, Israel, 10, 49–51, 61. *See also* Bureau of Internal Revenue

Knapp, Seaman, 129–131, 133
knowledge infrastructure, 65–67, 86, 178n14
Kolko, Gabriel, 158n8
Kramer, Paul, 190n2

landlords, 8, 45, 91, 93, 95, 98, 100, 142. *See also* growers
Larus and Brother Company, 146
Lawrence, William E., 18–19, 22, 24, 30, 35, 168n144. *See also* National Tobacco Association
leaf dealers, 41, 50, 55, 59, 63–64, 118, 135–137, 170n23, 175n95, 189n92; boards of trade and, 58; occupational licensing and, 36, 44–46, 107
Lebanon, 70
Le Duc, William, 116–117. *See also* Department of Agriculture, U.S.
Lewis, Joseph, 12–15, 17, 20, 25. *See also* Bureau of Internal Revenue
Liggett & Myers Tobacco Company, 135
Link, Stefan, 7
Liverpool, England, 65, 71, 76, 83, 118
lobbying, 17, 32, 39, 128, 136, 172n44
London, England, 65, 76
Lorillard, Pierre, 18, 22, 31–32, 34–35, 41, 56–58, 61, 63
Lost Cause, 78, 129–130, 133
Louisville, KY, 41–42, 75–76, 80–81, 83; Tobacco Board of Trade and, 52, 67
Lynchburg, VA, 36, 54, 80

Maggor, Noam, 7
Maier, Charles, 8, 68
Massachusetts, 18, 21
Mathewson, Ernest, 126, 132, 134–136
Mayo, Robert Atkinson, 29, 166n114
McAlpin, David Hunter, 18–19, 34
Mexico, 68
Miami River Valley, 21–22, 163n69
Mihm, Stephen, 164n77
Milov, Sarah, 144, 199n150
Mississippi, 137
Missouri, 16, 21–22, 65, 78, 126

Mitchell, Timothy, 72, 154n15, 179n21, 183n6, 198n130
monocropping, 92, 101, 108; one crop policy and, 94, 130
monopoly: government revenue systems and, 5, 10, 14, 20, 68–73, 85; revenue stamps and, 47–48, 51–53, 56, 63–64; Tobacco Trust and, 101, 135, 173n63; tobacconists and, 21–22, 27–29, 33–35
moonshine, 37, 43
Moore, Jason, 156n32, 184n14
Moore's Rural New Yorker, 15
Morrill, Justin, 28
Moss, Eugene, 131–138, 140–142

national debt of United States, 27–28, 58, 160n29
National Tobacco Association, 2, 13, 19, 35, 37–41, 49, 51–52, 58
National Tobacco Board of Trade, 128
National Tobacco Review, 75
North Carolina: Board of Agriculture and, 100, 131; Department of Agriculture, U.S., and, 129–136, 141; experiment stations and, 113, 125, 129; Farmers' Alliance and, 108, 110; Farmers Protective Association and, 109; fertilizer and, 96, 98, 100–102, 188n62; growers and, 56, 89, 91, 94–95, 109, 111, 139; Hoke County and, 136; leaf dealers and, 44; Person County and, 110; Piedmont and, 91, 124, 139, 140; Pitt County and, 91–92, 111; *The Progressive Farmer* and, 108, 139; Tobacco Growers' Protective Association and, 135; tobacconists and, 34, 43, 46, 59–60; warehouses and, 79, 93, 103–104, 106, 110; Wilson County and, 92, 104
New York, NY, 1, 12, 16, 18, 29, 47, 59, 141; Chamber of Commerce and, 85; consulate and, 73; exporters and, 83; Naval Stores and Tobacco Exchange and, 82; Tobacco Board of Trade and, 24, 30, 33, 36, 80, 85, 128; tobacconists and, 17, 172n40

New York Evening Post, 74
New York Herald, 31
The New York Journal of Commerce, 85
The New York Times, 26, 31
Newton, Isaac, 15. *See also* Department of Agriculture, U.S.
night riding, 110
No-Tobacco League, 145
Non-Smokers' Protective League, 145

Office of Tobacco Investigations, 5–6, 90, 113–115, 129, 131–139, 141–143, 146, 198n130, 199n150
Ohio, 76, 128–129, 163n69, 175n95; Board of Agriculture and, 15; exports and, 73–74; General Assembly and, 24, 159n16; tobacco grades and, 65–66; Tobacco Growers' Association and, 22
Ohio River Valley, 24, 163n69
Olmsted, Frank, 40, 42
Oregon, 121, 148
Osterhammel, Jürgen, 8
Ott, John, 88–90, 97, 110
Ottoman Empire, 68–69, 180n44
overproduction, 111, 120–121, 142
Oxford, NC, 63, 104, 134, 139
Oxford Public Ledger, 104

P. Lorillard & Company, 3, 10, 18, 31, 146, 179n23
packaging, 32, 34, 44, 47–48, 172n40
Paducah, KY, 73, 80
Panic of 1873, 2, 42, 47, 53, 55, 58, 170n24, 174n74
Patel, Raj, 156n32, 184n14
Pennsylvania, 18, 21, 43, 89, 128–129, 171n35
pensions, 53, 61–62, 174n74. *See also* veterans of the Civil War
pesticides, 92
petitions, 2, 6–7, 11–13, 21–22, 34, 36–37, 43, 52–53, 56, 63, 78, 112, 159n16
Petty, Adrienne Monteith, 189n87
Pfirshing, Charles, 29–30, 33
Philadelphia, PA, 30–31, 63, 128
Philippines, 68–69, 127

Pierce, W.B., 32
Pigou, Arthur Cecile, 147
plant disease, 92, 125–126, 131–134, 136
Poe, Clarence, 109, 139, 141, 199n140
Polk, Leonidas Lafayette, 108–109
Portugal, 68
potatoes, 94, 125, 131, 145
Prague, F.A., 29, 31–34
Prairie Farmer, 15
The Progressive Farmer, 108–109, 132, 139, 142
Prohibition, 145–148

Ragland, Robert, 53, 99–100, 107, 134, 186n38. *See also* Southern Fertilizing Company
Raleigh News & Observer, 141
Raleigh, NC, 110, 141
railroads, 5, 49, 76, 89–90, 94, 97, 102, 105–106, 112, 133
Rainey, Joseph, 54
Raum, Green Berry, 42–43, 46–49, 51, 56, 169n12, 170n17, 172n44. *See also* Bureau of Internal Revenue
Readjuster Party, 3, 54–55
Reidsville, NC, 111–112
Republican Party: Department of Agriculture, U.S. and, 116; sectionalism and, 12, 35; tariff and, 58, 61–62, 64; tobacco tax and, 3, 12, 15, 28–29, 54, 57; tobacconists and, 39
Reusens, George, 73, 75
revenue regimes, 66–71, 76, 80–83, 86–89
Reynolds, R.J., 124, 138
Rhode Island, 18
Rice, John McConnell, 37
Richmond Times Dispatch, 144
Richmond, VA, 1, 10, 29, 36, 43, 51, 56, 62–63, 70, 76, 78–80, 83, 86, 88, 96, 100, 102, 107, 136, 141
Richmond Whig, 53
Rockefeller, John D.: General Education Board and, 131
Roman, Frederick W., 145, 147. *See also* anti-tobacco movement

Romania, 68
Russia, 68–70

Sapiro, Aaron, 140
Schenck, Robert Cumming, 34–35
Scott, James C., 163n72
Scott, Tom, 105
Senate, U.S., 16–17, 55, 168n146; Agriculture Committee and, 15
Shamel, Archibald, 123, 126
sharecroppers, 1, 3, 44, 79, 133, 144, 189n84
Sherman, John, 15
Smalls, Robert, 54
Smith-Lever Act of 1914, 137, 198n129
snuff, 13, 36, 157n5, 159n15
soil: Department of Agriculture and, 6, 113–117, 123–130, 134, 136–137, 142, 193n53; tobacco culture and, 66, 92, 96–101, 105–106, 120, 178n9, 186n39
South Carolina, 89, 92, 96, 102, 113, 121, 129, 133, 136, 185n16, 186n39
Southern Fertilizing Company, 53, 96–97, 99–100, 107, 110, 187n43. *See also* Ott, John
Southern Planter and Farmer, 96
Southern Railway Security Company, 105
Southern Tobacco Journal, 106, 124
Spain, 68, 71
Spence, J.P., 25, 28, 32–35, 51. *See also* Association of the Tobacco Trade of Cincinnati
Spence, Thomas R., 34, 167n131
St. Louis, MO, 18, 61, 78
stamp tax system, 32–34, 39, 40, 47, 167n131, 172n46; free stamp proposal and, 35, 168n146
stock laws, 95, 107, 133–134, 186n37
Stoll, Steven, 2, 184n12, 186n35
sugar, 117, 177n6
Swanson, Drew, 178n9, 190n104

tariffs: government revenue and, 13, 58; postbellum politics and, 62, 64, 128; tobacco tax and, 4, 53, 57

taxation: Civil War and, 1; Congress and, 11–12, 15–16, 18, 159n15; evasion and, 17, 25, 42–44, 170n17; income and, 7, 13, 56; legibility and, 15–16; opposition and, 37–39, 50–64, 175n95; public revenue and, 14, 17, 37, 40, 121, 123, 174n74; Reconstruction and, 7; state development and, 8, 66, 79, 128, 179n21; states and, 77, 147–148; tariff and, 4; tobacconists and, 2–3, 10, 11, 13–14, 20–39, 158n10, 167n131. *See also* Bureau of Internal Revenue; growers; Pigou, Arthur Cecile; revenue regimes; stamp tax system
tea, 117
tenancy, 1, 91, 94–95, 100, 142, 199n150
Tennessee, 44, 56, 73, 76, 92, 101, 124, 181n62
Tilley, Nannie-Mae, 92, 163n68, 170n23, 185n22
tinfoil, 47–48, 172n40
Tobacco Association of the United States, 136
tobacco capitalists, 5, 89–90, 95–96, 101, 107–108, 112, 115, 123, 130, 132–133, 138, 149, 185n35
tobacco frontier, 5–6, 8, 86, 89–90, 98, 101–102, 106, 111, 122, 137, 139–140, 156n32, 177n8, 184n14, 185n24
Tobacco Leaf, 1, 11, 28–30, 33, 36–37, 39, 43–44, 47, 65, 70, 74–75, 84, 180n44. *See also* Pfirshing, Charles
Tobacco Merchants Association, 136, 146
Tobacco Trust, 1, 112, 129, 173n68. *See also* American Tobacco Company
tobacconists, 1–2, 4, 7, 10–13, 17–18, 21–22, 24–38, 41–44, 46–53, 55, 57–61, 63, 144, 146, 158n7, 161n48, 162n56, 164n77, 170n22, 172n46, 173n63. *See also* Republican Party; taxation
Tobacconists' National Association, 11, 22
Toel, Rose & Company, 73
Treasury Department, U.S., 20, 25, 31, 42, 58, 63, 116, 153n5, 180n37

Tri-State Tobacco Growers Cooperative Association, 135, 140–143, 199n150
Tucker, John Randolph, 55
Turkey, 68. *See also* Ottoman Empire

United States Tobacco Journal, 39, 41, 43, 49–50, 52, 58, 62, 64, 65, 84, 169n8

veterans of the Civil War, 53, 58, 61–62, 174n74
Virginia: Appomattox County and, 130; anti-tax politics and, 54–56; auctions and, 4, 46; Democratic Party and, 3, 55; Department of Agriculture, U.S., and, 113, 121, 129–131, 136; exports and, 65, 68, 73–74; factories and, 70; fertilizer and, 88–89, 96–100; General Assembly and, 86; growers and, 3, 21–23, 25, 41, 56, 91, 93–94, 106, 108, 140–141; inspection and, 77–79, 86; leaf dealers and, 44–45, 56; Louisa County and, 91; Nottoway County and, 80; Piedmont and, 91, 139; Prince Edward County and, 91; tobacco capitalists and, 101, 105; tobacconists and, 29, 32, 35, 53; warehouses and, 110
Virginia-Carolina Chemical Company, 97, 100–102, 111, 136
Volstead, Andrew, 145. *See also* Prohibition

W. Duke Sons & Company, 59, 101, 109. *See also* American Tobacco Company
W.T. Blackwell & Company, 43, 59–60, 105
Warehouse Act of 1916, 137–138, 141, 198n133
warehouses, 1, 5–7, 10, 20, 24, 35–36, 41, 46, 54, 66–67, 76–77, 79, 80–82, 89–91, 93–94, 96–98, 100–111, 121, 123, 127, 137–142, 183n6, 185n22, 186n38, 188n71, 189n87
Warner, Charles Dudley, 101–102, 108
Washington (state), 121
Washington Star, 31
Wells, David Ames, 22, 24–27, 30, 33, 165n88
Western Tobacco Journal, 39, 41, 51, 63, 65, 72
wheat, 53, 65, 90, 94, 120, 145, 177n6
Whitney, Milton, 125–126, 128–129. *See also* Bureau of Soils
Wiley, Harvey, 145. *See also* anti-tobacco movement
Wilson, James, 122, 131
wilt, 92, 130–131, 134
wine, 78, 117, 160n33
Wise, Peyton, 78–79
Wright, Gavin, 178n10, 189n84
Women's Christian Temperance Union, 145
World War I, 137, 139, 145

Patrick Mulford O'Connor is a history teacher at The Putney School in Putney, Vermont. He earned his doctorate in history at the University of Montana. *The Political Reconstruction of American Tobacco, 1862–1933* is his first book.

Reconstructing America
Andrew L. Slap, series editor

Hans L. Trefousse, *Impeachment of a President: Andrew Johnson, the Blacks, and Reconstruction.*

Richard Paul Fuke, *Imperfect Equality: African Americans and the Confines of White Ideology in Post-Emancipation Maryland.*

Ruth Currie-McDaniel, *Carpetbagger of Conscience: A Biography of John Emory Bryant.*

Paul A. Cimbala and Randall M. Miller, eds., *The Freedmen's Bureau and Reconstruction: Reconsiderations.*

Herman Belz, *A New Birth of Freedom: The Republican Party and Freedmen's Rights, 1861 to 1866.*

Robert Michael Goldman, *"A Free Ballot and a Fair Count": The Department of Justice and the Enforcement of Voting Rights in the South, 1877–1893.*

Ruth Douglas Currie, ed., *Emma Spaulding Bryant: Civil War Bride, Carpetbagger's Wife, Ardent Feminist—Letters, 1860–1900.*

Robert Francis Engs, *Freedom's First Generation: Black Hampton, Virginia, 1861–1890.*

Robert F. Kaczorowski, *The Politics of Judicial Interpretation: The Federal Courts, Department of Justice, and Civil Rights, 1866–1876.*

John Syrett, *The Civil War Confiscation Acts: Failing to Reconstruct the South.*

Michael Les Benedict, *Preserving the Constitution: Essays on Politics and the Constitution in the Reconstruction Era.*

Andrew L. Slap, *The Doom of Reconstruction: The Liberal Republicans in the Civil War Era.*

Edmund L. Drago, *Confederate Phoenix: Rebel Children and Their Families in South Carolina.*

Mary Farmer-Kaiser, *Freedwomen and the Freedmen's Bureau: Race, Gender, and Public Policy in the Age of Emancipation.*

Paul A. Cimbala and Randall Miller, eds., *The Great Task Remaining Before Us: Reconstruction as America's Continuing Civil War.*

John A. Casey Jr., *New Men: Reconstructing the Image of the Veteran in Late-Nineteenth-Century American Literature and Culture.*

Hilary N. Green, *Educational Reconstruction: African American Schools in the Urban South, 1865–1890.*

Christopher B. Bean, *Too Great a Burden to Bear: The Struggle and Failure of the Freedmen's Bureau in Texas.*

David E. Goldberg, *The Retreats of Reconstruction: Race, Leisure, and the Politics of Segregation at the New Jersey Shore, 1865–1920.*

David Prior, ed., *Reconstruction in a Globalizing World.*

Jewel L. Spangler and Frank Towers, eds., *Remaking North American Sovereignty: State Transformation in the 1860s.*

Adam H. Domby and Simon Lewis, eds., *Freedoms Gained and Lost: Reconstruction and Its Meanings 150 Years Later.*

David Prior, ed., *Reconstruction and Empire: The Legacies of Abolition and Union Victory for an Imperial Age.*

Sandra M. Gustafson and Robert S. Levine, eds., *Reimagining the Republic: Race, Citizenship, and Nation in the Literary Work of Albion W. Tourgée.* Foreword by Carolyn L. Karcher.

Brian Schoen, Jewel L. Spangler, and Frank Towers, eds., *Continent in Crisis: The U.S. Civil War in North America.*

Raymond James Krohn, *Abolitionist Twilights: History, Meaning, and the Fate of Racial Egalitarianism, 1865–1909.*

Hilary N. Green and Andrew L. Slap, eds., *The Civil War and the Summer of 2020*.

Ian Delahanty, *Embracing Emancipation: A Transatlantic History of Irish Americans, Slavery, and the American Union, 1840–1865*.

AnneMarie Brosnan, *A Contested Terrain: Freedpeople's Education in North Carolina During the Civil War and Reconstruction*.

Hilary N. Green, *Unforgettable Sacrifice: How Black Communities Remembered the Civil War*. Foreword by Edda L. Fields-Black.

Jonathan D. Neu, *Our Onward March: The Grand Army of the Republic in the Progressive Era*

Patrick Mulford O'Connor, *The Political Reconstruction of American Tobacco, 1862–1933*

www.ingramcontent.com/pod-product-compliance
Lightning Source LLC
Chambersburg PA
CBHW020405080526
44584CB00014B/1176